Anxiety as
Symptom and Signal

Anxiety as Symptom and Signal

edited by

Steven P. Roose

Robert A. Glick

THE ANALYTIC PRESS

1995   Hillsdale, NJ   London

Published by
The Analytic Press, Inc.
365 Broadway
Hillsdale, New Jersey 07642

Library of Congress Cataloging-in-Publication Data

Anxiety as symptom and signal / edited by Steven P. Roose, Robert A.
   Glick
          p.   cm.
      Includes bibliographical references and index.
      ISBN 0-88163-118-3
      1. Anxiety.   2. Psychotherapy.   I. Roose, Steven P., 1948–   .
II. Glick, Robert A., 1941–   .
      [DNLM: 1. Anxiety. 2. Psychoanalytic Therapy. WM 172 A63769
1995]
RC531.A639   1995
616.85'223—dc20
DNLM/DLC
for Library of Congress   94-44632
                                                              CIP

Printed in the United States of America
10 9 8 7 6 5 4 3 2 1

Contents

ANXIETY AS SIGNAL: THE TREATMENT SETTING

Contributors

Jeremy D. Coplan, M.D., Assistant Professor of Clinical Psychiatry, College of Physicians and Surgeons, Columbia University

Scott Dowling, M.D., Faculty, Cleveland Psychoanalytic Institute; Associate Clinical Professor of Psychiatry and Adjunct Associate Professor of Philosophy, Case Western Reserve

Gerald I. Fogel, M.D., Training and Supervising Psychoanalyst, Columbia University Center for Training and Research, Associate Clinical Professor of Psychiatry, College of Physicians and Surgeons, Columbia University

Abby J. Fyer, M.D., Associate Professor of Clinical Psychiatry, College of Physicians and Surgeons, Columbia University

Robert A. Glick, M.D., Admitting Psychoanalyst and Training and Supervising Psychoanalyst, Columbia University Center for Psychoanalytic Training and Research, and Clinical Professor of Psychiatry, College of Physicians and Surgeons, Columbia University

Jack M. Gorman, M.D., Professor of Clinical Psychiatry, College of Physicians and Surgeons, Columbia University, and Director, Department of Clinical Psychobiology, New York State Psychiatric Institute

Myron A. Hofer, M.D., Professor of Psychiatry, College of Physicians and Surgeons, Columbia University, and Director, Developmental Psychobiology, New York State Psychiatric Institute

Laszlo A. Papp, M.D., Associate Professor of Clinical Psychiatry, College of Physicians and Surgeons, Columbia University, and Director of Biological Studies Unit, New York State Psychiatric Institute

Morton F. Reiser, M.D., Albert E. Kent Professor Emeritus of Psychiatry, Yale University, and Training and Supervising Analyst, Western New England Psychoanalytic Institute

Owen Renik, M.D., Training and Supervising Psychoanalyst, San Francisco Psychoanalytic Institute, Editor-in-Chief, *Psychoanalytic Quarterly*, and Secretary of the Board of Professional Standards, American Psychoanalytic Association

Steven P. Roose, M.D., Associate Professor of Clinical Psychiatry, College of Physicians and Surgeons, Columbia University, and Faculty, Columbia University Center for Psychoanalytic Training and Research

Charles Spezzano, Ph.D., Training and Supervising Analyst, Psychoanalytic Institute of Northern California

Gloria J. Stern, M.D., Assistant Clinical Professor of Psychiatry, College of Physicians and Surgeons, Columbia University, and Training and Supervising Psychoanalyst, Columbia University Center of Psychoanalytic Training and Research

Preface

Psychoanalysis is a hybrid discipline that shares questions with the neurosciences about causes and mechanisms and with the humanities about meaning. To continue to be both a relevant theory of the mind and a clinically effective treatment, psychoanalysis must enjoy free access to knowledge from both of these disciplines. Both the explanatory and the therapeutic powers of psychoanalysis have foundered when causation has been attributed to intrapsychic conflict alone without regard for other knowledge. This has been apparent with such issues as character development, female psychosocial development, and male and female homosexuality and in regard to many major psychiatric disorders, including schizophrenia, panic attacks, and depression.

By contrast, interdisciplinary approaches have enriched modern psychoanalytic theory and treatment, leading to greater clinical relevance and effectiveness. In recent years psychoanalysis has, perhaps painfully but profitably, sacrificed some theoretical coherence for this new relevance. This transition is especially germane to the concept of anxiety, which has a uniquely central place in psychoanalytic theories of mind and treatment. We are creatures in pursuit of pleasure and safety, but forever fearing danger. Consequently we are principally concerned with threat: we live appraising and reacting to internal and external dangers, always asking the question, "Danger of what and from whom?" Data from the neurosciences and from pharmacological studies have compellingly challenged psychoanalytic models of anxiety, creating new ambiguities. Anxiety both organizes and disorganizes; it can be both a signal and a symptom. It is this new complexity that is the focus of this volume.

In his introductory chapter, "Freudian and Post-Freudian Theories of Anxiety," Robert Glick reviews the development of psychoanalytic

ix

theories of anxiety and the influence of infant research, brain studies, and clinical process.

In the first section, *Anxiety as Symptom*, Myron Hofer, in his chapter, "An Evolutionary Perspective on Anxiety," traces the connection between anxiety, danger, and survival and the important relationship between anxiety and learning. In "Neuroanatomy and Neurotransmitter Function in Panic Disorder" Jack Gorman and his colleagues consider the specific locus of brain function as connected to clinically observed types of anxiety with particular emphasis on the input of the cerebral cortex. In "Genetic and Temperamental Variations in Individual Predisposition to Anxiety" Abby Fyer addresses vulnerability to anxiety as the influence of brain systems on character development. This construct has implications for combined treatment approaches in clinical settings. Scott Dowling, in the chapter "The Ontogeny and Dynamics of Anxiety in Childhood," offers a developmental perspective on anxiety that has emerged from work with children with extraordinary physical conditions.

In the second section, *Anxiety as Signal*, psychoanalytic clinicians explore the meanings and functions of anxiety in clinical process. Gerald Fogel, in "Learning to Be Anxious," describes how a "new" experience of anxiety may be necessary for the working through of defenses against affective responses to early trauma. In the chapter "Anxiety and Resistance to Changes in Self-Concept," Gloria Stern examines cases of severe character pathology in which the transference provided an "antianxiety" effect that made possible the reintegration of primitive self and object representations. Owen Renick considers the dyadic and intersubjective dimension of the psychoanalytic situation in "The Patient's Anxiety, the Therapist's Anxiety, and the Therapeutic Process." Charles Spezzano, in "A Relational Perspective on Anxiety," presents a theoretical and therapeutic approach that is distinct from post-Freudian ego psychology. In his chapter, "Does Anxiety Obstruct or Motivate Treatment? When to Talk, When to Prescribe and When to Do Both" Steven Roose addresses how the different functions of anxiety as both symptom and signal can be incorporated into a therapeutic strategy. In the epilogue, Morton Reiser offers his perspective on the struggle to integrate concepts of mind and brain to yield a theoretically cogent and clinically useful model of anxiety.

1 Freudian and Post-Freudian Theories of Anxiety

Robert A. Glick

In 1932, the aged father of psychoanalysis wrote his *New Introductory Lectures in Psychoanalysis*. Too old and infirm to speak in public, he wrote in his conversations with posterity the following encouragement to those of us struggling in the field:

> What people seem to demand of psychology is not progress in knowledge, but satisfactions of some other sort; every unsolved problem, every admitted uncertainty is made into a reproach against it.
>
> Whoever cares for the science of mental life must accept these injustices along with it [Freud, 1933, p. 6].

In the development of affect theory (Shapiro and Emde, 1991), anxiety has been clinically and theoretically central, both as an affect and as a signal. An inescapable life experience, anxiety can painfully dominate and impoverish life. Yet as a signal of danger, rooted in our evolved psychobiology, anxiety gains deeply influential and adaptive, real and imagined, and conscious and unconscious meanings throughout our individual experience.

My purposes in this chapter are to explore the meanings and functions of anxiety in the evolution of psychoanalytic theory or theories and to suggest some of the challenges to those theories from infant development studies, neuroscience, and clinical process. In so doing, I hope to set the stage for the chapters that follow, examining both the history of psychoanalytic ideas and issues and the crucial influences on modern psychoanalytic understanding.

During the century since Freud's earliest conceptualization of hysteria up to the current theoretical pluralism, our understanding of anxiety has dramatically evolved and changed. As I shall describe,

1

theoretical concepts began with energies and mechanisms and with forces and agencies and have come to include the relations of selves and objects. At its core, the problem of anxiety deals with the nature and locus of threat to self or other; for the clinician and the theoretician, the question remains: the danger of what and whom?

Models of anxiety have always guided clinical psychoanalytic process. Using versions of the aforementioned question, analysts use theory to understand and interpret the mental life of a patient. However, there has been at times an ambiguously self-serving relationship between clinical observation and explanatory theory: the ways in which experience and explanation shape each other can include the danger of discovering what one seeks to find and of finding what one needs in order to confirm a theory. In addition, knowledge from outside psychoanalysis, from both the neurosciences and the social sciences, has not been easily integrated into psychoanalytic theoretical models.

Confronting all theories of anxiety, since the time of Freud's earliest efforts and remaining challenges today, are the dialectical relations of brain and mind and of constitutional and accidental. As suggested by this volume's title, *Anxiety: Symptom and Signal*, anxiety is both a disorganizer and an organizer in psychic development and in mental life; while as an affect anxiety painfully disrupts an individual trying to cope with overwhelming threat, anxiety as a signal reflects processes of internal appraisal and internal communication within the mind.

COHERENCE IN FREUDIAN AND
POST-FREUDIAN ANXIETIES

The concept of anxiety as an intrinsic adaptive reaction to danger originates not with Freud but with Darwin. By 1895, Freud (1895a,b) had concluded that the syndrome of anxiety hysteria—made up of conversion symptoms and phobias—had a psychological etiology, as a neuropsychosis of defense, and that it was a response of the mind to the threatened return of unpleasant emotions linked to unacceptable sexual memories. These were warded off and denied access to conscious awareness by means of repression, a psychological dynamic force. Anxiety emerged as the energic component of forgotten, repressed sexual ideas. Having the patient overcome amnesia and remember was both consistent with the etiological theory and effective as a treatment. In contrast, the syndrome of anxiety neurosis, comprising severe anxiety states and panic attacks, was a form of current or actual neurosis. Freud thought they had a somatic etiology; that is, the psychological experience of the somatic sexual drive was not fulfilled. For example, in coitus interruptus, when sexual excitation results in discharge, it never achieves adequate psychological satisfaction.

Freud always retained his deep respect for and fascination with the unknowable constitutional or biological determinants of anxiety; nonetheless he turned his attention to the psychical forms of anxiety that embodied the neurotic workings of failed repressions. Anxiety was for Freud both an affect and a metabolic product of sexual drive that had escaped repression but not achieved conscious satisfaction. The inadequately repressed libido would undergo a toxic modification into anxiety, "as vinegar is to wine" (Freud, 1905, p. 224). For Freud, the mind was ultimately a homeostatic and transformational system for the management of the psychic energy that flowed from the drives. The mental apparatus was governed by two regulatory principles: the homeostatic constancy principle, which sought to maintain a steady, low level of energy in the system, and the transformational pleasure–unpleasure principle, wherein increases of excitation are experienced as unpleasureable and decreases as pleasurable. Psychic dangers arose when the mind must safely contain or discharge the forces of unacceptable desires.

Within the next two and a half decades, psychoanalysis evolved into its true, high-classical form. With a sense of visionary passion, Freud and his disciples believed they were in possession of a revolutionarily new epistemological tool and scientific instrument that could both explain and explore virtually all aspects of human experience: character, illness, health, morality, religion, anthropology, history, and creativity. The repressed, wishful, infantile unconscious was the source of our lowest and highest qualities. Repressed unconscious wishes—derivatives of the unknowable instinctual drives—were recognized as *the* dangers—as *the* potential threats to the ego—whose principal task was the safe and acceptable expression of infantile sexuality. In the analytic situation, anxiety served as a beacon leading to the unconscious drives. Freud looked for it in his patients and offered them insight into its problematic, instinctual sources. Understanding of the sources would relieve the anxiety. Because his primary interest was in the drives, Freud had yet to appreciate the role of anxiety as an organizer and as an adaptive mental signal.

By 1926, the growth of psychoanalytic clinical experience and the limited explanatory power of the reigning theories prompted Freud's epic reformulation of anxiety theory. Freud (1926) set out much of what therapeutic process had taught him about the ego, the superego, and the unconscious structure of the major neuroses, the nature of defense, and the centrality of the Oedipus complex. He redefined the dynamic roles of anxiety—first, as a signal of danger, and second, as the initiator of defensive response. Originally, anxiety was the result of defensive response. Once Freud had defined the ego as the central executive agent of the mind, the signal function adaptively monitored the internal and external worlds for dangers. The ego samples the instinctual drive derivative—the wishful impulse—that threatens to evoke a dangerous situation of excessive excitation. Thus inoculated with the unpleasurable consequences of sampling a wish fulfillment, the ego draws on its individual and phylogenetic history of danger, invoking a defense mechanism to prevent the expression of the threatening impulse in action or in consciousness. Signal anxiety thus becomes the ego's most essential tool; signal anxiety makes it possible to remember, think, fear, and arbitrate drives, punishments, ideals, and reality. Imposing that central organizing role of anxiety onto his theories of psychological development—themselves portrayed as a series of dangers and potential trauma—Freud (1926) outlines the progression of possible anxieties:

> The danger of psychical helplessness . . . when his ego is immature; the danger of the loss of object . . . when he is still dependent on others; the danger of castration . . .; and the fear of the super-ego to the latency period. Nevertheless, all these danger-situations and determinants of anxiety can persist side by side and cause the ego to react to them with anxiety at a period later than the appropriate one [p. 142].

Within Freud's schema of profoundly influential terrors of childhood, the conceptual importance he placed on castration anxiety cannot be overstated. Castration anxiety links psychopathology and psychodynamics with theories of etiology, development, and structure and function of the mind. As the paramount organizing danger signal, castration anxiety sets in motion superego formation, guilt, conscience, morality, civilization, and neurosis. Through the therapeutic reconstruction of the history of infantile oedipal fixations and regressions, liberation from neurosis becomes possible. Patients are cured of neurosis once they understand the vicissitudes of their dangerous, wishful oedipal past. Signal anxiety guides the way to both the cure of the neurosis and the archaeological excavation of its sources.

At this point Freud's hunger for a profound unified theory of fundamental human nature seemed satisfied. Although his views of anxiety changed, Freud never gave up his conviction that repressed drives threaten our ego and our civilization. He believed that the history of the race and the history of the infant merged in the unconscious infantile fantasies of the neurotic adult. Likening himself to Sir Richard Burton, who discovered the source of the Nile, Freud thought he had found the biological basis for theories of mind, development, and psychopathology.

As a model of the mind, Freud's theory remained paternalistic and phallocentric. He had paid insufficient attention to the importance of mothering and the indelibility of early maternal, preoedipal experience. At that point Rank (1929) entered the scene with his theory of birth trauma. Rank, who had come to analysis from literature, envisioned the trauma of birth as the central organizing experience of anxiety. The primal real separation from the mother was for him the paradigm of all neurotic anxiety—not Freud's Oedipus complex. In Rank's formulation, all subsequent developmental fixations and regressions, including the Oedipus complex and castration anxiety, were secondary elaborations of the physical separation from the mother at birth. Clinical psychoanalytic process, according to Rank, would demonstrate in the transference the return of the repressed birth trauma and the singular role of the maternal authority prior to the paternal. Freud rejected that theory, which he regarded as a return to the abandoned theory of abreaction. The birth trauma represented an intolerable challenge to his sacrosanct doctrines of the primacy of the Oedipus complex, of the father's authority as the organizing force in mental life, and of the supreme paternal authority of Freud himself over one of his favorite analytic sons.

While Rank's theory offered an alternative biological (i.e., objective, scientific, theoretical) foundation, Rank's heresy posed political and conceptual problems. It reminded Freud of his struggle with Jung, whose defection from the primacy of sexuality as the scientific basis of psychoanalysis had been a bitter wound, and it stretched credibility, requiring a psychologically developed newborn. Much more important for the future direction of psychoanalytic thinking was Rank's (1929) (and Ferenczi's, 1924) anticipation of the importance of the preoedipal mother as a profound force on mental development, as a dynamic ambivalent unconscious object of the all-important drives, and as a paradigm for therapeutic analysis.

As a result of those contributions, Freudian coherence was gradually revealed to be inadequate to the larger spectrum of diagnoses and mental phenomena emerging as clinically significant. Several major theoretical fault lines, the kind of ambiguities and uncertainties that generated Freud's major ideological anxiety, would appear over the role and meaning of the real versus the fantasied and of trauma versus conflict and over the importance of oedipal experience and paternal internalization versus the preoedipal experience and maternal internalization.

Post-Freudian Anxieties

With Freud's death, there were to be significant tectonic shifts in the theories of essential psychic structure and of mental processes and contents; the metapsychological bedrock on which clinical experience was to rest would never again be so secure.

Following the path suggested by Rank, Klein (1964) radically redefined anxiety. Retaining anxiety as central, she argued for the importance of anxieties as signals of danger generated in the relationship with the internal maternal object over that of castration anxiety. Not only would Mother's importance usurp Father's, but aggression would take the place of libido as the core source of, and reason for, anxiety. Danger, still considered instinctual, was not quite economic or quantitative, as Freud postulated. It was no longer repressed libidinal excitation or unsatisfied sexual desire; "the danger arising from the inner working of the death instinct is the first cause of anxiety" (Klein, 1948, p. 116). With this, we leave the realm of psychophysics and enter that of mythic monsters.

Crucial here is a profound shift of emphasis. Freud had coined all the essentials: fear of loss of the object, guilt, aggression, and the death instinct. Klein's critical developmental chronology starts in the first months of life, years earlier than Freud's. In Klein's scheme, developmental anxieties arise in stages: there is the paranoid-schizoid position with its persecutory anxiety, including fears of the destruction of the ego/self by the devouring bad breast onto which infantile aggression is projected. Later, as the infant–toddler integrates split maternal representations, it attains the depressive position: the infant experiences depressive anxiety, fearing the destruction of the good, or at least ambivalently loved, object or its destructive retaliation.

The Kleinian vision of the mind has had profound impact on psychoanalysis. In Klein's theory as in Freud's second anxiety theory, anxiety remains an organizer. As in Freud, it is linked to the constitutional force of drive, now aggression more than libido. The Kleinian mind is composed of fantasied partial self and object relational units, of sexual parts and bodily products, not primarily agencies like id, ego, and superego in conflict. Kleinian anxieties signal the potential destruction of vital parts of one's internal world, more akin to mythic struggles than energic problems within a mental machine. In clinical reconstructions from the analyses of adults and children, these unconscious, nightmarish anxieties are evidence of developmental failures to resolve the universal, archaic, dangerous, and sadistic conflicts necessary for psychological growth. The nature and impact of the actual mother recede into the Kleinian shadows, behind the instinctual aggression. And role of the real object as influential in psychic development seems as secondary in Klein as it seemed in Freud.

While it is beyond my purpose here to review object relations theory (see Greenberg and Mitchell, 1983), I do note trends relevant to our interest in anxiety. Object relations theorists (e.g., Fairbairn, Winnicott, Guntrip) following Klein increasingly replaced the Freudian apparatus. Freud's mechanistic ego, with its structured set of functions constructed from incorporated need-satisfying objects, yields to a new vision of the self. Not easily defined, the self now refers to one's inner subjective experience. A larger, and more abstract, concept, the self is our unconscious and conscious sense of psychic agency, subsuming the processes of defense, identification, conflict resolution, and adaptation. Anxiety therefore reflects the state of the self, one's organizational integrity, and one's security and satisfaction. Crucial in that picture is the infant's relationship with the maternal object caring for it—gratifying and nurturing the growing I: self. Anxieties in this scheme point the way to real or imagined failures of the actual, real maternal object to protect and serve the infantile self. These early organizing anxieties set the stage for the meanings of danger in subsequent development. The vicissitudes of ties to the good and bad, gratifying and depriving maternal object are registered as fragmentation and separation anxieties of the ego-self, which in turn color all later dangers. For Klein, the dangers result from instinctually driven fantasies; for Fairbairn, Winnicott, and the others, the maternal failures are real, objective, and actual historical events. Absence of the protective and nurturant mother is the danger. A patient's anxiety signals structural defects in the ego/self, resulting from psychic deficiency states in development.

As elements of theories of the mind, the definitions of anxiety diverge. We stand at the junction of two major conceptual paths, each with differing goals and implications: Along one path, much of Freudian structuralism is abandoned. This is the path taken by those who focus increasingly on the self and self-experience, the self-psychologists, the intersubjectivists. Along the other path, the goal is the integration of Freudian ego psychology and object relations theory.

For those taking the first path, consisting of the truly post-Freudian paradigms, anxiety remains a signal of danger to the self. The organization of the self is vulnerable to disorganization or fragmentation experiences. Depending on one's history of internalized relationships, one risks falling apart if those relationships are severely flawed. For

Kohut (1971), the most influential advocate of that theoretical trend, the healthy narcissism of the self results from the successful internalization of real caregivers—what he calls the transmuting internalization of the selfobjects that have served as parts of the self. Real failures by real embodiments of selfobjects lead to pathological narcissism and narcissistic anxieties expressed in sexual and aggressive forms. Kohut (1971) insists that the central Freudian guilt-ridden man suffering from castration anxieties masks the genuine annihilation anxieties of the tragic man.

Along the other major theoretical path, the goal has been an integration of Kleinian and post-Kleinian object relations with Freudian and post-Freudian ego psychological metapsychology. Kernberg's (1976) theoretical schema incorporates a hierarchy of developmental processes that integrate Kleinian and ego psychological ideas. In Kernberg's structural classification, the severest degrees of character pathology are the result of events explicable through a modified Kleinian model and chronology. Kernberg places great emphasis on the turbulent relationship of primitive self and object representations and archaic destructive aggression. When these struggles are adaptively navigated, subsequent neurotic pathological character organization is best understood in terms of postoedipal, systemic structural organization. The ego, now subsuming integrated self and object representations, resolves conflicts among identifications, instinctual drives, superego dangers, and reality. Developmental history, psychodynamic structure, and psychopathology all form a coherent system. Anxiety is an organizer of constitutional and accidental factors, as well as a guiding set of signals in treatment.

In the modern pluralistic climate, psychoanalysts conceptualize analytic process by applying aspects of several models, as seems useful, without fear of either insufficient coherence or doctrinal heresy. As an essential theoretical glue, anxiety, though still important as a clinical beacon, has receded as the paramount integrating concept. Reflecting a widening of perspective, signals are sought about the state of psychic organization and of psychic reality. For the working analyst listening to patients, it is the unconscious and conscious fantasies that hold both the meaningful content of anxiety and the stuff of analytic clinical process (Compton 1972a,b, 1980) and from which fantasies the models of psychic organization and psychic reality are drawn. In that way, the internal mental events that we consider signals of anxiety no longer possess the same clarity and coherence that Freud suggested as organizing schemata about the workings of the mental apparatus. While we may comfortably retain the Freudian frame of reference and the structural language of analysis of defense, resistance, transference, and countertransference, we can no longer assume a confidence that we are explaining the workings of the mind—rather, only that we are interpreting a person's obscurely communicated experience. Without the conviction about the authoritative validity of a theory, there is a significant difference between interpreting and explaining.

QUESTIONS OF RELEVANCE: INFANTS, BRAINS, AND TREATMENT

Infantile Anxieties and Their Development

Observing infants is a risky business, offering new challenges to psychoanalytic theories of anxiety. We remain on the theoretical trail of the self, its formation, and its anxieties. If we picture an infant—a young I—in its alert state, we can imagine it taking notice of something, getting a signal, and asking, if you will, "What is it?" and "What happens next?" (Nilsson, 1977). We know that infants are intrigued by novelty, are curious, and thrive on new experience. According to Stern (1985), from the earliest weeks of life, infants seem to be processing experience in ways that suggest they are "predesigned to be aware of self-organizing processes." Stern proposes that this emerging infantile self (the "to whom" of our ideas of anxiety) "never experiences a period of total self/other undifferentiation."

As this emerging self is developing neurobiologically and experientially, it is also organizing experiences of self and other, inner and outer, subjective and objective (later to include real and unreal), and passive and active. All these processes include a hedonic quality—the pleasurable and unpleasurable nature of subjective experience—and are integrated within an evolving range of good and bad feelings. Freud was correct when he said that we consider as part of ourselves what feels good and reject what feels bad. That is how the self grows. From a developmental perspective, the moral self evolves out of moral emotions: in the beginning, what feels good or bad is good or bad.

How then does the infant become anxious? We assume that they have states of being alone with themselves, of quiescence, composure, equilibrium, quiet interest, and solitude, that alternate with periods or states of excitement, uncertainty, disequilibrium, dis-ease, and distress. In describing the progression to anxiety, Kagan (1984) speaks of the discrepancy principle:

The infant's emotional state is affected by his ability or inability to assimilate discrepant events. An event that can be assimilated after some effort produces excitement, but one that cannot be assimilated produces uncertainty. . . . Uncertainty is not synonymous with states of fear or anxiety, although it may precede them. If the infant continues to attempt assimilation of an event, remains unsuccessful, and additionally has no way to deal with the comprehension of failure, a different state is generated. Some psychologists call this subsequent state fear or anxiety [p. 38].

If we follow this idea—for an infant to be anxious, to have some internal experience such as Kagan (1984) describes—then there must be a growing capacity to register and retrieve representations of self and other. Associating these with states of pleasure and unpleasure, the infant begins to organize inner and outer worlds, as well as the realms of self and other.

Born with the capacity to respond to the human face with pleasure and alertness, born "knowing" the concept of face, the infant presumably uses it to build discriminations between self and other: good, manageable, interesting feeling states and bad, distressing ones. It recognizes the mother's face as the paramount source of pleasure and safety, not only as a signal of food supply. The infant comes to need the mother to feel safe, not just satisfied. Her presence soothes and restores equilibrium. Her distress distresses the infant. It would appear that the infant is not only at risk of helplessness precipitated by actual separation but, according to Stern, also at risk for problems of tuning in to the mother, of psychically connecting or attaching to organize experience. What Stern and others have discovered is that dangers can be communicated and experienced as internally generated through attachment processes as well as in separation processes. Optimally, that tuning-in process enables the infant to integrate what comes from within the self and what from without and to recognize and empathize with another self.

Our notion of trauma—the extreme of the accidental factors in the accidental-constitutional dialectic—rests on the preparedness of the infant to cope with degrees of distress and of disorganizing unpleasure. Especially before the phase of the verbal self, early trauma, severe loss, or chronic maternal anxiety and depression may have literally unspeakable effects on the emerging self. This is especially true for the manner in which the emergent self attunes and is attuned by relations with reliable and unreliable others. Erikson's (1950) concept of basic trust speaks to that problem. Separation anxiety reactions (Bowlby, 1960) and panic disorders seen in older children and adults may well be considered in terms of the limitations of the emerging self-organization to modulate and contain states of distress—states that interfere with subjective integrity and stability. What then is the impact of infant observation on theories of anxiety? The most important contributions appear to support object relations models that usefully integrate innate cognitive capacities in the structuralization of our internal world. What remains less clear are those elements of early psychoanalytic theory concerned with affective states and regulation. Here one needs to consider the influences on neurobiology on psychoanalytic understanding.

The Anxiety of Neurobiology

One of the most exciting challenges in psychoanalysis today is the relationship of the neurobiological brain and the psychoanalytic mind. Embracing Charles Darwin and anticipating Heinz Hartmann, James (1892) reassuringly reminds us that "our inner faculties are adapted in advance to the features of the world in which we dwell, adapted I mean, so as to secure our safety and prosperity in its midst. . . . Mind and world in short have evolved together, and in consequence are something of a mutual fit" (quoted in Kandel, 1983, p. 1281).

With this in mind, what can neuroscience usefully say to psychoanalysis about anxiety and the nature of danger?

Leaving Freudian motivational energics to history, modern neurobiology addresses motivation, adaptation, cognition, and memory, in the languages of information processing systems, of neuroelectrochemical events, of neural mapping, and so on. Although memories, wishes, feelings, fantasies, and ideas cannot be reduced to locations, substances, genetics, or neurobiologic processes, to ignore these influences on psychic life is to court irrelevant theories and ineffective treatments. When one regards psychological danger as the basis of anxiety, it becomes intriguing to consider how, from a neurobiological perspective, dangers are registered and processed. What influences the brain influences the mind, the nature of experience, and the meanings of anxiety and fear. For example, the locus coeruleus (a small nucleus in the brain stem) "may function as a part of an alarm-relay system which modulates the disagreeable and emotional side of pain . . . the evolutionary mechanism for elaboration of the anticipation of possible pain, into the emotions generally called fear or anxiety" (Reiser, 1984, p. 149).

Mental development, structure, and organization all influence and are influenced by functional neurobiology. We know that the brain is a source of extramental, noncontent, nonpsychological influence. For example, processes of affective dysregulation (what we call a predis-position to affective illnesses, including anxiety) impinge on the developing mind, coloring the meaning of experience and therefore the nature of mental structure. Neurobiological events, such as problems regulating emotional responses, become meaningful; that is, they acquire profound personal meanings that guide, organize, or distort psychological adaptation and subsequent emotional experience. Mood quality and stability—temperament—become the climate in which personality grows and adapts. It may be reasonable, from a neurobiological point of view, to suggest that one is a constitutionally anxiety-filled person and therefore experiences oneself as constantly facing unnamed threats and unanticipated dangers; such children will grow up imagining themselves constantly at risk, never safe and secure. They will always feel like a potentially fearful and angry victim.

Nature and nurture are mutually influential. Emotional events in development may also shape neurobiology for good or ill. Early enrichment of cognitive experience, for example, may alter cortical structuralization; severe acute and chronic psychic trauma, as in early profound object loss and recurrent separation, may alter the expression of intrinsic neurobiological processes, including gene expression. Appreciating the dialectic in brain–mind interaction, Reiser (1984) states:

> Actual expression of some genes does not occur in all individuals endowed with those genes. Intrauterine, neonatal, and postnatal influences, by shaping maturation and development throughout ontogeny, participate in determining what the actual, final functional and structural expression of the potentialities programmed in the genetic material will be [p. 199].

Summing up the clinical questions about neurobiology of anxiety, Cooper (1985) suggests that clinicians ask:

> What portions of the anxiety are, in their origins, relatively non-psychological, and what portions are the clues to psychic conflicts that are the originators of the anxiety? The neurobiological theory does not suggest that all anxiety is a non-mental content but rather a distinction must be made between psychological coping and adaptive efforts to regulate miscarried brain functions that create anxiety with no or little environmental input and psychological coping and adaptive efforts to regulate disturbances of the intrapsychic world that lead to anxiety and are environment sensitive [p. 1398].

Anxiety and Psychoanalytic Treatment

Finally, we return to the high plateau of the clinical therapeutic process. Clinical work offers the most useful and relevant test of our theories of anxiety. Freud (1930), in one of his late major writings, encourages us never to lose sight of anxiety:

Anxiety is always present somewhere or other behind every symptom; but at one time it takes noisy possession of the whole of consciousness, while at another it conceals itself so completely that we are obliged to speak of unconscious anxiety or, if we want to have a clearer psychological conscience, since anxiety is in the first instance simply a feeling, of possibilities of anxiety [p. 135].

When, for whatever reasons, anxiety is severely symptomatic and takes "noisy possession" we assess the patient's capacity for self-observation and for free association. Growing clinical experience strongly encourages that individuals with forms of affective dysregulation leading to chronic severe anxiety states and panic attacks receive concomitant treatment with medication; the medication allows patients to begin to observe themselves and to participate meaningfully in the therapeutic process.

Analytic work with such patients can then focus on the psychic meanings of those affective traumas. We begin to understand how preverbal traumas, registered in the mind before language, may lead to both anxiety disorders and such deformations of character structure that have resulted from the problematic defensive-adaptive responses to early symptoms. Severe childhood trauma at its worst can lead to dissociative states and other forms of severe character pathology that rely heavily on primitive defenses against disorganizing anxiety. Multiple personality disorder and certain forms of borderline character organization may reflect instances of adaptation to early severe trauma. Severe recurrent anxiety states during development may be later organized as fears of loss of control or fears of loss of sense of self. Anxiety can be interpreted as punishment for forbidden wishes or as a sense of self as bad, damaged, sick, or guilty; it may also represent the stigmata of martyrdom and the status of the exception, the coercive power of the victim, entitled to compensation. Today, with effective combined treatments, it is possible to analyze the characterological meanings and unconscious justifications that vulnerability to severe anxiety and panic states may produce.

By contrast, with Freud's "possibilities of anxiety," we have the heart of the psychological therapeutic process and what usefully remains of a theoretical signal anxiety concept; it refers to a guiding strategy, a compass direction for the analyst to pursue, and a major danger for the analysand to avoid and resist. These anxious possibilities—these signals of anxiety—may be usefully stirred in the analyst as well as the patient. Recognizing these countertransference reactions offers the analyst additional information about the unconscious interaction between the analyst and the patient, which guides exploration and interpretation of the patient's unconscious fantasies.

True affective signals of anxiety, such as uneasiness, uncertainty, discomfort, and apprehension, are in the clinical setting recognized, acknowledged, and associated to aloud by the patient and silently to himself or herself by the therapist. Here anxiety promotes meaningful self-exploration; it stimulates associations, recall, and reconstruction. Growing comfortable with being anxious, especially within the transference, sustains the intimacy, trust, and candor necessary for the treatment process. The patient's comfort level reflects a reorganization of tenacious character resistances, the deepening of the regressive transferential engagement, and the emerging self-reflecting, therapeutic alliance. What we seek—to return to our example of the anxious infant—is to foster a safe sense of novelty, curiosity, and tolerable discrepancy in the presence of the benevolent, benign therapist so that the patient can ask, "What is this?" and "What happens next?" without overwhelming or constricting anxiety, fears of shame and guilt, or helplessness and rejection. Freud saw that the ability to put into words to another person the aforementioned unspeakable memories, feelings, desires, and fears leads patients to the awareness of dangerous infantile fantasies and guides them to recover influential memories. The therapeutic process seeks this reworking and working-through of such anxious stories of danger, as they come alive in the room, in the transference space, and in the dynamic histories of early relationships.

CONCLUSION

From Freud's earliest work with hysteria, the discovery and creation of psychoanalysis grew out of the "problem of anxiety." Throughout his life and his work, Freud was eager to forge an internally consistent, coherent system that would describe the nature of the mind. He hoped such a system would embrace everything, from the conflicts of patients on his couch and the metabiological phylogenetic struggle of the titanic forces of life and death. Although his hopes are still unrealized, his inquiries into the nature of anxiety led him and all who followed down fruitful paths.

Of what then is anxiety a symptom? And what dangers does anxiety signal? And where or to whom is the signal intended to go? The answers remain elusive and challenging. We have come to see that our models of the mind—those maps we use to understand the mental events in our patient's (and our) mind—are no longer limited to forces or energies in conflict, or to drives and defense, or to self and objects, or to merging or battling, or to loving or hating. We interpret meaning in psychic life through lenses that accept the intrinsic and irreducible relations of constitution and accident and of organization and disorganization.

Our anxieties arise from both internal and external sources—sources that, be they neurobiological or experiential, remain inescapable. Our sense of ourselves, of who we are, and of how we got to be this way fashions itself from our anxieties and is revealed to us through anxiety.

REFERENCES

Bowlby, J. (1960), Separation anxiety. *Internat. J. Psycho-Anal.*, 41:89–113.
Compton, A. (1972a), A study of the psychoanalytic theory of anxiety: I: Development of Freud's theory of anxiety. *J. Amer. Psychoanal. Assn.*, 20:3–44.
——— (1972b), A study of the psychoanalytic theory of anxiety: II: Theory of anxiety since 1926. *J. Amer. Psychoanal. Assn.*, 20:341–394.
——— (1980), A study of the psychoanalytic theory of anxiety: III: Formulation of anxiety response. *J. Amer. Psychoanal. Assn.*, 28:739–774.
Cooper, A. (1985), Will neurobiology influence psychoanalysis? *Amer. J. Psychiat.*, 142:12, 1395–1402.
Erikson, E. (1950), *Childhood and Society*. New York: Norton.
Ferenczi, S. (1924), *Thalassa: A Theory of Genitality*. Albany, NY: Psychoanal. Quart. Books, 1938.
Freud, S. (1895a), Detaching syndrome of anxiety neurosis from neurasthenia. *Standard Edition*, 3:90–139. London: Hogarth Press, 1953.
——— (1895b), A reply to criticisms of my paper on anxiety neurosis. *Standard Edition*, 3:119–140. London: Hogarth Press, 1953.
——— (1905), Three essays on the theory of sexuality. *Standard Edition*, 7:130–245. London: Hogarth Press, 1953.
——— (1926), Inhibitions, symptoms and anxiety. *Standard Edition*, 20:87–172. London: Hogarth Press, 1959.
——— (1930), Civilization and its discontents. *Standard Edition*, 21:64–145. London: Hogarth Press, 1961.
——— (1933), New introductory lectures in psychoanalysis. *Standard Edition*, 22:5–182. London: Hogarth Press, 1964.
Greenberg, J. & Mitchell, S. (1983), *Object Relations in Psychoanalytic Theory*. Cambridge, MA: Harvard University Press.
Jones, W. (1892), *The Principles of Psychology, Vol. 1*. New York: Holt, 1893, p. 18.
Kagan, J. (1984), *The Nature of the Child*. New York: Basic Books.
Kandel, E. (1983), From metapsychology to molecular biology: Explorations into the nature of anxiety. *Amer. J. Psychiat.*, 140:10, 1277–1293.
Kernberg, O. (1976), *Object Relations Theory and Clinical Psychoanalysis*. New York: Aronson.

Klein, M. (1948), *A Contribution to the Theory of Anxiety and Guilt*. New York: McGraw-Hill.

———— (1964), *Contributions to Psychoanalysis, 1921–1945*. New York: McGraw-Hill.

Kohut, H. (1971), *The Analysis of the Self*. New York: International Universities Press.

Nilsson, A. (1977), System approach to adaptation: Relation to PSA model anxiety. *Internat. Rev. Psycho-Anal.*, 4:111–124.

Rank, O. (1929), *The Trauma of Birth*. New York: Harper & Row, 1973.

Reiser, M. (1984), *Mind, Brain, Body*. New York: Basic Books.

Shapiro, T. & Emde, R. (1991), Affect: Psychoanalytic perspectives. *J. Amer. Psychoanal. Assn.*, 39(Suppl.).

Stern, D. (1985), *The Interpersonal World of the Infant*. New York: Basic Books.

2 An Evolutionary Perspective on Anxiety

Myron A. Hofer

Since it is only by comparing that we can judge and since our knowledge rests entirely on the relations that things have with others that are similar or different ... if there were no animals, the nature of man would be even more incomprehensible.

—Georges-Louis Buffon
Histoire naturelle de l'homme, 1749

Of all the clinically important emotions, anxiety may be the one with the closest parallels in other species and with the most ancient evolutionary heritage. Presumably this is because natural selection depends so closely on strategies for avoidance of danger that elements of what we call anxiety have been built into the response repertoire of organisms from the time when they first evolved a means of moving about in their world. If we could follow the steps by which anxiety evolved from its earliest precursors, it might give us some new insights into anxiety's component units and how they function together in such complex organisms as ourselves. To see for a moment how nature put such a state together may give us the perspective from which to find new ways to understand and treat its disorders.

But how are we to do this? After all, there is no fossil record of the evolution of behavior. While preparing to write this chapter, I had a fantasy in which I was looking out over a vast territory containing innumerable species of animals ranging from single cells to large apes. They were arranged, by some magical intervention, according to the era during which they had first evolved. I could wander about among them, as if in a time machine that allowed me to travel back hundreds of millions of years in an instant. What struck me most was that although they resembled species I was familiar with, they were

17

not nearly so diverse. There seemed to be only one example of each major class. And then I realized that these were my ancestors—just those forms in a direct line of evolution.

The fantasy neatly solved the problem posed by the title of this chapter. In it I was shown which animals represent the major steps in human evolution, and thus my story was laid out before me, waiting to be told. Beginning with our oldest ancestors, I could find the earliest stage during which the essential elements for anxiety first appeared, and then I could move forward in time, as it were, through a series of steps as anxiety evolved toward the complex state of mind that we experience today. By contrast with reality, that fantasy reveals the problems we have in using contemporary animal studies to deduce the evolution of behavior. We cannot be sure which contemporary species most closely resemble our ancestors and whether in fact any close resemblance is at all likely in view of the evolutionary change that has taken place in all species since the time of our common ancestors.

Ten or fifteen years ago it was generally believed that evolutionary change was gradual and inevitable—a slow and continuous process by which species eventually became transformed into new ones. By that view of phyletic gradualism, none of our current species were likely to resemble our ancestors of millions of years ago. But Eldredge and Gould's (1972) findings and reanalysis of the fossil record have resulted in a very different view, now known as the theory of punctuated equilibria (for a less specialized treatment of this theory see Eldredge, 1989). The two have found strong evidence that once a species evolves, it rarely undergoes further change even over periods as long as several million years—the period of equilibrium. At some point, a small subpopulation (usually at the geographic border of the species' range, where selection pressures are likely to be strongest) gives rise to a new species in a relatively short (5,000- to 50,000-year) period. These sharp breaks are the punctuations in the equilibria. To put it in a concrete and more familiar form, 90% of the sea creatures immersed in Monterey Bay, California, today belong to species that were there three million years ago; the skeletal remains of the African antelope species, the Impala, and its distinctive horns in particular, have not changed for 8 million years (Eldredge, 1989).

This does not mean that we can simply assume that a rat or a marine invertebrate or a microbe that we study in the laboratory today is a precise replica of its ancient ancestors, for if we go back more than 10 million years in the fossil record, no evidence of species absolutely identical to those living today can be found. But organisms closely resembling certain contemporary species are abundant among fossils —as far back as a billion years in the case of single-celled organisms.

The conservative nature of evolution and the stability of anatomical structures and biochemical mechanisms over hundreds of millions of years tell us that by studying these diverse contemporary species, we are likely to open a revealing window into the workings of animals that lived many millions of years ago. The molecules and mechanisms that were effective for single cells have been retained and reused in countless species that have evolved since the earliest times.

Over the course of evolution, however, our ancestors have shared with other species the problems in living (e.g., securing protection, nutrition, reproduction) rather than sharing solutions (adaptations) to those problems. The resulting differences among animal species in the way they manage to avoid common dangers may be even more illuminating for our understanding of anxiety than the inherited similarities in the basic neural mechanisms underlying their behavior. This is the kind of perspective that I suspect Buffon, the great 19th-century naturalist, was referring to in the quotation that appears at the beginning of this chapter.

Darwin (1872) was perhaps the first to take a systematic evolutionary approach to the emotions and it is interesting to see how he viewed anxiety. Unlike the prevailing approach today, Darwin did not discuss anxiety in his chapter entitled "Surprise, Astonishment, Fear and Horror." Instead he linked anxiety to "Low Spirits, Grief, Dejection and Despair"—the title of another chapter—stating, "If we expect to suffer we are anxious, if we have no hope of relief, we despair." This view would seem to foreshadow by a century or more our contemporary interest in a link between anxiety and depressive disorders and in the association of anxiety with separation and loss.

In the same year that Darwin published his book on emotion, Douglas Spalding (1872) reported on the responses of young chicks raised by hand in a home laboratory on the estate of Bertrand Russell's parents, Lord and Lady Amberley:

A young turkey, which I had adopted when chirping within the uncracked shell, was on the morning of the tenth day of its life eating a comfortable breakfast from my hand when a young hawk in a cupboard just behind us gave a shrill chip, chip, chip. Like an arrow the young turkey shot to the other side of the room and stood there motionless and dumb with fear [p. 486].

Spalding was more than two generations ahead of Konrad Lorenz in observing what Lorenz (1935) would term an innate releasing mechanism for a fear response—what we call today a strong predisposition to respond to a specific signal of danger. The capacity of certain signals, originating from within as well as outside the animal, to elicit fearful states and behavior can be acquired through individual experience or through evolution of the species. Signal anxiety acquired through experience is readily understandable as a form of learned response. But animals cannot afford to learn all of the possible danger cues: certain signals for danger, particularly in the very young, have to be responded to when the animal first experiences them; otherwise, the animal would not live to reproductive age. Exactly how these highly specific stimulus–response mechanisms were established in evolution through natural selection, without any means for the inheritance of acquired characteristics, remains a puzzle.

Breuer and Freud (1895) cite Darwin as the source of their insight that "emotional expression consists of actions which originally had a meaning and served a purpose." Freud went on to develop and revise his ideas on the nature and origins of anxiety. But throughout he emphasized the role of memory in anxiety. "Affective states have become incorporated in the mind as precipitates of primeval traumatic experience" (Freud, 1926). Because Freud, like so many other scientists of his time, accepted the inheritance of acquired characteristics, that "primeval . . . experience" included that of our ancestors. But Freud emphasized birth and the early period of infant helplessness as the settings in which inevitable separations produce the first anxiety. Later in life, danger situations analogous to birth and early separation induce involuntary automatic anxiety, a more intense anxiety than signal anxiety, which he distinguished as being intentionally reproduced as a signal of danger and a cry for help.

The themes introduced by Darwin, Spalding, and Freud so long ago continue to help us understand the responses that are currently being studied in a variety of species as models of simpler forms of anxiety. The role of specific signal cues, the importance of memory for traumatic events, the occurrence of anxiety in the setting of early separation, and the adaptive value of states of enhanced attention to clues of danger are all illustrated in the examples that follow. I have chosen a single-celled organism, a bacterium; a marine invertebrate, the sea hare; a common vertebrate mammal, the rat; and "one of us," a primate. Using these examples, I hope to illustrate some of the aspects of anxiety that are likely to have evolved first and aspects appearing to be later acquisitions during stages in evolution taken by our ancestors over hundreds of millions of years.

MINIMAL NECESSARY CONDITIONS IN BACTERIA

The essential elements within which an anxiety state might evolve would consist of the following: a means to detect signals, a way to discriminate those that denote danger, and the capacity to initiate behavior that results in avoidance of that danger. Anxiety, as we currently understand it, occurs somewhere within the matrix of those capacities. Definitions of anxiety require several attributes in addition to these basic functions, but if we are looking within the whole sweep of phylogeny for the time the simplest forms of anxiety first appear, then organisms with this sort of basic equipment would be the place to start. Because of our use of such words as detect, discriminate, and initiate to refer to our own conscious processes, such capabilities would appear at first glance to require the evolution of animals with complex brains. But in reality, much simpler processes can be used to carry out the essential functions outlined—processes that can be found in single-celled organisms such as motile bacteria with thin, hairlike flagella. This places the starting point for our evolutionary search to the period between 2 billion and 600 million years ago (Margulis, 1993), before the great Cambrian explosion of life during which the major animal phyla first appeared, about 570 million years ago. Koshland's (1980) discovery of complex behavior in present-day typhoid and coliform bacteria and his elucidation of the underlying biochemical mechanisms provide a vivid demonstration of adaptive behavior that does not require consciousness or even a brain.

Motile bacteria are each equipped with five to seven whiplike flagellae that drive them forward through the fluids that surround them. The flagellae are attached to the cell membrane in a way that enables them to rotate like propellers. Koshland (1980) found that these cell membranes also contain up to 30 receptors. Flagellae and receptors are both widely distributed over the surface of the cell membrane and are functionally linked through a series of intracellular biochemical pathways that are enzyme regulated. The receptors respond to specific molecules and control the actions of the flagellae so that the bacterium can either move forward or stop. For example, in response to certain molecules in the water acting at the membrane receptors, the flagellae all rotate in the same direction, forming a tight bundle that effectively drives the bacterium forward with a single corkscrewlike action. In response to other molecules, the flagellae alternately rotate clockwise and counterclockwise. This causes the flagellae to fly apart and then exert inconsistent and discordant forces at the various individual flagellar attachment sites on the cell membrane so that the bacterium stops and then tumbles in place.

This simple system lets the bacterium move forward in a relatively straight line, then stop, and then move off again in what is likely to be a new direction determined randomly by the orientation of the bacterium at the moment uniform flagellar rotation resumes. This allows the bacterium not only to approach sources of one kind of molecular signal (e.g., sugar) but also to stop and change direction when another kind of specific signal molecule (e.g., a toxin) binds to a receptor. By trial and error it will thus gradually move away from the source of a signal that it is predisposed to avoid. The receptor, its transmembrane protein linkage, and its intracellular signaling mechanism embody the components that are familiar to us as the basis for communication within the brain by neurotransmitter molecules. In the bacterium, they directly control the behavior of the cell in which they exist.

Koshland (1980) found that some of the membrane receptors are constitutive and do not change with the environment, whereas others are inducible by exposure of the bacteria to high concentrations of certain molecules. Nine genes play a role in the formation of receptor types. Thus, responses of the cell are affected by hereditary, environmental, and probabilistic factors in the life processes of cell division, mobility, and replication of the organism. For bacteria in a given culture can be shown to have highly individual response properties despite being identical in heredity and general environment, and such differences have been found to remain for the lifetime of the cell.

The presence of multiple receptors and time-dependent intracellular enzyme systems allows a limited degree of integration and flexibility in responses. For example, when both attractant and repellent molecules are present, bacteria respond as an algebraic function of both influences. After weak stimuli, a return to previous functioning is more rapid than after strong stimuli, and suppression of tumbling in response to positive (e.g., nutrient) gradients is long-lasting, whereas initiation of tumbling in response to negative (e.g., toxic) gradients is extremely rapid in onset. However, the only form of learning appears to be habituation, and bacterial memory is extremely short—about half a second.

Clearly, a single-celled organism has evolved the machinery for an organized behavioral repertoire with some fairly sophisticated capabilities. It can approach weak stimuli that are beneficial, and it can flee from very strong stimuli and those that signal danger. When it stops and tumbles in response to loss of a positive signal or the presence of a negative signal, is it anxious? Certainly we would not want to say so, even though the mental picture of a tumbling creature with flagellar hairs standing on end may be intuitively persuasive. A change in behavioral state has taken place in the bacterium—a state that differs from anxiety primarily in the simplicity of the information and memory processes taking place and in the narrowness of the repertoire of responses available. We have a scaled-down, highly simplified prototype for anxiety that is capable of producing some of the behaviors seen in anxious humans. The presence of these behaviors in so primitive an organism gives us an idea of how basic some state resembling anxiety has been in promoting the survival of life forms.

TWO TYPES OF ACQUIRED ANXIETY IN AN INVERTEBRATE

By traveling forward in time hundreds of millions of years, we reach the origins of the marine invertebrates in the Cambrian period, 500 million years ago. By this time there had evolved organized systems of highly specialized cells, a modern representative of the class being *Aplysia californicus*, the sea hare, studied with such success by Eric Kandel (1983) and his colleagues. Based on specialization of cellular function, organization of groups of these cells into component organs, and integration of the organs into a self-contained system, evolution has increased enormously the variety of behaviors and the range of signals available. That complex organization now has different functional states that are specialized for responding to certain types of signals and for carrying out one or another set of behaviors. Examples of such states are hunger and sexual arousal. After some consideration, we may want to call these motivational or emotional states. The range of signals has been expanded by a crucial new addition—the registration of contingencies between signals and events: learning. By means of the organization of groups of cells specialized for signal processing, this simple nervous system is now capable of responding to an event in terms of its past experience as well as its current environmental input.

The sea hare normally flees from contact with its natural predator, the starfish—a response also carried out (less reliably and less efficiently) by the typhoid bacillus in response to a similar chemical signal. Kandel and coworkers (reviewed in Kandel, 1983) showed that a chemical stimulus that *Aplysia* normally ignored—shrimp juice—could be made to signal an escape response by associating it repeatedly with electric shock, the laboratory equivalent of a starfish attack. But they went further than that by showing that after such an experience, shrimp juice, when encountered a second time, induced a state change in *Aplysia* during which other defensive responses (not involved in the original training) were enhanced, such as gill withdrawal and the release of protective clouds of ink. This state change also involved a reduction in appetitive behaviors such as feeding. An innocuous event had thus become a signal eliciting an anticipatory state in which responses to threat were intensified and in which what we might call pleasurable behaviors were inhibited; a simple form of anticipatory anxiety had been induced.

The sea hare in the previous experiments behaved normally after training when shrimp juice was not present. In the second procedure, a prototype of chronic anxiety was produced in which the animal showed a persistent state of altered responsiveness similar to that induced by shrimp juice but without requiring a danger signal. A series of unavoidable electrical shocks were used (sensitization), which produced a change in response repertoire over a period of several weeks following the traumatic events. During this persistent state, defensive and escape responses were exaggerated, and responses to positive events, blunted; an abnormal behavioral repertoire had been established that resembled a form of chronic diffuse anxiety.

These two simple paradigms—one for anticipatory, signaled anxiety and the other for chronic, generalized anxiety—have become the focus of intense efforts to work out the neural and molecular mechanisms for the altered states and their novel behavioral responses. The strategy has been to concentrate on one of the associated response systems—the one mediating enhanced gill withdrawal—because the nerve cells and connections underlying this response have been well worked out. The changes induced by both procedures have been traced to a single connection within the relatively simple wiring diagram of the animal. It is within the terminals of the sensory neurons, where they synapse upon the motor neurons for the gill withdrawal response, that increased release of the familiar neurotransmitter serotonin (as a result of the conditioning) sets in motion a process called presynaptic facilitation. Two general classes of molecular events have been identified as responsible for this facilitation: the short-term changes induced by the learned signal are the product of a biochemical cascade within the nerve terminal that alters membrane channels upon which neurotransmitter release on to the motor cell depends. The long-term changes involve the same biochemical cascade within the cell, but also involve altered gene activity and new protein synthesis, resulting in structural enlargement of the synaptic area between sensory and motor cells. Each of these different mechanisms enhances the likelihood and intensity of motor cell activity in response to a given intensity of sensory stimulation.

Study of the structural and gene activity changes underlying long-term facilitation has been aided by the development of methods for studying identified neurons maintained in dissociated cell culture (Mayford et al., 1992). Although long-term effects depend on new protein synthesis, and the signaled anticipatory learning does not, the mechanisms for the two types of synaptic change appear to be linked.

The intracellular trigger for the altered gene activity responsible for the long-term changes appears to be a portion or subunit of the same protein kinase enzyme that is at the center of the short-term biochemical cascade. This subunit is transported within the cell to the nucleus, where it interacts with regulatory genes and initiates the synthesis of new protein for the structural changes.

The neurotransmitter serotonin, the components of the biochemical cascade, and the enzyme protein kinase are all conserved by evolution and are key elements underlying brain activity in higher animals, including humans. In *Aplysia*, the short- and long-term presynaptic facilitation that was found to underlie anticipatory and chronic anxiety-like states has become a particularly promising model for understanding the molecular mechanisms for memory. This is a turn of events that Freud would have enjoyed, considering his emphasis on the role of remembered states in human anxiety.

SEPARATION ANXIETY IN A SMALL MAMMAL

Turning the clock forward again rapidly, we come to the age of the dinosaurs, 100 million to 200 million years ago, when our ancestors—small terrestrial mammals—were to be found on dry land, scurrying through the undergrowth of the forest floor out of sight of the great reptiles. Only the most adaptive of them survived the great extinction of species that brought an end to the age of the dinosaurs 65 million years ago. Of today's small mammals, one of the most successful orders consists of the rodents, and a domesticated strain—the laboratory rat—is the species we know the most about next to the human. For this reason I have chosen this animal to represent our early mammalian ancestors.

MacLean (1985) studied the probable evolution of the brain that accompanied the splitting off of mammals from reptilian ancestors 250 million years ago. He argues that the evolution of the limbic system of the mammalian brain distinguishes mammals from all modern reptiles, endowing mammals with sets of novel behaviors as well as this novel brain structure. According to MacLean, the three crucial behavioral attributes that evolved in mammals are play, parental behavior, and the separation cry, all of which he points out are absent in modern-day reptiles. MacLean provides neuroanatomical and neurophysiological evidence supporting his theory that the presence of these behaviors in modern-day mammals is made possible by the specialized neural networks of the limbic system and their connections to the cerebral cortex and the midbrain. The evolution of social relationships based on mutual attachment in mammals provides a new set of behaviors, motivational systems, and dangers within which a new variant of anxiety can evolve. The infant's separation cry is a communication to the mother with adaptive value; it is also the manifestation of a state of distress that may constitute the first innate anxiety state to have evolved.

Here the cues are not learned as they are by the sea hare; rather, rat infants respond to their very first experience of separation. Evolution has endowed mammalian infants with a response to a set of cues (separation) that represent the potential for a number of actual dangers. The uncertain nature of the danger and the lack of control inherent in the loss of the parent and of familiar surroundings add new dimensions to this form of anxiety that were not present in the simpler forms of anxiety elicited in marine invertebrates in the previous example. Thus the evolution of prolonged immaturity of offspring, together with the related period of close parental care created the basis for a new form of anxiety in this relatively primitive mammal, a form that seems to resemble the separation anxiety we are familiar with in children and even in adult humans.

In 1956 Austrian ethologist Wolfgang Schleidt and his student Zippelius discovered that young mice emitted short bursts of ultra-high-frequency sound, similar to the recently discovered ultrasonic pulses of bats that had provided an animal analog for the sonar used so effectively by the Allies for antisubmarine patrol in World War II. Zippelius and Schleidt (1956) found that these sounds were readily produced by removing a mouse pup from its home nest and placing it on a laboratory bench top in front of the special microphone and amplifiers needed to record ultra-high-frequency sound (higher than 20,000 cycles/sec). However, these ultrasounds did not appear to be involved in echolocation as they were in bats, and Schleidt proposed that they might provide directional cues for the mother to locate young accidentally displaced from the nest. This was soon shown to be one of the functions of those calls. But their relation to separation from social companions or to a separation anxiety state was not immediately apparent to researchers.

The emphasis of early research on this phenomenon was on the environmental events (such as cold, rough handling, altered substrate odor, and texture and novelty) that rat or mouse infants were responding to when they initiated calling. I became interested in this behavior after I found that rat pups showed other behavioral and physiological responses to separation from their mother. I obtained a bat detector from England, which by selective tuning and electronic processing transduces any form of sound between 15 and 100 kilohertz to the frequency range of human hearing—between 2 and 10 kHz. In a series of studies, my colleague Harry Shair and I (Hofer and Shair, 1978) found that a pup emitted these calls, even in the home cage nest, if all of the littermates and the mother were removed, showing that separation from social companions was a key element in eliciting such vocalizations. Next, we found that a pup alone in an unfamiliar place would greatly reduce or cease calling if a littermate or the mother were placed with it, even if the mother were completely passive (anesthetized).

We now had a behavioral indicator for a state induced rapidly by separation, one that could be roughly quantified. And we had a means of rapidly terminating the state by what appeared to be a form of contact comfort. Because the separation-induced state depended on the effect social companions had on pups, we embarked on a search for the cues to which the pup was responding during contact comfort responses and the sensory pathways by which the pup was sensing those cues (Hofer and Shair, 1980, 1991). We found that after the neonatal period, pups appeared to be responding to texture, odor, and temperature in a cumulative fashion, with contour and size being additional factors. Artificial-model surrogates with the greatest number of these modalities were the most effective in reducing call rate and in eliciting contact. Pups appeared to use their snout and vibrissal sensory hairs to process thermal and textural cues provided during contact and to use their highly developed olfactory senses to respond from greater distances. It was sufficient that the pups have only one of those senses intact in order to show a normal quieting response—an example of parallel sensory processing. When both pathways were interrupted, the contact comfort response was absent.

By this time we had a better idea of how the pup recognized its social companions and some understanding of the sensory processes by which it could become aware of separation from them. The rate of calling in these situations, we thought, might give us a rough quantitative estimate of the intensity of the state induced by the experience of separation. Evidence from other lines of research supported the inference that these ultrasonic calls indicated a state of distress. Cold, rough handling, electric shock, and cessation of regular reward in a learning task (Amsel et al., 1977) elicited ultrasonic calls; oral delivery of sugars or milk (Blass and Fitzgerald, 1988), as well as warmth, markedly quieted pups.

But as scientific skeptics, we would like to ask whether rat pups really experience separation negatively and whether the state induced by separation involves a change in the way the pup responds to new information, as was found during the state induced by sensitization in

Aplysia and as is familiar to us from our own experiences with anxiety. Experiments by researchers interested in early learning have given affirmative answers to both of those questions. Isolated rat pups will learn difficult maze problems in order to get back to their mother, and for a separated pup, merely experiencing short periods of contact with the mother acts as a powerful reinforcer. Furthermore, cues associated with separation are strongly avoided when encountered subsequently. These findings show us that rat pups dislike separation and are strongly predisposed to respond to cues associated with reunion. In addition, Spear, Kucharski, and Hoffman (1985) found a variety of associations, discriminations, and tasks that rat pups learn less well when they are separated from their home cage than when they are provided with familiar nest cues during the learning experience. This was not a simple generalized interference with functioning, however. As in human anxiety, rat pups form some associations *more* readily when isolated. They learned to associate novel tastes and odors with illness and then to avoid those cues (taste-aversion learning) two to three times more strongly when separated than when the learning was carried out in the home cage.

These striking effects of separation and of home cage contextual cues on learning are not seen in older juvenile or adult rats, which also do not show the vocalization response to separation. Thus there is growing evidence of altered information processing in young rats during separation. It appears that perceptual and cognitive alterations are characteristic of the state of anxiety; they are present in a simple form in *Aplysia*, and evolve more complex manifestations in animals such as the rodent and primate with more elaborate brains.

For those most interested in the neurobiological mechanisms of anxiety, studies on drugs and neuropeptide modulators have provided the most compelling evidence that the isolation distress state of young rats provides a useful animal model of anxiety (for a recent review see Miczek, Tornatsky, and Vivian, 1991). In studies during the past 5 or 6 years, it has been found that most major classes of drugs that are useful in human anxiety have powerful and selective inhibitory effects on isolation-induced ultrasonic calls in rat pups, without affecting other behaviors or inducing signs of sedation. Even more convincing, synthetic compounds known to produce severe anxiety in human volunteers (such as pentylenetetrazol and the inverse agonist benzodiazepines) greatly increase the call rate in isolated pups and can even elicit calling in the home cage with littermates (Carden, Bortot, and Hofer, 1993).

The benzodiazepines were the first anxiolytics found to be effective on isolation distress in rat pups, and Insel, Gelhard, and Miller (1989) found autoradiographic evidence that an endogenous ligand at the GABA-benzodiazepine receptor complex in the cerebral cortex and hippocampus may play a role in rat pup isolation distress. Morphine and more recently synthesized specific mu and delta opiate receptor ligands decrease calling, whereas a specific kappa receptor ligand increases calling in isolated pups (Carden, Barr, and Hofer, 1991). Kappa opiate receptor activation even causes pups in contact with littermates in the home cage nest to vocalize vigorously. From this it seems possible that endogenous opiates play a role in both the initiation and the reduction of isolation distress vocalization. This possibility is strengthened by our finding that naltrexone, an opiate receptor blocker, acting primarily as mu receptors, prevents companion comfort response to littermates in young rats (Carden and Hofer, 1990). This finding suggests that social companions exert some of their comforting effect by stimulating endogenous mu opiate release in young that have become displaced from the nest.

Winslow and Insel (1990) have shown that rat pups respond to clinically effective anxiolytic drugs that are active primarily on the serotonin system, such as the reuptake inhibitor clomipramine and the 5HT1A receptor agonist buspirone. Finally, neuropeptides such as cholecystokinin, implicated in human satiety following ingestion of food, reduce ultrasonic calling in young rats (Weller and Blass, 1988). More recently, Insel (1992) has proposed oxytocin as a neuropeptide underlying a broad range of affiliative behaviors. Oxytocin is present in maternal milk and may well be absorbed by nursing pups. When given to isolated rat pups, it reduces calling.

There are, however, some neurochemical differences between the separation anxiety state in young rats and that in adult humans. For example, drugs effective on central adrenergic systems underlying anxiety in humans and adult rats, such as clonidine and yohimbine, have paradoxical effects in infant rats (clonidine enhancing and yohimbine reducing vocalization rates). Only after 17 days of age, when the infant separation distress response is waning and the juvenile period begins, do these drugs have the effects on vocalization that would be expected on the basis of their actions in adult models of anxiety in rats and humans (Kehoe and Harris, 1989). It is believed that late maturation of one component of the central adrenergic system (the autoreceptors) underlies this developmental drug response change.

From the evidence we have to date, it seems reasonable to view the isolation calls of the infant rat as indicating a simple form of separation anxiety. Because the subject is readily approachable experimentally, we can ask questions that cannot be posed in the human. For example, we can focus on the underlying neural systems at the microanatomical, cellular, and molecular levels. Such research should begin to tell an interesting story in the months and years to come.

But other issues are also of interest, such as the nature and extent of early experience required for the acquisition of these responses. We used an artificial rearing procedure and found that rat pups raised from birth in single styrofoam cups floating in a warm-water bath and fed through implanted gastric cannulas showed high rates of calling (even higher than normal) when separated from their familiar artificial nest (Hofer, Shair, and Murowchik, 1989). This is consistent with a wealth of other evidence that infants of several species, including humans, form attachments to their inanimate surroundings. We expected, however, that these pups, reared without social companions, would show no contact comfort response. And we planned to be able to introduce certain kinds of social and feeding interactions as supplements to the limited experience of artificial rearing in order to learn which developmental events were necessary to establish the contact comfort response. To our surprise, we found that 2-week-old pups with no prior experience with their mother since the day of their birth, showed highly effective contact comfort responses on their first encounter with her. However, they were not unchanged by their socially deprived rearing experience; their isolation response call rate was twice as high as normal. In following them to adulthood, these artificially reared pups continued to show appreciable levels of isolation-calling in the juvenile and especially the pubertal periods, whereas in normal rat pups, as in other species, separation cries occur only during infancy.

It seems likely then that a strong predisposition exists in rat pups to respond to certain olfactory, thermal, and tactile cues reducing or terminating a separation anxiety state. Whether this is indeed an innate response or whether very early experiences (e.g., birth and the first nursing bout) may be necessary for its expression remain to be discovered. In that connection, it is worth noting that British ethologist Peter Hepper (1986a,b), has established that rat pups can discriminate from strangers their own littermates, their own mother, and even close kin (e.g., father, siblings) they have never interacted with. They accomplish this by olfaction, a sense capable of distinguishing genetically coded odorant molecules. Clearly, the advanced capabilities of rodent olfaction allow even greater specificity of kin selection than that available to the human, thus strengthening the possibility of an innate specific attachment system in this species.

Because this chapter concerns evolutionary processes, we should ask: how might vocalization have first evolved as a manifestation of the separation state, so that the mother's retrieval behavior could then act selectively to enhance survival of vocal young and establish this important mother–infant communication system? A possible answer to the question involves the close natural association of cold temperature with displacement from mother and home nest in small mammals, for exposure to cold is known to be a major cue for the elicitation of ultrasonic calls in isolated rat pups. Our language represents a long-standing appreciation of that connection in such phrases as "left out in the cold," "cold fear," and "shivering with terror." Warmth is connected with emotions of attachment and closeness. We have recently found that when rat pups are made severely hypothermic (25°C below normal) and recover at room temperature (a routine surgical anesthesia procedure), they start to emit ultrasound while still comatose—at surgical levels of anesthesia (Hofer and Shair, 1992). These hypothermic ultrasounds are produced by the same laryngeal mechanism as isolation calls and have similar acoustic properties. Although they are emitted at a slower tempo than isolation calls, due to the slow respiratory rates of pups at such low temperatures, rat mothers respond to hearing such calls by searching, and then use them as directional cues (Brunelli, Shair, and Hofer, 1994). However, vocalizing may not have originated as a signal to the mother, but rather in a physiological role. We found that when hypothermic pups were devocalized (by cutting the nerves to the larynx or bypassing the larynx with a small plastic tube), they did not rewarm nearly as fast as vocal pups: they developed fluid in their lungs (pulmonary edema), and some failed to recover if left alone. A physiologic role for ultrasonic vocalization in supporting thermoregulatory response was first proposed in 1990 by Blumberg and Alberts, but has since been shown to be inconsequential at more normal body temperatures (Hofer and Shair, 1993).

From this set of findings one can speculate that the pulmonary, laryngeal, and neural systems underlying the separation cry may have had an earlier role in evolution as part of a physiological defense against severe cold. The central position of words connoting warmth in descriptions of close social relationships, as well as words connoting cold in descriptions of separation and the anxiety that accompanies separation and loss, may be testimony to the ancient role of the separation cry during periods in our evolution when severe thermal stresses were unavoidable (e.g., the ice ages) and when the underlying physiological effects of laryngeal activity conferred a strong selective advantage.

If early experiences constitute the first anxiety in our lives and if anxiety in adulthood reevokes those early experiences, as Freud and

others have supposed, then knowledge about this relatively simple
form of anxiety in rat pups may help us understand the more complex
forms and manifestations of anxiety in primates such as our own
species. Already in the rat pup this state involves a range of cognitive
changes, a communicative role for the affect display and a neural substrate involving all of the major systems known to mediate clinical
anxiety. The central role of separation responses in early social development and attachment raises a number of interesting questions about
the early development of anxiety states, some of which will be taken
up in a new species in the next and last example.

THE DEVELOPMENT OF ANXIETY IN MONKEYS

We now advance our time control to a more recent period, 5 million to
10 million years ago, when our ancestors could finally be classified as
primates. The following example involves the bonnet macaque monkeys studied by Rosenblum and his coworkers (Rosenblum and
Paully, 1984; Andrews and Rosenblum, 1991). Rosenblum has worked
with nonhuman primates both in the laboratory and in the field for
many years, and in the studies I will describe, he drew on his field
experience to create a set of conditions in the laboratory that altered
mother–infant interaction over a prolonged time period in such a way
as to reliably produce an abnormally anxious juvenile monkey. This
effect involved separation but added to it certain qualities of relationship that acted on the development of systems that mediate anxiety.
This brings us to the kinds of issues and the level of complexity that
we are familiar with in clinical work with anxious patients.

The brain of the primate is of course distinguished from other
mammals by the size of the cerebral cortex, which has made possible
a degree of complexity in social organization not seen in other mammals. Primate mother–infant interaction involves a bewildering array
of subtle behavioral responses based on exquisite timing, complex
remembered expectations, and coordination resulting in such qualities
as synchrony, harmony, and attunement. Conversely, disruptions can
result in subtle forms of missed contingencies, unmatched behavioral
intensities, and failed expectations. The infant's emotional states of
pleasure and unpleasure appear to be linked to these aspects of the
relationship and not simply to the presence or absence of contact, as in
the rat. Degrees of uncertainty in expectation and ambiguity of meaning can be generated in such interactions and remembered within the
enlarged memory stores of the primate cerebral cortex. The early nonverbal interactions between members of other primate species are

strikingly similar to those between humans, so that studies of these behaviors in an animal model may enable us to understand much more precisely how alterations in its workings might lead to the development of anxiety states in offspring.

What Rosenblum and his colleagues (Rosenblum and Paully, 1984; Andrews and Rosenblum, 1991) did was simply to change the way food was offered to the monkey mothers of young infants. In addition to the usual laboratory situation in which food was always freely available (low foraging demand), another condition was created (high foraging demand) in which the food crackers were buried in 6 inches of wood shavings in pans behind a number of different access holes. There was always enough food, but in the high-foraging-demand situation, it required that the monkey mothers spend a total of about 2 hours of the day searching to obtain the food, a minimal total time requirement. Some interesting differences emerged between groups housed under stable low- or high-foraging demands, but no marked disruptions were produced by the foraging requirement. However, when the monkeys were subjected to unsignaled changes between high- and low-demand conditions in which 2-week periods of each condition were alternated without external cues, major changes emerged in adult interactions, in the mother–infant relationships, and in the infants themselves. Among adults, there was less mutual grooming and more dominance-related behavior, creating a quality of increased tension in the group. Contact between mothers and infants was increased overall, but the number of times contact was broken and then reestablished increased sharply. This pattern was found to be the result of heightened levels of maternal efforts to separate from their infants and of infants' efforts to reestablish contact. In the variable foraging-demand situation, infant play levels gradually fell behind infants in the stable-demand groups, and those infants also showed lower levels of object exploration when away from their mother. When with their mother, they showed increased clinging and less playful interactions. Immediately after maternal departures, only infants in the variable-demand group showed periods of self-clasping and a passive hunched position reminiscent of the depressive response seen after many hours of complete separation. After 14 weeks, dyads from low- and variable-foraging-demand groups were challenged by being placed in novel environments. The decrease in episodes of infants leaving their mother that is usually induced by novel surroundings was much more pronounced in infants in the variable-demand situation, and they did not recover with time as did the others. These infants also explored inanimate objects less and played hardly at all. In general, young monkeys that had experienced 3 to 4 months of anxious attachment appeared to respond as if they had become chronically anxious.

The foregoing primate model of experimental genesis of an anxiety state in early development clearly involves factors similar to those that have been inferred from clinical studies of human infants and mother–infant relationships (e.g., unpredictable outside demands and lack of control). In addition, the behavioral and psychological processes likely to explain the observed behaviors are at a level of complexity found in humans. Yet the events are reproducible, can be studied for a few months in the laboratory, and are available for analytic experiments capable of revealing the underlying behavioral and neurochemical mechanisms. Such work is in its early stages, but already, intriguing differences have been found in the responses of anxious juveniles to pharmacologic probes in the adrenergic and serotonergic receptor systems. The relationship of those early experiences to anxiety in adulthood, among many other issues, remains to be explored.

CONCLUSIONS AND PERSPECTIVE

By examining these few examples from widely diverse life forms, we gain an appreciation of the differences that have evolved in how organisms successfully utilize a behavioral state—anxiety—in avoiding threats to their survival. In the course of trying to understand how our ancestors may have accomplished this, we challenge our own concepts of anxiety. Readers should notice I did not offer a definition of anxiety but rather let the description of the behavioral processes at work in the four examples give readers a basis for forming their own definition. The examples show how the underlying information processing machinery available to the organism alters the definition of anxiety that one can propose at each level of evolutionary complexity. The examples also show how the evolution of prolonged parental care during early development in our ancestral small mammal predecessors plays a crucial role in shaping today's ideas of what is essential to an understanding of anxiety in humans.

This long view of phylogeny seems to tell us that there are many forms of anxiety. Correspondingly, because individual humans are so different from each other, it seems likely that even within our species, anxiety is likely to exist in a variety of forms. But in order for the word "anxiety" to be useful to us, we must have some sense of its irreducible core meaning. And here again, an evolutionary behavioral approach is useful, for it provides us with a graded series of examples, each of which has one or two or several of the basic components and we can try out various alternatives. I have described only one of the very early forms and asked whether the tumbling of bacteria might represent the first anxiety state to evolve. If readers were inclined to agree with that notion earlier in this chapter, they should now consider the fact that bacteria tumble also once they have arrived in an area with optimal concentration of a familiar nutrient. In that case they actively metabolize the substrate and avoid moving away from the location where such metabolizing is most efficiently carried out. Therefore we would have to infer that tumbling represented an intensely pleasurable state. Clearly, even for bacteria, any definition of anxiety cannot simply depend on a description of ongoing behavior; it also requires some consideration of context.

Anxiety would appear to represent a stage in the process by which an individual adapts to the presence of threats to its survival. That stage is omitted when it comes to the rapid responses to imminent injury, which are mediated by sensorimotor reflex pathways. As soon as animals evolved more than one kind of response to danger and receptors that could detect cues in advance of imminent injury, it became advantageous for them to enter an intervening state between stimulus and response during which information processing and response thresholds could be specialized for assessing and responding to those cues for danger. That state enabled individuals to make responses that were well suited to a variety of different dangers and timed to be maximally effective. The very early evolution of highly specific information processing capability in the form of the membrane receptors of bacteria emphasizes the central role of evaluative processes as forerunners of altered cognitive processing in anxiety. And as early as the marine invertebrates, there evolved a pattern of selective enhancement of certain behavioral responses with inhibition of other behaviors as part of their intervening anxiety state.

The very early appearance of learning and memory in the simple neural networks of the first marine animals is now widely appreciated. That combination of capacities both to learn and to enter a specialized information processing and motor response state is likely to have been a basic prerequisite for survival since early stages of evolution. It marks the origin of the capacity for the state we call anxiety as being very old indeed. One could say that all that has happened in the course of our own evolution is represented by the addition of massive degrees of complexity to each element in the simple invertebrate system outlined earlier. But such vast increases in complexity have a way of creating new, emergent properties: The evolution of increasingly complex social structure added a whole new host of dangers that are not present for bacteria or sea hares. The evolution of the limbic system of the brain made possible the enormous amplification of the possible kinds of intervening emotional states, creating a variety of qualitatively different anxieties. The evolution of the cerebral cortex vastly expanded the capabilities for learning and memory so that long-past experiences as well as recent ones play important roles in eliciting anxiety and in shaping information processing during the state. The extent of parallel processing that became possible in the primate brain increased the extent of self-regulation within the system to the point that self-awareness and what we call consciousness emerged. Those evolutions created a whole new order of response to anxiety, namely, the experience of it. Finally, the advent of symbolic communication in language made it possible for us to communicate that experience to each other, which in turn led to a whole new order of interactions that can alleviate or perpetuate anxiety and can avoid or create new dangers. It is small wonder that our own experience of anxiety, when it reaches our conscious mind, is deeply imbued with uncertainty, ambiguity, and a sense of being overwhelmed or losing control.

An evolutionary perspective would thus seem to lead us to a sense of the core meaning of anxiety as a behavioral state that occurs in response to signals of danger and that entails a special set of response tendencies that have resulted in avoidance of similar dangers during events in the organism's past development and in the evolution of the species. The nature of the signals, of the dangers, of the responses, and of the events in the individual's past history changes during evolution and varies across species and even across individuals. As humans evolved, the capacities of our ancestors for remembering and reflecting on previous experience increased enormously. Most recently, our ancestors developed an inner awareness that they could represent in language and then communicate to others. Finally now, in preparing this volume, we are trying to use our abilities to learn, our cultural heritage of accumulated knowledge, and our ability to communicate with each other not only to avoid dangers but also to understand anxiety itself and thus overcome its pathological manifestations.

REFERENCES

Amsel, A., Radek, C. C., Graham, M. & Letz, R. (1977), Ultrasound emission in infant rats as an indicant of arousal during appetitive learning and extinction. *Science*, 197:492–495.

Andrews, M. W. & Rosenblum, L. A. (1991), Attachment in monkey infants raised in variable- and low-demand environments. *Child Dev.*, 62:686–693.

Blass, E. M. & Fitzgerald, E. (1988), Milk-induced analgesia and comforting in 10-day-old rats: Opioid mediation. *Pharmacol. Biochem. Behav.*, 29:9–13.

Blumberg, M. S. & Alberts, J. R. (1990), Ultrasonic vocalizations by rat pups in the cold: An acoustic by-product of laryngeal braking? *Behav. Neurosci.* 104:808–817.

Breuer, J. & Freud, S. (1895), Studies on Hysteria. *Standard Edition*, 2. London: Hogarth Press, 1955.

Brunelli, S. A., Shair, H. N. & Hofer, M. A. (1994), Hypothermic vocalizations of rat pups (Rattus Norvegicus) elicit and direct maternal search behavior. *J. Compar. Psychol.*, 108:299–303.

Carden, S. E., Barr, G. A. & Hofer, M. A. (1991), Differential effects of specific opioid receptor agonists on rat pup isolation calls. *Dev. Brain Res.*, 62:17–22.

——— Bortot, A. T. & Hofer, M. A. (1993), Ultrasonic vocalizations are elicited from rat pups in the home cage by pentylenetetrizol and U50,488, but not by Naltrexone. *Behav. Neurosci.*, 107:851–859.

——— & Hofer, M. A. (1990), Socially mediated reduction of isolation distress in rat pups is blocked by naltrexone but not by RO 15-1788. *Behav. Neurosci.*, 104:457–463.

Darwin, C. (1872), *The Expression of the Emotions in Man and Animals* (repr.) Chicago: University of Chicago Press, 1965.

Eldredge, N. (1989), *Time Frames.* Princeton, NJ: Princeton University Press.

——— & Gould, S. J. (1972), Models in paleobiology. In: *Punctuated Equilibria*, ed. T. J. M. Schopf. San Francisco: Freeman, Cooper, pp. 82–115.

Freud, S. (1926), Inhibitions, symptoms and anxiety, *Standard Edition*, 20:87–172. London: Hogarth Press, 1959.

Hepper, P. G. (1986a), Parental recognition in the rat. *Quart. J. Exper. Psychol.*, 38B:151–160.

——— (1986b), Kin recognition: Function and mechanisms. *Biol. Rev.*, 61:63–93.

Hofer, M. A. & Shair, H. N. (1978), Ultrasonic vocalization during social interaction and isolation in 2-week-old rats. *Dev. Psychobiol.*, 11:495–504.

——— & ——— (1980), Sensory processes in the control of isolation-induced ultrasonic vocalization by two-week-old rats. *J. Compar. Physiol. Psychol.*, 94:271–279.

——— & ——— (1991), Trigeminal and olfactory pathways mediating isolation distress and companion comfort responses in rat pups. *Behav. Neurosci.*, 105:699–706.

——— & ——— (1992), Ultrasonic vocalization by rat pups during recovery from deep hypothermia. *Dev. Psychobiol.*, 25:511–523.

——— & ——— (1993), Ultrasonic vocalization, laryngeal braking and thermoregulation in rat pups: A reappraisal. *Behav. Neurosci.*, 107:354–362.

——— ——— & Murowchik, E. (1989), Isolation distress and maternal comfort responses of two-week-old rat pups reared in social isolation. *Dev. Psychobiol.*, 22:553–566.

Insel, T. R. (1992), Oxytocin—a neuropeptide for affiliation: Evidence from behavioral, receptor autoradiographic and comparative studies. *Psychoneuroendocrinology*, 17:3–35.

——— Gelhard, R. E. & Miller, L. P. (1989), Rat pup isolation distress and the brain benzodiazepine receptor. *Dev. Psychobiol.*, 22:509–525.

Kandel, E. R. (1983), From metapsychology to molecular biology: Explorations into the nature of anxiety. *Amer. J. Psychiat.*, 140:1277–1293.

Kehoe, P. & Harris, J. C. (1989), Ontogeny of noradrenergic effects on ultrasonic vocalizations in rat pups. *Behav. Neurosci.*, 103:1099–1107.

Koshland, D. E. (1980), Bacterial chemotaxis in relation to neurobiology. *Ann. Rev. Neurosci.*, 3:43–75.

Lorenz, K. (1935), The conspecific as the eliciting factor for social behaviour patterns. In: *Studies in Animal and Human Behaviour, Vol. 1*, ed. K. Lorenz (trans. R. Martin). Cambridge, MA: Harvard University Press, 1976, pp. 10–258.

MacLean, P. D. (1985), Brain evolution relating to family, play and the separation call. *Arch. Gen. Psychiat.*, 42:405–417.

Margulis, L. (1993), *Symbiosis in Cell Evolution*. New York: Freeman.

Mayford, M., Barzilai, A., Keller, F., Schacher, S. & Kandel, E. R. (1992), Modulation of an NCAM-related adhesion molecule with long term synaptic plasticity in *Aplysia*. *Science*, 256:638–644.

Miczek, K. A., Tornatsky, W. & Vivian, J. (1991), Ethology and neuropharmacology: Rodent ultrasounds. *Adv. Pharmacol. Sci.*, 1991:409–429.

Rosenblum, L. A. & Paully, G. S. (1984), The effects of varying environmental demands on maternal and infant behavior. *Child Dev.*, 55:305–314.

Spalding, D. (1872), On instinct. *Nature*, 6:485–486.

Spear, N., Kucharski, D. & Hoffman, H. (1985), Contextual influences on conditioned taste aversions in the developing rat. *Ann. N.Y. Acad. Sci.*, 443:42–53.

Weller, A. & Blass, E. M. (1988), Behavioral evidence for cholecystokinin-opiate interactions in neonatal rats. *Amer. J. Physiol.*, 255:R901-R907.

Winslow, J. T. & Insel, T. R. (1990), Serotonergic and catecholaronergic reuptake inhibitors have opposite effects on the ultrasonic isolation calls of rat pups. *Neuropsychopharmacology*, 3:51–59.

Zippelius, H.-M & Schleidt, W. M. (1956), Ultraschall-laute bei jung en mausen [Ultrasonic vocalization in infant mice]. *Naturwissenschaften*, 43:502.

3 Neuroanatomy and Neurotransmitter Function in Panic Disorder

Jack M. Gorman
Laszlo A. Papp
Jeremy D. Coplan

Although the idea that panic attacks are a distinct form of anxiety is more than 30 years old, it is only since the 1980s that scientists and clinicians have regarded panic disorder as an actual diagnostic entity. Even today, many maintain that panic attacks are merely an extreme form of generalized anxiety; this position is especially prevalent in the United Kingdom. A few clinicians and investigators also believe that panic disorder is simply a complication of depression.

The view taken by the DSM-III and DSM-III-R in the United States, however, is that the panic attack is a unique phenomenon. Patients who experience four or more panic attacks in a 4-week period are given the diagnosis of panic disorder, as are patients who have a single panic attack followed by at least a month of continuous anxiety about the possible occurrence of further attacks. A panic attack must include several purely physical symptoms, such as rapid heartbeat, difficulty breathing, gastrointestinal upset, and faintness, as well as a subjective sense of terror and impending doom. Between attacks, patients with panic disorder may have anticipatory anxiety, fearing the next attack. Attacks themselves generally last from 10 to 30 minutes.

Panic disorder is distinguished from generalized anxiety disorder (GAD), which involves continuously high levels of worry and anxiety without panic attacks for a period of months. Even though it is true that many patients with GAD go on to develop panic disorder, there are important distinctions between the two conditions. Most notably, patients with panic disorder are far more preoccupied with physical symptoms, whereas patients with GAD are more concerned with cognitive symptoms. Panic disorder patients typically first present to nonpsychiatric physicians, often in emergency rooms, insisting that they are in the midst of a catastrophic medical event such as a heart attack or stroke. GAD patients, on the other hand, are more likely to present to a mental health professional complaining of worries, tension, and the inability to relax.

Another important distinction must be made between panic disorder and depression. There is no doubt that panic patients are at high risk to develop depression during their lifetime and that many depressed patients experience panic attacks. Most antipanic medications are also antidepressants, and several studies have shown a possible genetic overlap between depression and panic. Nevertheless, panic disorder patients frequently do not meet clinical or research criteria for depression, lacking the consistently depressed mood, anhedonia, and vegetative signs necessary to a diagnosis of affective disorder. Some studies actually suggest that high levels of depression make a panic disorder patient less likely to respond to antidepressant medication, and several family studies clearly demonstrate the distinction between panic and depression. It is important to watch for depression among panic patients, but equally important not to lump the two conditions together.

Begun in the late 1960s by Donald Klein, the original movement to separate panic disorder from generalized anxiety disorder came about from three sources of information. First, it was noted that panic attacks responded to the tricyclic antidepressant drug imipramine. At the time, it was thought that benzodiazepines such as diazepam (Valium) are effective for GAD but not panic attacks. Hence, the idea of a pharmacological dissection of panic from GAD arose. As we shall see, that idea must now be modified. Second, it was discovered that panic attacks could be provoked in the laboratory in patients with panic disorder but not in normal volunteers by infusion of sodium lactate. This appeared to indicate that the panic attack was a unique, chemically responsive phenomenon, an idea that still holds. Finally, phenomenologists noted that panic attacks, but not GAD, frequently lead to phobic avoidance in which the patient feared situations in which panic attacks might occur and access to emergency help be limited. Complete phobic avoidance is known as agoraphobia, first described by the Viennese psychiatrist Westphal.

For almost 20 years, most research into panic disorder focused on the search for a biological abnormality. Investigators likened panic attacks to seizures, certain they would ultimately locate a part of the brain that malfunctioned and thereby triggered the attacks. Anticipatory anxiety and phobic avoidance were seen as learned behavior consequent to the attacks themselves. At first, the main line of research consisted in the attempt to understand why lactate infusion provoked panic. Later, it was discovered that stimulation of the brain neurotransmitter noradrenaline also provoked attacks, and so a noradrenergic hypothesis for panic was developed. The brain's center of noradrenergic activity is a small area of the brain stem called the locus coeruleus. Proponents of the noradrenergic hypothesis posited that the locus coeruleus is the panic center of the brain and that it fires abnormally to provoke attacks.

More recently, psychotherapy theorists have advanced sophisticated hypotheses linking panic attacks to learning and psychoanalytic theory. They note that no discrete biological lesion has yet been convincingly proven to be involved in panic and that panic patients display a particular set of cognitive errors and unconscious conflicts that may have etiological significance.

It has been our contention that anxiety disorders represent an exquisite interplay of both higher and lower brain function. Higher brain function, located in the frontal cortex, mediates cognition and complex associative learning. Lower brain function, located in the brain stem and limbic cortex of the brain, mediates visceral function such as heart rate and respiration as well as memory. What, in our opinion, is often labelled psychological really represents cortically mediated events, and what is often labelled biological represents brain stem– and limbic lobe–mediated events. A comprehensive theory of panic disorder, therefore, should include careful reference to both. This chapter therefore presents our most current thinking on brain function in panic disorder.

THE NEUROANATOMICAL HYPOTHESIS

Gorman et al. (1989b) presented a theory to explain the manifold clinical presentations of panic disorder and the curious observation that both medication and psychotherapy treatments effectively block panic attacks. The theory essentially holds that panic attacks themselves originate in hypersensitive loci within the brain stem, that anticipatory anxiety is a kindled effect of limbic lobe origin, and that phobic avoidance is a higher-order cognitive function originating in the prefrontal cortex. In the past several years, a number of experimental studies provide evidence confirming some tenets of the neuroanatomical hypothesis, but others require modification. The current neuroanatomical and neurotransmitter data are reviewed in this chapter.

The two principles that originally motivated creation of the neuro-anatomical theory remain in force as follows.

1. Although the central clinical feature of panic disorder is the acute panic attack, manifestation of the illness is highly variable among patients through the course of the disorder. Classically, patients first experience panic attacks and then develop a chronic state of apprehensive expectation between attacks, called anticipatory anxiety. About two-thirds of patients then develop phobic avoidance, fearing development of an attack in a place or situation in which help is not immediately available. Treatment usually blocks attacks first, with subsequent reduction in anticipatory anxiety and then in phobic avoidance. This pattern does not occur in all patients, however, and, in addition, it changes over time for individual patients until they receive treatment. Some patients, for example, continue to have recurrent attacks without developing phobias; others maintain phobias for years after panics themselves subside. The critical phenomenological point is that panic attacks themselves are not the most clinically important manifestation of panic disorder throughout the course of the illness. Although our current understanding is that most cases begin with panic attacks, in time the dominant feature of the disorder often becomes anticipatory anxiety or phobic avoidance. A theory of panic disorder must therefore account for the variability in clinical course.

2. It was once believed that the only way to eliminate panic attacks themselves was to administer antipanic medication. Behavioral psychotherapy was believed necessary only for patients whose phobic avoidance persisted even after antipanic medication blocked their attacks. In such cases, the recommendation was to give brief, in vivo hierarchical desensitization while maintaining the patient on medication. More recently, however, evidence mounts that behavioral and cognitive psychotherapies may be effective in stopping panic attacks (Clark, 1986; Barlow et al., 1989; Welkowitz et al., 1991).

A four-site collaborative study, funded by the National Institute of Mental Health, is currently under way to compare the efficacy of medication and behavioral psychotherapy in blocking panic attacks among patients who do not have substantial amounts of phobic avoidance in the first place. Until completion of the study it is probably premature to assert that psychotherapy is equal to medication in blocking panic, but the evidence that psychotherapy is effective is already impressive based on studies by Barlow et al. (1989), Clark (1986), and Welkowitz et al. (1991), among others. Nevertheless, any comprehensive theory about panic disorder must answer the fundamental question, How can a single illness respond to treatments as seemingly divergent in neurobiologic effect as psychotherapy and medication?

By assignment of different clinical features of the panic disorder syndrome to different neuroanatomical loci, it is possible to account for the aforementioned phenomenological and treatment observations. Following is a review of the neuroanatomical argument.

Panic attacks originate in hyperactive brain stem loci. An abundance of data implicate aberrant autonomic nervous system function, regulated at the level of the brain stem, in the pathogenesis of panic attacks. First, clinical studies consistently show that the important characteristic that differentiates panic from generalized anxiety is the degree to which the patient complains of autonomic nervous system-related symptoms (Hoehn-Saric, 1982; Anderson, Noyes, and Crowe, 1984). The panic patient presents with physical complaints: the heart is not beating properly, there is chest pain, it is difficult to breathe. That list is distinct from that of the generalized anxiety disorder patient, who presents with more cognitively mediated complaints. The latter patient is preoccupied with incessant worries and tension rather than the persistent feeling that his or her body is functioning abnormally. The panic patient's clinical complaints are largely referable to the autonomic nervous system.

Subjective complaints receive support from studies indicating that panic patients do indeed manifest overactive autonomic responses to relatively trivial stimuli. In the laboratory and while at rest, panic patients demonstrate faster heart rate and minute ventilation than do controls (Liebowitz et al., 1985; Gorman et al., 1990b). They also show greater variance in the tidal volume component of respiration even when they report no subjective anxiety (Gorman et al., 1988a), indicating aberrant respiratory regulation. Other evidence of respiratory dysregulation at rest includes lower serum phosphate level in a subgroup of patients (Gorman et al., 1986) and, in one study (Papp and Gorman, 1990) but not another (Balon, Pohl, and Yeragani, 1991), elevated urinary bicarbonate level. In addition to elevated heart rate, panic patients have exaggerated cardiovascular response to standard autonomic stressors such as standing up, tilt, and the Valsalva maneuver (Weissman et al., 1987; Hoehn-Saric, McLeod, and Zimmerli, 1991). Panic patients have also shown an increased number of atrial and ventricular ectopic beats in a 24-hour ambulatory monitoring study (Shear, 1986). Finally, patients with panic disorder are approximately twice as likely as controls to have mitral valve prolapse (Gorman et al., 1988b). We now know that the prolapse common to panic patients is not the autosomal dominant form that results in calcification of the valve itself but a more common, acquired form that does not involve calcification and may even disappear over time. Studies suggest that that functional type of mitral valve prolapse may be part of a broad syndrome of dysautonomia. We have shown that mitral valve prolapse is not the cause of panic attacks and that actually the reverse may be the case: mitral valve prolapse appears to go away after successful pharmacological treatment of panic (Coplan et al., 1992b). Hence, prolapse of the mitral valve may represent an effect of hyperactive autonomic nervous system tone common to panic disorder patients.

Evidence exists linking panic attacks to dysfunction in three parts of the brain stem: the respiratory centers in the medulla, the noradrenergic nucleus locus coeruleus in the pons, and the serotonergic neurons of the midbrain raphe. There is theoretical reason to believe that all three are linked in the pathophysiology of panic attacks.

VENTILATORY FUNCTION IN PANIC

Evidence for the prominent role of respiratory physiological disturbance in panic disorder comes from the aforementioned studies in which panic patients have elevated minute ventilation, and tidal volume variance, reduced serum phosphate as well as increased urinary pH level compared with controls. During sodium lactate–induced panic there is a significantly greater drop in arterial pCO_2 and greater increase in minute ventilation and lactate level compared with subjects who do not panic during the infusion (Gorman et al., 1988c). This indicates that during a laboratory-induced panic there is a strong stimulus to hyperventilation. We found that patients lower the pCO_2 during panic attacks provoked by sodium bicarbonate (Gorman et al., 1989a) and sodium-d-lactate (Gorman et al., 1990a) infusion as well. In the former case, this is especially remarkable because sodium bicarbonate infusion produces profound metabolic alkalosis, which should decrease ventilation; panic overrides this usual physiological response, however, and the patient hyperventilates. A few patients have had attacks in our laboratory during the placebo infusion that ordinarily precedes lactate infusion; once again, there was a striking degree of hyperventilation in these patients beginning minutes before the panic was reported (Goetz et al., 1993). Many of the agents now used in various laboratories to provoke panic attacks in susceptible patients are known respiratory stimulants, including isoproterenol (Keltz, Samortin, and Stone, 1972), caffeine (D'Urzo et al., 1990), and cholecystokinin (Bradwejn et al., 1992). Taken together, these studies suggest that panic attacks are commonly accompanied by substantial ventilatory stimulation.

This evidence led us and others to directly assess ventilatory function in panic using the technique of carbon dioxide stimulation. The resulting studies show that panic patients are indeed behaviorally hypersensitive to the effects of inhaled carbon dioxide, which cannot be explained simply by the dyspneogenic effect of carbon dioxide (Papp et al., 1993). Further evidence, although controversial, indicates that at least a subgroup of panic patients have hyperactive response of the medullary chemoreceptor to carbon dioxide (Papp et al., 1989). Hence, not only is it clear that patients with panic disorder become more anxious than controls during carbon dioxide inhalation, but also there is reason to believe that they have centrally mediated hypersensitivity.

NORADRENERGIC HYPERACTIVITY IN PANIC

Interestingly, stimulation of the medullary chemoreceptors that detect carbon dioxide leads to stimulation of the pontine nucleus locus coeruleus (Elam et al., 1981). The locus coeruleus contains most of the brain's noradrenergic nuclei and through afferent fibers influences most of the central nervous system including the limbic and frontal cortices. The locus coeruleus appears to mediate attentional behavior in animals; artificially stimulating the locus coeruleus in an experimental animal leads to an alerting response, which some have likened to anticipatory anxiety and, as discussed later, a paniclike response in some species of nonhuman primate. In humans, the symptoms of opiate withdrawal are believed to be produced by firing of the locus coeruleus. Because of this, patients undergoing heroin or methadone detoxification are often given medications such as clonidine that block locus coeruleus firing. It is also clear that stimulation of the locus coeruleus leads to an increase in heart rate and blood pressure, which are autonomic nervous system features of panic as well.

Beginning with classical experiments by Redmond (1977), it has been shown that stimulation of the locus coeruleus—which increases brain noradrenergic activity—causes an anxiogenic reaction in monkeys. We have recently done studies (Coplan et al., 1991) that call into question whether animals' reaction is a reasonable model of human panic; nevertheless, it is clear that stimulating the noradrenergic center in animals produces an acute anxiogenic reaction.

In humans, Charney, Heninger, and Breier (1984) elegantly demonstrated that yohimbine hydrochloride, a locus coeruleus stimulant, produces panic in patients with panic disorder but not controls or patients with other psychiatric illness. MHPG is the major metabolite of noradrenaline, and subgroups of patients with especially frequent attacks have an exaggerated plasma MHPG response when they panic after yohimbine administration. Patients with panic disorder also show abnormal responses to administration of clonidine, a drug with effects directly opposite to those of yohimbine (Charney and Heninger, 1986; Nutt, 1986; Middleton, 1990). Panic patients show greater decrease in blood pressure and anxiety level and blunted release of growth hormone than normal controls after clonidine. We have shown (Coplan et al., 1992c) that the blunted growth-hormone response to clonidine in panic patients persists even after clinical remission. Thus, blunted growth-hormone response to clonidine may be a characteristic trait of panic disorder patients.

When the locus coeruleus is stimulated, the subject experiences increases in heart rate and blood pressure and becomes hypervigilant —all common occurrences during panic. Stimulation of the medullary chemoreceptor by carbon dioxide causes secondary stimulation of the locus coeruleus. Therefore, it seems likely that activation of the locus coeruleus is involved in the generation of acute panic.

SEROTONERGIC INVOLVEMENT IN PANIC

One potential problem for the noradrenergic hypothesis of panic disorder is an accumulation of evidence for involvement of a different brain neurotransmitter—serotonin. Studies have indicated that panic patients are hyperresponsive to serotonergic stimuli such as MCPP (Kahn et al., 1988) and fenfluramine (Targum and Marshall, 1989). More important, it is now clear that medications that appear to affect only serotonin receptors—so-called selective serotonin reuptake inhibitors (SSRIs)—are also effective antipanic medications (Gorman et al., 1987; Coplan et al., 1992a). These drugs, which include fluoxetine and sertraline, do not have acute effects on noradrenergic transmission but nevertheless block panic attacks. The question arises, therefore, whether the noradrenergic hypothesis is tenable given the efficacy of drugs that do not have apparent effect on the noradrenergic system.

Actually, the serotonergic and noradrenergic systems are highly interrelated within the central nervous system (Pickel, Joh, and Reiss, 1978). In general, stimulation of the serotonin system causes a decrease in noradrenergic transmission. SSRIs, when given for several weeks, lead to an overall net increase in serotonergic transmission, which might depress noradrenergic function. Indeed, we recently showed (Coplan et al., 1992c) that successful fluoxetine treatment led to a decrease in plasma MHPG level, suggesting that an SSRI may work via noradrenergic influence in relieving panic. Further studies, however, examining 24-hour urinary metabolites of norepinephrine are required before this latter view can be regarded as definitive. It is also of interest that depletion of serotonin in experimental animals leads to hyperventilation, whereas increase in serotonergic function decreases respiratory sensitivity (Lundberg, Mueller, and Breese, 1980). Therefore SSRIs may have an antipanic effect both by decreasing noradrenergic transmission and by decreasing the sensitivity of the medullary respiratory sensors.

These lines of evidence converge to suggest that one or more inter-related brain stem loci are likely to be the generator of the acute panic attack. All of the associated autonomic symptoms of the attack can be explained on the basis of aberrant firing of those loci. Medications with antipanic effect have in common the ability to increase the threshold for firing of the loci.

Anticipatory anxiety originates in the limbic area of the brain, and takes time to develop. But with each successive panic attack, the patient becomes increasingly nervous about the likelihood that another one will occur. Eventually, minimal provocation—the barest reminder of a previous attack—becomes sufficient to generate extremely high levels of generalized anxiety.

This phenomenon has the appearance of a kindled effect (Uhde and Post, 1984). Kindling, which involves the ability to provoke a neuronal reaction with progressively smaller amounts of stimulation, is especially related to the limbic area of the central nervous system (Goddard, 1983). Interestingly, it has been shown (Goddard et al., 1986) in experimental animals that repeated brain stem stimulation leads to a secondary kindling of limbic lobe neurons. Many primitive but learned anxiety responses, including the fear-potentiated startle response, appear to have origin in the limbic lobe, in this case specifically within the amygdala (Davis, 1992). Gray (1977) argued that generalized anxiety is a hippocampal phenomenon. Penfield (1958), by means of classic neurosurgical experiments, observed that electrical stimulation of the temporal-limbic area caused fear in human subjects undergoing surgical treatment for intractable epilepsy.

Two clinical observations are compatible with the idea that anticipatory anxiety arises in limbic areas of the brain. First, Reiman and colleagues (1984) conducted positron-emission tomography on panic disorder patients immediately before sodium lactate infusion. They found that patients who went on to have panic attacks once the lactate infusion was started showed abnormal asymmetry of blood flow through a limbic structure—the parahippocampal gyrus. As the patients were *about* to have lactate infusion when the tomography was performed, it is reasonable to surmise that they were in a state of high anticipatory anxiety.

Second, it has long been observed that only high-potency benzodiazepines, such as alprazolam, lorazepam, and clonazepam, are capable of blocking panic attacks. However, ordinary doses of the low-potency benzodiazepines, such as diazepam, relieve both generalized anxiety and the anticipatory anxiety of panic disorder patients. The limbic lobe is especially rich in benzodiazepine receptors (Mohler and Richards, 1983), and it has been shown experimentally that benzodiazepines prevent kindling in the limbic lobe (Racine, Livingston, and Joaquin, 1975). All benzodiazepines are capable of decreasing anticipatory anxiety, but it may take the high-potency types to affect areas of the brain, such as the brain stem, that are relatively poor in number of benzodiazepine receptors.

Hence, we have concluded that panic attacks originating in the brain stem kindle limbic lobe structures, probably in the hippocampus and amygdala, which leads to a generalized and chronic state of anticipatory anxiety. Benzodiazepines are effective in relieving this second component of the panic disorder syndrome.

Phobic avoidance originates in the prefrontal cortex. Avoidance of noxious stimuli is a learned phenomenon that can be induced in primitive animals. It would seem at first, therefore, that phobic avoidance in panic disorder patients should involve a relatively primitive part of the central nervous system. Yet there is a striking feature of agoraphobia that differentiates it from avoidance behaviors produced by conditioning paradigms in lower animals. Even nonhuman primates will eventually extinguish an avoidance behavior if too long a period of time elapses after the previous presentation of the noxious stimulus. Humans with agoraphobia, however, often maintain avoidance forever, even if no panic attacks ever occur again. For example, it is not uncommon for a patient to report having had a single panic attack while driving in a car over a specific bridge in a traffic jam many years ago. Despite the fact that the patient has never had a panic again in a similar circumstance, the patient still refuses to drive on the bridge or in traffic jams. It is not simply that the patient associates the bridge with the panic attack, for such a pairing would mimic the kind of avoidance paradigms seen in animal experiments. Rather, the mechanism by which that patient maintains phobic avoidance despite the lack of reinforcement involves a complex set of cognitions. Usually, the patient reasons that a panic attack occurring in the car on a bridge in a traffic jam would be especially dangerous because help would be difficult to obtain. Even a companion would be unable to get the patient to an emergency room in time in such a situation. Hence, the patient believes there is a high likelihood that the panic attack could result in a catastrophe such as serious physical harm or complete loss of control.

The point here is that careful examination of phobic avoidance in panic patients indicates that such behavior requires complex and higher-order cognitions that could not occur even in our nearest intellectual relatives, the nonhuman primate. Bringing the aforedescribed patient near the bridge begins a cascade of thoughts that are replete with what cognitive psychologists call probability overestimations and catastrophic cognitions. Even in the absence of panic attacks, the patient can quickly and in time almost automatically conjure those cognitions. The cognitions in turn actually appear capable of secondarily triggering panic.

Because these complex thoughts are uniquely human, we posit that they must originate in the uniquely human part of the central nervous system, the prefrontal cortex. Of great interest is the fact that the corticoreticular tracts that carry neuronal impulses from the frontal cortex to the brain stem end on nuclei of the medulla that control respiration (Rossi and Brodal, 1956). Thus, anxious cognitions provoked by presentation of a phobic stimulus can, through descending neuronal pathways, provoke the hyperactive brain stem nuclei previously described and can trigger all of the autonomic features of a panic attack. It is especially noteworthy that respiratory control appears to have a central place in the scheme. Alone among autonomic functions, respiration is easily controlled either voluntarily and consciously or automatically. It is nearly impossible for people to willfully lower their heart rate by 10 beats per minute but trivial to lower their respiratory rate by any number of breaths per minute. Yet respiration is easily transferred to the brain stem for control as soon as one forgets about breathing. This dual control for respiration accords with the theory that panic disorder is dually controlled by both lower (brain stem) and higher (prefrontal cortical) centers in the brain.

We hypothesize, therefore, two ways by which a panic attack can occur. The first involves the spontaneous firing of hyperactive brain stem nuclei. This eventually kindles the limbic lobe and anticipatory anxiety occurs. Later, fear of having a panic attack in a situation in which help is not readily available leads to phobic avoidance, a learned phenomenon involving higher cortical processes in the brain stem. The second involves the generation of anxious cognitions upon presentation of a phobic stimulus. This leads, via descending pathways, to stimulation of abnormally sensitive brain stem nuclei.

The model can be used to handle the clinical problems highlighted in the beginning of this discussion. Depending on the relative involvement of brain stem, limbic area, and frontal cortex, a patient will experience different amounts of panic, anticipatory anxiety, and phobic avoidance. In addition, there is no difficulty understanding how drugs and psychotherapy both might work. Drugs decrease brain stem and limbic hyperactivity; psychotherapy decreases anxiogenic cognitions. Depending on the current state of the individual patient, one or the other may be more effective. It is likely, although not proven, that a combination of antipanic medication and psychotherapy represents the most efficient treatment because it addresses the psychopathology of panic disorder at different levels. According to that reasoning, medication and psychotherapy should usually be complementary; the sometimes proffered notion that medication in some way detracts from the psychotherapy response would have no basis in experimental fact.

Several theorists have attempted to apply psychodynamic observations and theories to panic disorder (Nemiah, 1981; Cooper, 1985). The exact nature of the unconscious conflicts that play a role in panic etiology have not yet been specifically characterized, but the current neuroanatomical hypothesis could easily accommodate psychodynamic data. Unconscious conflicts would work in much the same way as abnormal, conscious cognitions: they would originate in the prefrontal cortex and cause stimulation of lower brain stem loci via the descending tracts. Freud (1900) originally placed great emphasis, in fact, on the role of disordered respiration in anxiety states (p. 194). It is entirely plausible, although not documented, that unconscious mental processes could provoke hyperventilation in a manner analogous to what happens when we perform lactate infusion or administer carbon dioxide inhalation.

THE ROLE OF GENES AND ENVIRONMENTAL TRAUMA

The neuroanatomical hypothesis assumes that the primary lesion in panic disorder consists of abnormally sensitive brain stem autonomic nervous system regulators. There are two, nonexclusive ways in which this could occur in an individual.

The first and most obvious is by way of inheritance. There is some evidence from twin studies that the tendency to have panic attacks is in part genetically mediated. Thus, Torgersen (1983), for example, found a higher concordance rate for panic attacks—but not the full syndrome of panic disorder—among monozygotic (identical) than among dizygotic (fraternal) twins, suggesting that what might be inherited is the autonomic hyperactivity that predisposes to panic. There is also evidence that the tendency to be timid and behaviorally inhibited and to have autonomic dysfunction may be a stable and enduring trait that predisposes to anxiety disorder. Kagan, Reznick, and Snidman (1987) identified as early as 4 months of age a group of individuals termed "behaviorally inhibited to the unknown." Such individuals remain shy and withdrawn over many years of observation, have higher heart rate and lower heart rate variability than controls when presented with novel stimuli, are often the offspring of parents with anxiety disorder (Biederman et al., 1990), and tend themselves to develop anxiety disorder (Coll, Kagan, and Reznick, 1984). This again suggests the possibility that autonomic hyperactivity is an inherited function.

The second way abnormally sensitive brain stem function could develop is by early trauma. Evidence already exists that adults suffering from posttraumatic stress disorder are hypersensitive to two agents that cause panic in panic disorder patients—sodium lactate (Rainey et al., 1987) and yohimbine (Southwick, Krystal, and Charney, 1990). There are data indicating that adults with panic disorder often suffered from separation anxiety and school phobia as children (Gittelman-Klein and Klein, 1971). Imipramine, an excellent antipanic agent, has been shown effective in treating school phobia as well (Gittelman-Klein and Klein, 1971). Adults with panic disorder are more likely to panic when alone; the threshold for panic increases when such adults are surrounded by familiar figures. Finally, some studies have suggested that perceived, threatened, or actual separations may precede the onset of panic attacks (Last, Barlow, and O'Brien, 1984; Breier, Charney, and Heninger, 1986; Charney and Heninger, 1986).

The evidence that early trauma and separation responses may be linked to panic is strengthened by animal experiments. Panksepp and colleagues (1988) showed that stimulation of areas of the brain that produce distress vocalizations in infant mammals separated from their mother also produces hyperventilation. Decrease in noradrenergic function represents one way of decreasing such distress vocalizations. Coplan et al. (1992d) experimentally varied the degree of attachment between mothers and infant nonhuman primates. By one year of age, the infants raised with insecure attachment to the mother showed behavioral abnormalities such as timidity and withdrawal that are strikingly similar to those observed in Kagan's behaviorally inhibited children. When the infants were grown they manifested hyperactive response to yohimbine and hypoactive response to the serotonergic stimulant MCPP.

We suggest, therefore, that very early traumatic events, especially insecure infant–parent attachment, may produce neurobiological changes that ultimately lead to panic susceptibility. Early evidence reveals that both adults with panic disorder and adult nonhuman primates who were raised under conditions of insecure maternal attachment manifest abnormal sensitivities toward noradrenergic and serotonergic probes. Therefore, it is plausible that some combination of genetic predisposition and traumatic life events creates the autonomic nervous system climate in which panic disorder can occur.

SUMMARY

Our speculations are supported in part by a large body of research. Neurobiologists, psychopharmacologists, psychotherapists, and cognitive and behavioral psychologists have contributed to the literature on which the neuroanatomical, neurotransmitter, and developmental hypotheses presented here are based. Nevertheless, there are many areas in which we have gone beyond what experimentally derived evidence has actually shown. For instance, a great deal remains to be learned about the developmental aspects of panic, including further work on animal models and childhood precursors of panic. We also look forward to more research on higher cortical function in anxiety disorders, including studies of psychodynamic hypotheses.

Our strongest recommendation, however, is that research studies and theories be designed to accommodate the obvious fact that pathological anxiety—including panic—is not simply a disorder of small groups of neurons and single neurotransmitters. Rather, we are convinced that a comprehensive approach to the study and treatment of panic must consider numerous complexities of human neurological development and psychological function.

REFERENCES

Anderson, D. J., Noyes, R., Jr. & Crowe, R. R. (1984), A comparison of panic disorder and generalized anxiety disorder. *Amer. J. Psychiat.*, 141:572–575.
Balon, R., Pohl, R. & Yeragani, V. K. (1991), Urine pH and panic disorder (letter). *The Lancet*, 337:1351.

Barlow, D. H., Craske, M. G., Cerny, J. A. & Klosko, J. S. (1989), Behavioral treatment of panic disorder. *Behav. Ther.*, 20:261–282.

Biederman, J., Rosenbaum, J. F., Hirshfeld, D. R., Faraone, S. V., Bolduc, E. A., Gersten, M., Meminger, S. R., Kagan, J., Snidman, N. & Reznick, J. S. (1990), Psychiatric correlates of behavioral inhibition in young children of parents with and without psychiatric disorders. *Arch. Gen. Psychiat.*, 47:21–26.

Bradwejn, J., Koszycki, D., Payeur, R., Bourin, M. & Borthwick, H. (1992), Replication of action of cholecystokinin tetrapeptide in panic disorder: Clinical and behavioral findings. *Amer. J. Psychiat.*, 149:962–964.

Breier, A., Charney, D. S. & Heninger, G. R. (1986), Agoraphobia with panic attacks: Development, diagnostic stability, and course of illness. *Arch. Gen. Psychiat.*, 43:1029–1036.

Charney, D. S. & Heninger, G. R. (1986), Abnormal regulation of noradrenergic function in panic disorders. *Arch. Gen. Psychiat.*, 43:1042–1054.

—————— ———— & Breier, A. (1984), Noradrenergic function in panic anxiety: Effects of yohimbine in healthy subjects and patients with agoraphobia and panic disorder. *Arch. Gen. Psychiat.*, 41:751–763.

Clark, D. M. (1986), A cognitive approach to panic. *Behav. Res. Ther.*, 24:61–471.

Coll, C. G., Kagan, J. & Reznick, J. S. (1984), Behavioral inhibition in young children. *Child Devel.*, 55:1005–1019.

Cooper, A. M. (1985), Will neurobiology influence psychoanalysis? *Amer. J. Psychiat.*, 142:1395–1402.

Coplan, J. D., Rosenblum, L. A., Friedman, S., Bassoff, T. & Gorman, J. M. (1991), Behavioral effects of oral yohimbine in differentially reared nonhuman primates. *Neuropsychopharmacology*, 6:31–37.

—————— Gorman, J. M. & Klein, D. F. (1992a), Serotonin-related function in panic disorder: A critical overview. *Neuropsychopharmacology*, 6:189–200.

—————— Papp, L. A., King, D. L. & Gorman, J. M. (1992b), Mitral valve prolapse amelioration in panic disorder patients following antipanic treatment. *Amer. J. Psychiat.*, 149:1587–1588.

—————— ———— Martinez, J., Rosenblum, L. A. & Gorman, J. M. (1992c), *Noradrenaline: Serotonin interaction in panic disorder.* New Research Program, American Psychiatric Association, Washington, D.C.

—————— Rosenblum, L. A., Friedman, S. T., Bassoff, T. B., & Gorman, J. M. (1992d), Noradrenaline and serotonin function in nonhuman primates. New Research Program, American Psychiatric Association, Washington, DC.

Davis, M. (1992), The role of the amygdala in fear-potentiated startle: Implications for animal models of anxiety. *Trends Pharmacolog. Sci.*, 13:35–41.

D'Urzo, A. D., Khirad, R., Jenne, H., Avendano, M. A., Rubinstein, I., D'Costa, M. & Goldstein, P. S. (1990), Effect of caffeine on ventilatory responses to hypercapnia, hypoxia, and exercise in humans. *J. Appl. Physiol.*, 68:322–328.

Elam, M., Yoa, J., Thoren, P. & Svensson, T. H. (1981), Hypercapnia and hypoxia: chemoreceptor-mediated control of locus coeruleus neurons and splanchnic, sympathetic nerves. *Brain Res.*, 222:373–381.

Freud, S. (1900), Extracts from the Fliess papers. *Standard Edition*, 1:175–280. London: Hogarth Press, 1966.

Gittelman-Klein, R. & Klein, D. F. (1971), Controlled imipramine treatment of school phobia. *Arch. Gen. Psychiat.*, 25:204–207.

Goddard, G. V. (1983), The kindling model of epilepsy. *Trends Neurosci.*, 6:275–279.

—— Dragunow, M., Maru, E. & Macleod, E. K. (1986), Kindling and the forces that oppose it. In: *The Limbic System*, ed. B. K. Doane & K. F. Livingston. New York: Raven Press, pp. 95–108.

Goetz, R. R., Gully, R., Dillon, D., Kahn, J., Liebowitz, M. R., Klein, D. F. & Gorman, J. M. (1993), Panic attacks during laboratory placebo procedures: Physiology and symptomatology. *Arch. Gen. Psychiat.*, 50:280–285.

Gorman, J. M., Battista, D., Goetz, R. R., Dillon, D. J., Liebowitz, M. R., Fyer, A. J., Kahn, J. P., Sandberg, D. & Klein, D. F. (1989a), A comparison of sodium bicarbonate and sodium lactate infusion in the induction of panic attacks. *Arch. Gen. Psychiat.*, 6:145–150.

—— Cohen, B. S., Liebowitz, M. R., Fyer, A. J., Ross, D., Davies, S. O. & Klein, D. F. (1986), Blood gas changes and hypophosphatemia in lactate induced panic. *Arch. Gen. Psychiat.*, 43:1067–1075.

—— Fyer, M. R., Goetz, R., Askanazi, J., Martinez, J., Liebowitz, M. R., Fyer, A. J., Kinney, J. & Klein, D. F. (1988a), Ventilatory physiology of patients with panic disorder. *Arch. Gen. Psychiat.*, 45:31–39.

—— Goetz, R. R., Dillon, D., Liebowitz, M. R., Fyer, A. J., Davies, S. & Klein, D. F. (1990a), Sodium D-lactate infusion of panic disorder patients: Preliminary report. *Neuropsychopharmacol.*, 3:181–189.

—— Goetz, R. R., Fyer, M. R., King, D. L., Fyer, A. J., Liebowitz, M. R. & Klein, D. F. (1988b), The mitral valve proplase–panic disorder connection. *Psychosom. Med.*, 50:114–122.

—— Goetz, R. R., Uy, J., Ross, D., Martinez, J., Fyer, A. J., Liebowitz, M. R. & Klein, D. F. (1938c), Hyperventilation occurs during lactate-induced panic. *J. Anx. Disorders*, 2:193–202.

—— Liebowitz, M. R., Fyer, A. J., Goetz, D., Campeas, R. B., Fyer, M. R., Davies, S. O. & Klein, D. F. (1987), An open trial of fluoxetine in the treatment of panic attacks. *J. Clin. Psychopharmcol.*, 7:319–332.

—— Liebowitz, M. R., Fyer, A. J. & Stein, J. (1989b), A neuroanatomical hypothesis for panic disorder. *Amer. J. Psychiat.*, 146:148–161.

—— Papp, L. A., Martinez, J., Goetz, R. R., Hollander, E., Liebowitz, M. R. & Jordan, F. (1990b), High dose carbon dioxide challenge test in anxiety disorder patients. *Biol. Psychiat.*, 28:743–757.

Gray, J. A. (1977), Drug effects on fear and frustration: Possible limbic site of action of major tranquilizers. In: *Handbook of Psychopharmacology, Vol 8, Drugs*, ed. L. L. Iversen, D. D. Iversen & S. H. Snyder. New York: Plenum Press, pp. 443–529.

Hoehn-Saric, R. (1982), Comparison of generalized anxiety disorder with panic disorder patients. *Psychopharmacol. Bull.*, 18:104–108.

—— McLeod, D. R. & Zimmerli, W. D. (1991), Psychophysiological response patterns in panic disorder. *Acta Psychiat. Scand.*, 83:4–11.

Kagan, J., Reznick, J. S. & Snidman, N. (1987), The physiology and psychology of behavioral inhibition in children. *Child Devel.*, 58:1459–1473.

Kahn, R. S., Wetzler, S., Van Praag, H. M., Asnis, G. M. & Strauman, T. (1988), Behavioral indications for serotonin hypersensitivity in panic disorder. *Psychiat. Res.*, 25:101–104.

Keltz, H., Samortin, T. & Stone, D. J. (1972), Hyperventilation: A manifestation of exogenous beta-adrenergic stimulation. *Amer. Rev. Resp. Dis.*, 105:637–640.

Last, C. G., Barlow, D. H. & O'Brien, G. T. (1984), Precipitant of agoraphobia: Role of stressful life events. *Psychol. Rep.*, 54:567–570.

Liebowitz, M. R., Gorman, J. M., Fyer, A. J., Levitt, M., Dillon, D., Levy, G., Appleby, I. L., Anderson, S., Palij, M., Davies, S. O. & Klein, D. F. (1985), Lactate provocation of panic attacks, II: Biochemical and physiological findings. *Arch. Gen. Psychiat.*, 42:709–719.

Lundberg, D. B. A., Mueller, R. A. & Breese, G. R. (1980), An evaluation of the mechanism by which serotonergic activation depresses respiration. *J. Pharmacol. Exp. Ther.*, 212:397–404.

Middleton, H. C. (1990), An enhanced hypotensive response to clonidine can still be found in panic patients despite psychological treatment. *J. Anx. Disorders*, 4:213–219.

Mohler, H. & Richards, J. G. (1983), Benzodiazepine receptors in the central nervous system. In: *The Benzodiazepines*, ed. E. Costa. New York: Raven Press, pp. 93–116.

Nemiah, J. C. (1981), A psychoanalytic view of phobias. *Amer. J. Psychoanal.*, 41:115–120.

Nutt, D. J. (1986), Increased central alpha 2-adrenoreceptor sensitivity in panic disorder. *Psychopharmacology* (Berlin), 90:268–269.

Panksepp, J., Normansell, L., Herman, B., Bishop, P. & Crepeau, L. (1988), Neural and neurochemical control of the separation distress call. In: *The Physiological Control of Mammalian Vocalization*, ed. J. D. Newman. New York: Plenum.

Papp, L. A., Goetz, R., Cole, R., Klein, D. F., Jordan, F., Liebowitz, M. R., Fyer, A. J., Hollander, E. & Gorman, J. M. (1989), Hypersensitivity to carbon dioxide in panic disorder. *Amer. J. Psychiat.*, 146:779–781.

———— & Gorman, J. M. (1990), Urine pH in panic: A possible screening device (letter). *The Lancet*, 335:355.

———— Martinez, J., Klein, D. F., Jordan, F., Liebowitz, M. R. & Gorman, J. M. (1993), The diagnostic and substance specificity of carbon dioxide induced panic. *Amer. J. Psychiat.*, 150:250–257.

Penfield, W. (1958), Functional localization in temporal and deep sylvian areas. *Res. Publ. Assoc. Res. Nerv. Ment. Dis.*, 36:210–226.

Pickel, V. M., Joh, T. H. & Reiss, D. J. (1978), Immunocytochemical evidence for serotonergic innervation of noradrenergic neurons in nucleus locus coeruleus. In: *Interactions between Putative Neurotransmitters in the Brain*, ed. S. Garattini, J. F. Pujal & R. Samanin. New York: Raven Press, pp. 369–399.

Racine, R., Livingston, K. & Joaquin, A. (1975), Effects of procaine hydrochloride, diazepam and diphenylhydantoin on seizure development in cortical and subcortical structures in rats. *Electroencephalogr. Clin. Neurophysiol.*, 38:355–365.

Rainey, J. M., Jr., Aleem, A., Ortiz, A., Yeragani, V., Pohl, R. & Berchou, R. (1987), A laboratory procedure for the induction of flashbacks. *Amer. J. Psychiat.*, 144:1317–1319.

Redmond, D. E. (1977), Alterations in the function of the nucleus locus coeruleus: A possible model for studies of anxiety. In: *Animal Models in Psychiatry and Neurology*, ed. I. Hanin & E. Usdin. Oxford: Pergamon Press, pp. 293–304.

Reiman, E. M., Raichl, M. E., Butler, F. K., Herscovitch, P. & Robins, E. (1984), A focal brain abnormality in panic disorder: A severe form of anxiety. *Nature*, 310:683–685.

Rossi, G. F. & Brodal, A. (1956), Corticofungal fibers to the brain stem reticular formation: An experimental study in the cat. *J. Anat.*, 90:42–62.

Shear, M. K. (1986), Pathophysiology of panic: A review of pharmacologic provocation tests and naturalistic monitoring data. *J. Clin Psychiat.*, 47:18–26.

Southwick, S. M., Krystal, J. H. & Charney, D. S. (1990), Yohimbine in post traumatic stress disorder. *New Res. Abstr.*, 143rd Annual Meeting, American Psychiatric Association, New York.

Targum, S. D. & Marshall, L. E. (1989), Fenfluramine provocation of anxiety in patients with panic disorder. *Psychiat. Res.*, 28:295–306.

Torgersen, S. (1983), Genetic factors in anxiety disorders. *Arch. Gen. Psychiat.*, 40:1085–1089.

Uhde, T. W. & Post, R. M. (1984), Carbamazepine treatment of neuropsychiatric disorder. In: *Anticonvulsants in Affective Disorders*, ed. H. M. Emrich, T. Okuna & A. A. Muller. New York: Elsevier.

Weissman, N. J., Shear, M. K., Kramer-Fox, R. & Devereux, R. B. (1987), Contrasting patterns of autonomic dysfunction in patients with mitral valve prolapse and panic attacks. *Amer. J. Med.*, 82:880–888.

Welkowitz, L. A., Papp, L. A., Cloitre, M., Liebowitz, M. R., Martin, L. Y. & Gorman, J. M. (1991), Cognitive-behavior therapy for panic disorder delivered by psychopharmacologically oriented clinicians. *J. Nerv. Ment. Dis.*, 179:473–477.

4 Genetic and Temperamental Variations in Individual Predisposition to Anxiety

Abby J. Fyer

This chapter considers the question of whether anxiety can exist not only as a product of interpersonal or intrapsychic conflict but also as a physiological product of brain function that creates a context within which psychic conflict and personality development take place. In this book, anxiety has been understood primarily as a result of the interaction between the self and other, wish and conflict, or ego and id. Implicit in this is the assumption that all individuals begin at the same starting point: with a similar potential for anxiety. In this chapter we reverse the perspective and ask instead whether the starting point itself can differ; that is, are there inherited or otherwise constitutional variations among individuals that, given equal circumstances, make some more likely than others to become anxious or develop anxiety disorders?

This question, though important from the vantage point of both clinicians and theorists, has not been easily amenable to empirical investigation. Study designs that can distinguish the effects of nature versus nurture not only are complicated and costly but also often rely on experimental manipulations (such as infant–mother separations), which are inappropriate in human populations. Even more problematic is that we have very little information about the form that predisposition to anxiety might take, in terms of either clinical presentation or biological substrate. Despite these difficulties, three areas of research provide definite evidence of individual variation in predisposition to anxiety: (1) studies of infant and childhood temperament, (2) genetic studies of adult personality, and (3) genetic studies of pathological anxiety (anxiety symptoms and disorders).

STUDIES OF INFANT AND CHILDHOOD TEMPERAMENT

The word "temperament" is generally used to describe variations in the behavioral styles or reactivity of infants, which are inherited or constitutional and thought to be relatively stable over the course of development. In this chapter the term "inherited" is meant in its narrower sense (i.e., referring to genetic transmission). "Constitutional" refers to enduring characteristics that are the result of nongenetic influences prior to birth (Greenacre, 1941; Escalona, 1984). For example, in utero exposure to higher levels of certain neurochemically active drugs (e.g., nicotine, caffeine) or to a virus may lead to altered reactivity after birth.

Prospective longitudinal studies of human infants have identified a wide range of human temperamental characteristics, including stability of mood, threshold for and intensity of response to external stimuli, level of motor activity, soothability, and reactivity (i.e., approach/avoidance) to unfamiliar people, objects, or situations (Kagan and Moss, 1962; Plomin and Rowe, 1979; Thomas, Chess, and Korn, 1982).

Though it is easy to imagine that variability in almost any of these dimensions might affect an individual's propensity to anxiety, only one temperamental characteristic—reactivity to the unfamiliar—has been studied in this regard.

Research addressing this problem can be divided into two main types. The first is a series of experimental studies of behavioral inhibition in children conducted by Kagan and colleagues (1991) at Harvard University during the past 20 years. The second is a group of behavioral genetic studies of shyness or hesitancy in social response to unfamiliar people carried out in large part by Buss, Plomin, and Willerman (1973) at the University of Colorado.

Behavioral Inhibition to the Unfamiliar

In the early 1960s, Kagan and Moss (1962) noted that the most stable and predictive behavioral characteristic of children first assessed at age three and followed up in their 20s was the tendency to be extremely shy, withdrawn, and inactive when encountering unfamiliar people, objects, or situations.

Behavioral reactivity to the unfamiliar is measured by observer assessment of a child's behavior in two or more laboratory situations. Although the types of unfamiliar situations created vary somewhat with the child's age, most assessments include a play situation with an unfamiliar peer; exposure to unfamiliar toys, objects, and rooms; playing with or being tested by an unfamiliar adult; and separation from the mother. Critical variables include the extent to which the child approaches or retreats from each situation, the time from initial exposure to spontaneous approach or verbalization, the total number of the child's spontaneous verbalizations during exposure, and the amount of reassurance sought from the mother. Inhibited children demonstrate retreat or slow approach, may be silent or speak only late in the session, and often cling to their mothers. Uninhibited children display an opposite pattern of behaviors.

In a prospective study, Kagan found that about 15% of two- and three-year-olds exhibit an extreme form of this trait, which he and his colleagues have named behavioral inhibition to the unfamiliar (Kagan, Reznick, and Snidman, 1987). In contrast another 15% of children demonstrated a diametrically opposed pattern; these uninhibited toddlers responded to new situations with spontaneous activity and exploration. They quickly initiated interaction with new people and did not appear to require ongoing reassurance from or proximity to their mothers. Somewhat surprisingly, neither the inhibited, uninhibited, nor midrange groups were distinguishable from each other when encountered on their familiar home territory.

These two temperamental categories (inhibited and uninhibited) appear to be discernible during infancy, remain reasonably stable throughout early childhood, and are associated with distinct physiological characteristics (Hirshfeld, et al., 1992). Three-quarters of the toddlers first assessed at 21 or 30 months of age had retained their initial temperament classification when reevaluated at 5½ and 7½ years old (Kagan, 1989). In addition, in four-month-old infants, high versus low levels of motor activity and crying as reactions to unfamiliar stimuli predicted behavioral inhibition at age 21 months (Kagan and Snidman, 1991).

At all ages, inhibited children also exhibited greater levels of sympathetic nervous system arousal on exposure to the unfamiliar than did their uninhibited counterparts: higher and stabler heart rates, higher peripheral cortisol levels, greater pupillary dilation, and greater vocal chord muscle tension (Garcia-Coll, Kagan, and Reznick, 1984). As sympathetic nervous system arousal is characteristic of both normal fear and certain types of pathological anxiety states, the foregoing observation forms another potential link between behavioral inhibition and anxiety. For example, extreme sympathetic arousal is a hallmark of the classic fight-or-flight reaction. It is also seen in social and simple phobics (except blood/injury) who are forced to confront their feared situations (Barlow, 1988). Symptoms of chronic sympathetic hyperactivity have been reported as part of generalized anxiety disorder (Hoehn-Saric, McLeod, and Zimmerli, 1989) and in children with anxiety or depressive disorders or both (Rogeness et al., 1990). Moreover, in Kagan's (1989) sample, inhibited children who consistently demonstrated higher sympathetic nervous system arousal to the unfamiliar over time were also more likely to evidence consistency in temperament.

Evidence for a Genetic Contribution to Behavioral Inhibition

The data suggest that severe behavioral inhibition is a moderately stable temperamental characteristic of children that is associated with specific behavioral (withdrawal and timidity) and neurophysiologic (sympathetic arousal) responses to the unfamiliar. However, with respect to our central hypothesis (that variation in predisposition to anxiety begins before birth), two questions remain unanswered: (1) Is there a genetic contribution to behavioral inhibition? and (2) Is there a relationship between behavioral inhibition and anxiety?

With respect to the first question, none of the observations presented so far, despite their suggestiveness, establishes or requires a genetic or constitutional etiology. Genetic—that is, twin, adoption, or DNA marker linkage studies of behavioral ihibition have not been carried out in humans, but supportive evidence for genetic etiology is available from studies of animal models of behavioral inhibition.

There are several animal models of genetically determined variation in reactivity to the unfamiliar (Scott and Fuller, 1965; Blizard, 1981). In each of these the more reactive strain, similar to Kagan's (1989) inhibited children, exhibits higher levels of behavioral distress and neurophysiologic arousal. The data most relevant to our argument come from breeding and cross-fostering experiments carried out by Suomi (1987) in two behaviorally distinguished strains (high vs. low reactive) of rhesus monkeys. Detailed discussion of these data is presented here because of the striking similarities between these strains and Kagan's (1989) inhibited versus uninhibited temperamental categories.

The high-reactive strain of rhesus monkeys is very similar to severely inhibited children in regard to the behavioral and the neurphysiological responses of both to unfamiliar situations or social environments. For example, when placed in an unfamiliar playpen, high-reactive monkeys become relatively immobile, stopping their normal vocalizations and play. In addition, like inhibited human counterparts, they exhibit neurophysiologic signs of activation of the hypothalamic-pituitary-adrenal axis, including elevated stable heart rate, higher peripheral cortisol levels, and increased turnover of norepinephrine in their cerebrospinal fluid (Higley et al., 1992; Suomi, 1981). In contrast, low-reactive monkeys (similar to uninhibited children) respond to new situations with exploration, vocalization, and minimal physiologic change. Though these differences are relatively stable, they are apparent only in confrontation with unfamiliar stimuli. In familiar home territory, high- and low-reactive strains are indistinguishable.

Suomi and colleagues (1987) have conducted several experiments to begin to investigate relative genetic and environmental contribution to low and high reactivity. In the first of these, animals reared in the author's breeding colony were first categorized behaviorally by reactivity to the unfamiliar. The classifications were then organized according to extent of genetic relationship between individuals. Full and half siblings were found to be much more likely to have the same reactivity classification than were individuals who were less closely (e.g., cousins) or not genetically related. Parental (or caretaker) influence was considered to be an unlikely source of similarity because most of the monkeys had been removed from their mothers at birth and reared in the laboratory under identical conditions. A second experiment compared development of infants born to high- versus low-reactive pedigrees who were (1) placed at birth with foster mothers who had either the same or different reactive histories and then (2) transferred at adolescence to a peer group environment. Adult foster mothers were also further subdivided according to their previous child-rearing practices as either nurturant or punitive.

Outcome at six months suggested that the infant's pedigree was the dominant predictor of response to stress during adolescence. Individuals from high-reactive pedigrees were much more distressed and impaired in response to separation than were those from low-reactive pedigrees regardless of maternal caregiving style. In contrast the child's functioning in the daily home environment reflected the quality of maternal caretaking rather than reactivity pedigree. In the home environment, infants from high-reactive pedigrees who were raised by nurturing mothers did just as well as those from low-reactive pedigrees.

In summary, comparison of these studies of temperament in humans and primates supports a genetic contribution to behavioral inhibition in human children in that: (1) the temperamental characteristic of high reactivity in rhesus monkeys is an extremely accurate animal model for behavioral inhibition in human children, (2) genetic modeling and cross-fostering (i.e., adoption) studies indicate genetic contributions to the development of high-reactive temperament in monkeys. Because these two temperamental characteristics are so similar in all other attributes, it is highly likely that they share etiologic features as well and that genetic factors contribute to the development of behaviorally inhibited temperament in human children. However, twin and adoption studies of human children are needed to confirm this view.

Is there a Relationship between Behavioral Inhibition and Anxiety?

The data we have reviewed so far suggest that behavioral inhibition is a genetically influenced, longitudinally stable temperament, which is characterized by predisposition to behavioral and physiologic responses that overlap with some of those we commonly associate with so-called anxiety. Even so, linking behaviorally inhibited temperament to genetic predisposition to anxiety requires several further steps. For example, one important question is whether behavioral inhibition includes the subjective emotional experience of anxiety. While the behavior of inhibited children in unfamiliar situations is similar to that often observed to be associated with subjective reports of anxiety, studies connecting the observational data to self-report of subjective emotional experience are not yet available.

A second important step is to study behavioral inhibition outside the laboratory to learn if and how it may play a role in a child's day-to-day anxieties. One recent study carried out by a member of Kagan's (Gersten, 1989) group suggests that the traits characterizing behaviorally inhibited children in the laboratory are consistent with their response in daily life. In that study, children classified as behaviorally inhibited or uninhibited from age 21 months on were observed on repeated occasions in their kindergarten classrooms by a rater blind to temperamental classification. Information was also gathered from structured interviews with teachers. On the basis of both types of data, behaviorally inhibited children were more often shy, withdrawn, or isolated from their peers and were less likely to volunteer answers to the teacher's questions or to participate in activities.

These observations suggest an association between behavioral inhibition and social behaviors we connect with anxiety. Given our current level of etiologic knowledge about emotions and behavior, further empirical clarification of how this association takes place is unlikely in the near future. Still, it is of some interest in terms of the central questions of this chapter to consider one speculative approach to the problem, as offered by Kagan and Snidman (1991). In considering the possible mechanisms underlying school phobia in a behaviorally inhibited child, Kagan and Snidman (1991) suggest the possibility that "for some individuals on some occasions, the brain generates a physiological state that provokes the mind to invent some basis for the change in feeling tone" (p. 861).

How might this occur? The current working hypothesis to explain the temperamental differences between behaviorally inhibited and uninhibited children is that these reflect genetically determined variations in the threshold for excitability of neural pathways in the amygdala and the sympathetic nervous system. Inhibited children are thought to have a lower threshold for excitability of those neural pathways and therefore to experience more internal distress and subsequent difficulty in adapting to new situations. Given that premise, the authors suggest that temperamentally based excitability may lead to spontaneous discharge of those pathways. The emotional distress or anxiety provoked by that discharge may then be mistakenly attributed to coincidentally associated situations—in this case, the school.

Is there a Relationship between Behavioral Inhibition and Anxiety Disorders?

A third step in linking behavioral inhibition and anxiety is to establish whether there is a relationship between this temperament and clinical anxiety disorders. Are behaviorally inhibited children more vulnerable to anxiety disorders? Are there manifestations of this temperament that in themselves meet diagnostic criteria for anxiety disorder(s)?

Several recent studies have begun to address this question. However, results must be regarded as preliminary because of small sample sizes. In addition, the designs of the studies currently available can indicate an association; they cannot clarify whether the observed association involves a causal relationship. However, the findings do provide an initial link between this temperament and clinical anxiety. For example, in Kagan's (1991) longitudinal study sample, both phobias and a lifetime diagnosis of more than one anxiety disorder were more common in inhibited compared with uninhibited children (Biederman et al., 1991). Seven of the 22 inhibited children but only one of the 19 uninhibited ones suffered from phobias ($p < .04$). One-fourth of the inhibited but none of the uninhibited children had multiple anxiety diagnoses. Multiple anxiety disorders were also more common among the parents of inhibited children than among those of uninhibited or normal control children (Rosenbaum et al., 1991).

From the reverse perspective, a more specific relationship has also been suggested between behavioral inhibition and panic disorder with agoraphobia. Rosenbaum et al. (1988) compared the prevalence of behavioral inhibition among children with at least one agoraphobic parent to prevalence among children with a parent who was psychiatrically ill but did not have agoraphobia. Three-fourths of the children of agoraphobics compared with only one-third of the children of the psychiatric controls met the Kagan criteria for behavioral inhibition ($p < .01$).

Shyness

A second group of developmental researchers concentrated its efforts on using twin and adoption studies to assess the relative contributions of heredity and environment to the etiology of one specific aspect of reactivity to the unfamiliar: social response to unfamiliar people. The term "shyness" is used here to describe the fearful end of this spectrum, that is, timid, withdrawn, and avoidant behavior on initial exposure to a new, unfamiliar person. In contrast, children who are not shy are at ease and express interest in the company of strangers.

Even though there is obviously overlap between the definitions and Kagan's inhibited versus uninhibited categories, it is important to clarify that shy individuals may be but are not necessarily, inhibited in situations that do not involve new social encounters.

A number of twin studies of shyness in toddlers and young children are consistent in indicating moderate genetic contribution to this trait (Plomin and Daniels, 1986; Goldsmith, 1983; Goldsmith and Gottesman, 1981). In each case, members of monozygotic twin pairs, who share identical genetic material, are significantly more alike in their response to new persons than are members of dizygotic twin pairs; the genetic overlap between of dizygotic twins is similar to that between regular siblings. However, while the genetic contribution to shyness is robust, it is not exclusive. Only about a third of the variation in shyness between twins is genetically explained. Moreover, initial results of an adoption study suggest an equally relevant environmental contribution derived from the social behavior of caregivers (Plomin, 1990).

The longitudinal course of this type of early childhood shyness has not been well studied. Therefore its possible implications for social functioning later in life are not known.

Genetic Studies of Adult Personality Traits

A number of twin studies have used self-report questionnaires to examine possible genetic contributions to adult personality traits. In this section we review work in two areas: neuroticism and social ease versus social anxiety.

One of the most consistent findings in personality research is the significant genetic contribution to a relatively common and stable trait named variously, neuroticism, anxiety, or stress reaction. Individuals exhibiting this trait complain of frequent feelings of nervousness and somatic anxiety symptoms, are easily upset about variations in normal routine, and have a tendency to worry (Eysenck, 1967). A genetic contribution to neuroticism is indicated by results of several studies that compared the correlation between neuroticism scores in members of genetically identical (monozygotic) and genetically non-identical (dizygotic) twin pairs (Young, Fenton, and Lader, 1971; Carey et al., 1978; Eaves, 1978; Slater and Shields, 1969). Correlations between scores of members of the genetically identical monozygotic twin pairs were consistently and significantly higher. Moreover, the pattern held true even when the monozygotic twins were reared apart. For example, Shields (1962) studied 110 twin pairs: 43 monozygotic pairs reared apart, 42 monozygotic pairs reared together, and 25 dizygotic pairs reared together. Correlations for neuroticism scale scores were actually higher among monozygotic twins reared apart (.58) than either of the other two groups (monozygotic reared together, .38; dizygotic, .11). The inclusion of a group of monozygotic twin pairs whose members were reared separately clarifies the distinction between genetic and environmental influences on development (i.e., nature vs. nurture). If both members are reared together, then it could be monozygotic twins are more alike than dizygotic twins because their identical appearance evokes a greater similarity of response from caretakers. This interpretation is not possible if the members of monozygotic twin pairs are reared separately. Developmental similarities are more likely to reflect genetic influence.

A second anxiety-related adult personality trait that has shown evidence of genetic influence is the diathesis ranging from social ease to social anxiety. Studies of self-report of anxiety in adult twins in situations involving interaction with strangers show a pattern of moderate genetic heritability. For example, one twin study of adult males demonstrated genetic contribution to self-report scores on a seven-item scale related to social ease. The scale was drawn from the California Psychological Inventory (Horn, Plomin, and Rosenman, 1976) and included items related to enjoyment of social notice, mixing well with people, and ability to influence others. Scale scores of monozygotic twins were more similar than those of dizygotes. Similar results were found by this scale in several studies of high school students (Goldsmith, 1983; Plomin and Daniels, 1986).

Additional corroboration of genetic contribution to this diathesis is provided by a second set of twin studies conducted by investigators in

Norway (Torgersen, 1979) and in the Midwestern United States (Rose et al., 1981; Rose and Ditto, 1983). In this work, social functioning is approached from the opposite point of view by assessing the presence of social fears (e.g., performance anxiety, fears of negative evaluation or ridicule by others) rather than social ease. In those studies, social anxiety was measured by asking individuals to rate their fear of a number of specific social situations using a four-point scale (none to panic) on a standardized self-report questionaire that included social and nonsocial fears. Types of social fears assessed included those of public speaking, being watched eating, writing or working, and talking to strangers.

Results of each of these studies indicated genetic contribution to self-report of irrational social fears. There was significantly greater similarity between the social fear scores of members of monozygotic twin pairs than of members of dizygotic pairs.

GENETIC STUDIES OF ANXIETY DISORDERS

The data we have reviewed so far indicate there are a range of heritable or constitutional temperaments and behavioral styles associated with patterns of behavior and and arousal we consider connected to anxiety. In this section we consider the further question of whether there are heritable predispositions not only to anxiety but to anxiety disorders as well. Evidence of genetic contribution to etiology has been established for several of the DSM-III-R anxiety disorders. However, detailed review of that area is outside the scope of this chapter. Instead, we limit the discussion to two examples: phobias and panic disorder. Both are common illnesses whose etiology has been shown to be at least partially genetic.

Phobias

Family and family history studies of phobia patients have consistently indicated that these disorders run in families (Burglass et al., 1977; Carey and Gottesman, 1981; Marks, 1987; Reich and Yates, 1988; Fyer et al., 1990, 1993). Evidence of genetic contribution to the etiology of phobias is provided by two methodologically rigorous twin studies, discussed below. However, whether the unit of genetic transmission is vulnerability to a specific type of phobic disorder, a general phobia proneness, or a combination of the two remains unresolved.

Kendler and colleagues (1992) recently completed a large, epidemiologically sampled twin study of anxiety disorders. Over 1,000 female twin pairs from the Virginia Twin Registry were clinically interviewed and diagnosed according to DSM-III-R criteria. The findings of their study indicate definite genetic contribution to each of the four types of phobias assessed: social phobia, simple phobia, situational phobia, and agoraphobia. Interestingly, these data also suggest there are two types of genetic influences involved in the etiology of phobias. The first is a common phobia proneness, which predisposes an individual to *any* phobic disorder. The second comprises several individual genetic factors each of which is specific to a particular disorder. In this study the relative importance of each type of genetic contribution and of environmental factors differed across the four phobia types. For example, in this model, simple phobias were influenced by the genetic factors common to all phobias and by phobia-specific environmental events (e.g., stuck in an elevator, bitten by a dog). In contrast, specific genetic factors were the stonger influence in the etiology of agoraphobia.

A second twin study of phobias was conducted by Carey and Gottesman (1981) using a sequential series of patients admitted to the Maudsley Clinic for phobic neurosis. Patients in all of the current DSM-III-R phobia categories were included, though there was a predominance agoraphobics. Twice as many of the monozygotic as the dizygotic twin pairs reported concordance for any phobic symptom (with or without impairment or treatment or both). When the diagnostic threshold was raised to include only clinically significant phobias, however, there was no difference between concordance in the two types of twin pairs, suggesting that the occurrence of irrational phobic fear is genetically influenced but that other, nongenetic factors are involved in extent of impairment and treatment seeking.

In summary, available family and twin study data are consistent in indicating heritable contribution to the etiology of phobias. However, whether that contribution occurs in terms of an inherited general predisposition (e.g., fearful temperament), a specific malfunction or a combination of the two remains unresolved.

Panic Disorder

Panic disorder is perhaps the best-studied anxiety disorder with respect to heritability. A series of direct interview family studies conducted during the past 40 years has consistently indicated a four- to sevenfold increased risk for panic disorder among first-degree relatives of panic disorder patients compared with relatives of controls (Cohen et al., 1951; Noyes et al., 1986; Crowe et al., 1988; Maier, 1990; Weissman et al., 1993).

Evidence of genetic contribution to etiology is provided by two twin studies. By cross-indexing the Norwegian Twin and mental health clinic registries, Torgersen (1983) identified twin pairs in whom at least one individual was affected with an anxiety disorder. There were 13 monozygotic and 16 dizygotic twins who had panic disorder. Among the co-twins of the 13 monozygotes, two (15%) also had panic disorder, and another two (15%) had panic attacks but did not meet DSM-III-R criteria for panic disorder. In contrast, none of the co-twins of the 16 dizygotes had either panic disorder or panic attacks. This was a relatively small sample. Still, the significantly higher concordance for panic attacks among genetically identical compared with nonidentical twins (4/13 compared with 0/16) strongly supports genetic contribution to the disorder. This pattern was not found for anxiety disorders not characterized by panic attacks.

In a second, much larger epidemiologically sampled study, Kendler and colleagues (1993) reported on prevalence of panic disorder in more than 1,000 female twin pairs from the Virginia Twin Registry. Results of that study indicated definite genetic contribution to the heritability of panic disorder. Almost all of the heritability of panic disorder appeared to result from genetic factors. However, in this study, overall heritability of panic disorder, from combined genetic and environmental sources, was more modest than that suggested by previous twin and family studies. For example, as mentioned earlier, family studies have found a four- to sevenfold increased risk for panic disorder among first-degree relatives of panic patients compared with relatives of controls. Torgersen (1983) found only a modest increased risk for strictly defined panic disorder in his monozygotic pairs. However, when the diagnostic threshold was lowered to include all co-twins with recurrent panic attacks, the difference between monozygotic and dizygotic pairs approached that predicted by the family studies. In contrast, the proband-wise concordance for panic disorder in the work of Kendler et al. (1993) was only about twice as great in monozygotic compared with dizygotic twins (24% versus 11%) and did not increase even when several types of lower thresholds were considered.

Such differences may reflect variations in sampling or methodology. For example, a clinical sample is more likely to have a higher proportion of severely ill individuals than is a sample drawn from the general population. More severe forms of disorder are also sometimes associated with increased familial risk. That type of sampling difference could account for the lower familial/genetic contribution observed in the Kendler et al. study (1993) compared with previous investigations. Kendler et al. (1993) conducted the first epidemiologically based twin or family study of panic disorder.

It is also possible that the variations indicate genetic heterogeneity (Durner, Greenberg, and Hodge, 1992). In that case there may be two or more types of panic disorder that are clinically similar but genetically distinct. If two different study samples include different proportions of each of these etiologically distinct types, then discrepancies in family and twin study findings can result. Unfortunately, at present there are insufficient data to resolve the problem.

Several studies have attempted to fit observed patterns of prevalence of panic disorder in families to those predicted by different models of transmission, but results have been inconsistent and inconclusive. In common with most behavioral disorders, the pattern of intergenerational transmission of panic disorder does not appear to follow that predicted by simple Mendelian models (i.e., single dominant or recessive gene). Analyses in one family study data set (Noyes et al., 1986) suggest that the disorder is transmitted as a single dominant trait (Pauls et al., 1979, 1980). Those from a second study are more consistent with a single locus recessive model (Vieland et al., 1993). In contrast, Kendler's (1993) twin study suggests combined effect from multiple genes.

Taken as a whole the available data indicate definite genetic contribution to panic disorder. However, as in the case of phobias discussed here, the questions of what is transmitted and the process by which the disorder develops remain unanswered.

CONCLUSIONS

The data indicate the need for a dual conceptualization of anxiety, including its roles as both a determinant and a consequence of personality development. Traditionally, anxiety has been understood primarily as a consequence of intrapsychic or interpersonal conflict. As we have seen, however, anxiety can also occur as a genetically or constitutionally derived brain-generated state that has a major influence on the ways that different aspects of reality are experienced by different individuals (Ohman, 1986; McLeod et al., 1990). This second type of anxiety—that is, anxiety conceptualized as temperament—is not simply a product of psychic conflict but rather a critical determinant of the structure and form of psychic content itself.

This model of anxiety has two implications for psychoanalytic treatment. The first is in the field of interpretation. For the most part, the appearance of the affect of anxiety during treatment is understood as the signal of an area of psychic conflict and the need for interpretation. If the interpretation is accurate, then the anxiety diminishes.

However, anxiety deriving from genetic or constitutionally determined temperament or disorder is not likely to respond to this type of intervention. Instead, in that case, it is probably more helpful to clarify the temperament itself to the patient, that is, to make the patient aware that rather than being inherent in the reality itself, this anxiety is part of a specific way in which he/she experiences reality. This clarification is reassuring, for it means that the world is a less dangerous place than the patient had believed. Moreover, once the distinction is understood, the patient can learn to filter the effects of temperament and develop a more realistic assessment of events as they occur.

A second implication concerns indications for combined (medication plus psychotherapy) treatment. Over the past decade it has been shown that certain types of anxiety and, specifically, clinical anxiety disorders respond well to specific medication treatments. For individuals whose anxiety arises from both temperament and intrapsychic conflict, the most effective treatment is often sequential use of the two modalities. When a patient presents with such coexisting anxiety syndromes, the presence of both may be obvious. However, the exact boundaries of each and the extent to which symptoms are a result of their interaction is ususally unclear. To help clarify the situation, and because its main effects have a relatively rapid and defined time frame, medication is usually begun first. Once medication has taken effect, the patient is reevaluated, and psychotherapeutic goals are set on the basis of the changed condition.

REFERENCES

Barlow, D. H. (1988), *Anxiety and Its Disorders*. New York: Guilford.
Biederman, J., Rosenbaum, J. F., Hirshfeld, D. R., Faraone, S. V., Bolduc, E. A., Gersten, M., Meminger, S. R., Kagan, J., Snidman, N. & Reznick, J. S. (1991), Psychiatric correlates of behavioral inhibition in young children of parents with and without psychiatric disorders. *Arch. Gen. Psychiat.*, 47:21–26.
Blizard, D. A. (1981), The Maudsley reactive and nonreactive strains. *Behav. Genet.*, 11:469–489.
Burglass, D., Clarke, J., Henderson, A. S., Kreitman, M. & Presley, A. S. (1977), A study of agoraphobic housewives. *Psychol. Med.*, 7:73–86.
Buss, A. H., Plomin, R. & Willerman, L. (1973), The inheritance of temperaments. *J. Pers.*, 41:513–524.
Carey, G., Goldsmith, H. H., Tellegen, A. & Gottesman, I. I. (1978), Genetics and personality inventories: The limits of replication with twin data. *Behav. Genet.*, 8:299–313.
———— & Gottesman, I. I. (1981), Twin and family studies of anxiety, phobic, and obsessive disorders. In: *Anxiety*, ed. D. F. Klein & J. Rabkin. New York: Raven Press, pp. 117–136.

Cohen, M. E., Badal, D. W., Kilpatrick, A., Reed, E. W. & White, P. D. (1951), The high familial prevalence of neurocirculatory asthenia (anxiety neurosis, effort syndrome). *Amer. J. Hum. Genet.*, 3:126–158.

Crowe, R. R., Noyes, R., Persico, T., Wilson, A. F. & Elston, R. C. (1988), Genetic studies of panic disorder and related conditions. In: *Relatives at Risk for Mental Disorder*, ed. D. L. Dunner, E. S. Gershon & J. E. Barrett. New York: Raven Press, pp. 73–84.

Durner, M., Greenberg, D. A. & Hodge, S. E. (1992), Inter- and intrafamilial heterogeneity: Effective sampling strategies and comparison of analysis methods. *Amer. J. Hum. Genet.*, 51:859–870.

Eaves, L. J. (1978), Twins as a basis for the causal analysis of human personality. In: *Twin Research*, ed. W. Nance, G. Allen & P. Parisi. New York: Liss, pp. 151–174.

Escalona, S. K. (1984), Social and other environmental influences on the cognitive and personality development of low birthweight infants. *Amer. J. Ment. Deficiency*, 88:508–512.

Eysenck, H. J. (1967), *The Biological Basis of Personality*. Springfield, IL: Thomas.

Fyer, A. J., Mannuzza, S., Chapman, T. F., Liebowitz, M. R. & Klein, D. F. (1993), A direct interview family study of social phobia. *Arch. Gen. Psychiat.*, 50:286–293.

——— ——— Gallops, M. S., Martin, L. Y., Aaronson, C., Gorman, J. M., Liebnowitz, M. R. & Klein, D. F. (1990), Familial transmission of simple phobias and fears: A preliminary report. *Arch. Gen. Psychiat.*, 47:252–256.

Garcia-Coll, C., Kagan, J. & Reznick, S. J. (1984), Behavioral inhibition in young children. *Child Devel.*, 55:1005–1019.

Gersten, M. (1989), Behavioral inhibition in the classroom. In: *Perspectives on Behavioral Inhibition*, ed. S. J. Resnick. Chicago: University of Chicago Press, pp. 71–91.

Goldsmith, H. H. (1983), Genetic influences on personality from infancy to adulthood. *Child Devel.*, 54:331–355.

——— & Gottesman, I. I. (1981), Origins of variation in behavioral style: A longitudinal study of temperament in young twins. *Child Devel.*, 52:91–103.

Greenacre, P. (1941), The predisposition to anxiety. *Psychoanal. Quart.*, 10:66–94, 610–638.

Higley, J. D., Thompson, W. T., Champoux, M., Goldman, D., Hasert, M. F., Kraemer, G. W., Scanlan, J. M., Suomi, S. J. & Linnoila, M. (1992), Paternal and maternal genetic and environmental contributions to CSF monoamine metabolites in rhesus monkeys (*Macaca mulatta*). *Arch. Gen. Psychiat.*, 49:436–441.

Hirshfeld, D. R., Rosenbaum, J. F., Biederman, J., Bolduc, E. A., Faraone, S. V., Snidman, N., Reznick, J. S. & Kagan, J. (1992), Stable behavioral inhibition and its association with anxiety disorder. *J. Amer. Acad. Child Adolesc. Psychiat.*, 31:103–111.

Hoehn-Saric, R., McLeod, D. R. & Zimmerli, W. D. (1989), Somatic manifestations in women with generalized anxiety disorder: psychophysiological responses to psychological stress. *Arch. Gen. Psychiat.*, 46:1113–1119.

Horn, J. M., Plomin, R. & Rosenman, R. (1976), Heritability of personality traits in adult male twins. *Behav. Genet.*, 6:17–30.

Kagan, J. (1989), Temperamental contributions to social behavior. *Amer. Psychol.*, 44:668–674.

——— & Moss, H. A. (1962), *Birth to Maturity*. New Haven, CT: Yale University Press, 1983.

——— Reznick, J. S. & Snidman, N. (1987), Temperamental variation in response to the unfamiliar. In: *Perinatal Development*, ed. N. A. Krasnegor, E. M. Blass & M. A. Hofer. New York: Academic Press, pp. 421–440.

——— & Snidman, N. (1991), Temperamental factors in human development. *Amer. Psychol.*, 46:856–862.

Kendler, K. S., Neale, M. C., Kessler, R. C., Heath, A. C. & Eaves, L. J. (1992), The genetic epidemiology of phobias in women: The interrelationship of agoraphobia, social phobia, situational phobia, and simple phobia. *Arch. Gen. Psychiat.*, 49:273–281.

——— Neale, M. C., Kessler, R. C., Heath, A. C. & Eaves, L. J. (1993), Panic disorder in women: A population based twin study. *Psychol. Med.*, 23:397–406.

Maier, W. (1990), Are panic and depression transmitted independently in families? Presented at annual convention of the American College of Neuropsychopharmacology, San Juan, Puerto Rico.

Marks, I. (1987), The development of normal fear: A review. *J. Child Psychol. Psychiat.*, 28:667–697.

McLeod, D. R., Hoehn-Saric, R., Zimmerli, W. D., DeSouza, E. B. & Oliver, L. K. (1990), Treatment effects of alprazolam and imipramine: Physiological versus subjective changes in patients with generalized anxiety disorder. *Biol. Psychiat*, 28: 849–861.

Noyes, R., Crowe, R. R., Harris, E. L., Hamra, B. J., McChesney, C. M. & Chaudhry, D. R. (1986), Relationship between panic disorder and agoraphobia. *Arch. Gen. Psychiat.*, 43:227–232.

Ohman, A. (1986), Face the beast and fear the face: Animal and social fears as prototypes for evolutionary analyses of emotion. *Psychophysiology*, 23:123–145.

Pauls, D. L., Bucher, K. D., Crowe, R. R. & Noyes, R. (1980), A genetic study of panic disorder pedigrees. *Amer. J. Hum. Genet.*, 32:639–644.

——— Crowe, R. R. & Noyes, R. (1979), Distribution of ancestral secondary cases in anxiety neurosis (panic disorder). *J. Affect Dis.*, 1:287–290.

Plomin, R. (1990), The role of inheritance in behavior. *Science*, 248:183–188.

——— & Daniels, D. (1986), Genetics and shyness. In: *Shyness*, ed. W. H. Jones, J. M. Cheek & S. R. Briggs. New York: Plenum Press, pp. 63–80.

——— & Rowe, D. C. (1979), Genetic and environmental etiology of social behavior in infancy. *Devel. Psychol.*, 15:62–72.

Reich, J. & Yates, W. (1988), Family history of psychiatric disorders in social phobia. *Compr. Psychiat.*, 29:72–75.

Rogeness, G. A., Claudio, C., Macedo, C. A., Fischer, C. & Harris, W. R. (1990), Differences in heart rate and blood pressure in children with conduct disorder, major depression, and separation anxiety. *Psychiat. Res.*, 33:199–206.

Rose, R. J. & Ditto, W. B. (1983), A developmental-genetic analysis of common fears from early adolescence to early adulthood. *Child Devel.*, 54: 361–368.

——— Miller, J. Z., Pogue-Geile, M. F. & Cardwell, G. F. (1981), Twin-family studies of common fears and phobias. In: *Twin Research 3; Intelligence, Personality, and Development*, ed. K. Gedda, P. Parisi & W. Nance. New York: Liss, pp. 169–174.

Rosenbaum, J. F., Biederman, J., Gersten, M., Hirshfeld, D. R., Meminger, S. R., Herman, J. B., Kagan, J., Reznick, J. S. & Snidman, N. (1988), Behavioral inhibition in children of parents with panic disorder and agoraphobia: A controlled study. *Arch. Gen. Psychiat.*, 45:463–480.

———— Biederman, J., Hirshfield, D. R., Bolduc, E. A., Faraone, S. V., Kagan, J., Snidman, N. & Reznick, J. S. (1991), Further evidence of an association between behavioral inhibition and anxiety disorders: Results from a family study of children from a non-clinical sample. *J. Psychiat. Res.*, 25:49–65.

Scott, J. P. & Fuller, J. L. (1965), *Genetics and the Social Behavior of the Dog*. Chicago: University of Chicago Press.

Shields, J. (1962), *Monozygotic Twins Brought up Apart and Brought up Together*. London: Oxford University Press.

Slater, E. & Shields, J. (1969), Genetical aspects of anxiety. *Brit. J. Psychiat.*, Special pub. #3:62–71.

Suomi, S. J. (1981), Genetic and maternal contributions to individual differences in rhesus monkey biobehavioral development. In: *Perinatal Development*, ed. N. A. Krasnego, E. M. Blass & M. A. Hofer. New York: Academic Press, pp. 397–419.

———— (1987), Genetic, maternal, and environmental influences on social development in rhesus monkeys, In: *Primate Behavior and Sociobiology*, ed. A. B. Chiarelli & R. S. Corruccini. New York: Springer, pp. 81–87.

Thomas, A. & Chess, S. (1982), The reality of difficult temperament. *Merrill-Palmer Quart.*, 28:1–20.

———— ———— & Korn, S. J. (1982), The reality of difficult temperament. *Merrill-Palmer Quart.*, 28:1–20.

Torgersen, S. (1979), The nature and origin of common phobic fears. *J. Psychiat.*, 134:343–351.

———— (1983), Genetic factors in anxiety disorders. *Arch. Gen. Psychiat.*, 40:1085–1089.

Vieland, V. J., Hodge, S. E., Lish, J., Adams, P. & Weissman, M. M. (1993), Segregation analysis of panic disorder. *Psychiat. Genet.*, 3:63–71.

Weissman, M. M., Adams, P., Lish, J., Wickramaratne, P., Horwath, E., Charney, D., Woods, S. W., Leeman, E. & Frosch, E. (1993), The relationship between panic disorder and depression: New family study. *Arch. Gen. Psychiat.*, 50:767–780.

Young, J. P. R., Fenton, G. W. & Lader, M. H. (1971), Inheritance of neurotic traits: A twin study of the Middlesex Hospital Questionnaire. *Brit. J. Psychiat.*, 119:393–398.

5 The Ontogeny and Dynamics of Anxiety in Childhood

Scott Dowling

CASE 1

I begin by relating a case vignette drawn from my clinical work with infants and children. It concerns normative developmental issues, the relationship of fear to anxiety, and the place of anxiety in early childhood.

I had been caring for Bill, a 3-year-old boy, in the role of combined pediatrician/developmental adviser for a year when his sister, Karen, was born. Both children had congenital insensitivity to pain, a condition in which awareness of pain is completely absent. As a result, not only did Bill show no aversive response to imposed injury such as falls or burns, but also he repeatedly damaged his own body, mutilating fingers, tongue, cheek, and skin—with teeth that knew no difference between mouthing and biting and with bloody fingers that knew no difference between touch and scratch. When Karen was born with the same disorder, the parents and I were determined to do everything possible to anticipate and prevent self-injuring behavior. Karen responded to the pangs of hunger and thirst and to tactile discomfort with the restlessness or crying that is common to all infants. In contrast, the pain that accompanies cuts, piercing of the skin, and pressure on tendons and viscera was absent. Through supportive discussion about her concern, anxiety, and guilt, I helped Karen's mother provide active, responsive mothering. I emphasized the importance of directly soothing Karen through touch, speech, singing, and vestibular stimulation. Karen's familiarity with her mother through such bodily responses as molding and modification of reflexive feeding reactions was quickly evident, for she was soon expressing her need for the familiar mother with crying demand. To her parents' sorrow and dismay, however, there was daily evidence of her utter indifference to needle sticks, tendon pressure, and other forms of both superficial and deep pain. Her parents' pleasure in the infant was clouded by the anticipation of a hopeless future of unpreventable injury. They described their dilemma: "How are we going to keep her from getting hurt? We spank Bill, but it does no good. He may cry when we shake him, but we don't want to do that and it makes little difference."

Their anxiety for Karen was self-evident and well-founded. Karen was a happy, responsive infant, but when her teeth appeared, her sucking, mouthing, and chewing soon included maceration and laceration of fingers, arms, and tongue. Judging from the experience with Bill, her parents feared that the danger to Karen's somatic integrity would increase rapidly once she started crawling and walking. Hot stoves, radiators, and running water that had burned his skin, collisions with furniture and floor that had bruised or lacerated his skin or broken his bones or teeth; and adventitious injuries from pinching, sharp objects, or angry playmates did not cause Billy to protect himself or avoid harmful actions. Such injuries, painful to other children, had little or no effect on his behavior. In fact, parental confusion—vividly, if ineffectively, expressed in crescendos of physical discipline—elicited only temporary fear responses in Bill, often followed by his teasing repetitions of the prohibited activity.

Karen's mother and I took a different approach with Karen. Under my tutelage, her mother showed love and care for Karen's body in exaggerated, though heartfelt, expressions of attention and concern expressed vocally and by body contact. She talked about Karen's beautiful hands and arms, her lovely legs and toes, her exquisite face and hair. The attention and vocalization gave Karen pleasure, as did other aspects of her warm relationship with her mother. During the first year, Karen was engaged in games of "Pretty Baby," which involved stroking her own arms and hands as well as those of her doll. As the self-inflicted injuries mounted during the second six months, the mother's expressions concomitantly turned into ones of distress and the actions ones of care and repair. Puzzled at first, Karen soon joined in her mother's distress; by 1 year of age she was showing her mother the injured part and initiating the expressions of concern. When Mother expressed concern, say, for an injured finger, Karen did so too. The expressed concern was more effective for body parts she could see, such as a finger, than for those she couldn't, such as her tongue. She looked to her mother for indications about the safety of an object or activity and expressed anxiety when a body part was injured. After 12 months she showed distress independent of Mother's attitude: she became visibly and vocally anxious and avoidant with injury and when an object was termed hot or not safe. Similar developments had been lacking with Bill.

I have described the work with Karen and her mother to make three points: a general one—that distress, not anxiety, is the typical negative affect of the infant during much of the first year—and two specific ones—first, distress and anxiety can be effectively contagious from mother to child and, second, that anxiety, within a strongly affectionate relationship, can be far more effective than fear in influencing infant behavior. Thus anxiety can, as in this case, *replace* physical pain as a modulator of behavior. We see that anxiety, contrasted with distress, arises in an interpersonal context. In the relationship with the caregiver, the ingredient of *meaning*—initially, nonverbal meaning and later, verbalizable meaning—is added to the previous state of distress. Karen's case confirms, and takes us beyond, the Freudian content of infantile anxiety (i.e., loss of Mother and loss of Mother's love); here it includes loss or change of what Mother loves: her child's intact body.

I define *anxiety* as a peculiarly uncomfortable mental experience, an apprehension that something harmful is about to happen. Like other affects, anxiety comprises both an emotion, with its autonomic underpinnings, and ideational content, that is, a script or an associated fantasy, which may be either conscious or unconscious or both. It also includes a name. Affect becomes the handmaiden of the personality when it is named and thereby more delimited than when it cannot be communicated about in words (Katan, 1961).

What can we learn from children about the experience of anxiety that is unavailable from adults? It is possible to describe typical settings of anxiety and forms of anxiety expression throughout development. It is of greater value to grasp the psychological content of anxiety and the significance of the changes that usher in the developmental steps. We can expect to find a changing blend of emotion and ideation as we progress from infancy to adulthood. In early infancy, the emotion corresponds to *nonspecific distress*. Later it is anxiety of varying intensity, blended with other emotions. The associated ideation has both content—the familiar sequence of danger situations outlined by Freud (1926) in "Inhibitions, Symptoms and Anxiety"—and form—determined, or at least limited, by the cognitive maturity of the child.

CASE 2

This case demonstrates the effects of cognitive development on the content and thus on the experience of anxiety in a 3-year-old child. It also illustrates the importance of the world of experienced events and especially of object relationships in determining an individual's experience of anxiety.

Betty had congenital absence of the left arm just above the elbow. She and her parents had visited me at intervals of 2 weeks to a month since she was 5 months old. She was the firstborn; both parents realized that their grief, concern, and confusion were shaping their attitudes and behavior with their daughter. They wanted both to understand their own and Betty's reactions to the anomaly and to plan their child rearing with those reactions in mind.

This we had done. Betty, at 3, was a lively, determined, intelligent child with excellent physical skills: she skillfully manipulated objects by using her left arm in association with the right arm and the feet. Even more impressive were her social skills, stressed by the seemingly unending series of anxious, curious, staring children and adults at supermarkets, wading pools, and ice cream parlors. Betty treated her arm with cheerful indifference, either with or without a cosmetic prosthesis (her "mitt"), which she wore on parental request. She talked about her arm freely and directly with parents and others. She asked questions and defended herself from the importuning children. With friends and neighbors she was an active playmate, a bit more aggressive than most, but by all appearances an untroubled child.

The only fly in the ointment was the still uncertain status of Betty's bowel training. She had been teasingly oppositional but, finally, at age 3, was using the toilet regularly.

Also at 3 she acquired a new sister, Millie, who had no congenital anomalies.

At 3 years 2 months Betty approached her mother and, speaking with great seriousness and finality, said that she would like her mother to get her a new arm, like Millie's arm, *now*.

Her manner of speaking was straightforward and without doubt. Her voice, her mother explained to me, was full of urgency but also was charged with confident expectation. She wanted her arm now. She wanted it right away. She knew her mother could get it for her. Her mother stated, as she had many times before, that Betty had a very nice arm but that it would never be like her other arm or like Millie's or like her playmates'. It could not be changed.

As the talking went on that day and for the next day or two, Mother noted a striking change. Betty's face became worried and pinched, and the cheerfulness was gone. Her voice was first more strident and then hesitant, as she now anxiously, very anxiously, but also very persistently, pursued her wish for an arm and met her mother's steady and reiterated, but empathic, statement that this was not possible.

In the ensuing days there were several more changes. For one thing, the anxiousness receded. Betty became more withdrawn and her attitude quieter; some of the life seemed to have emptied out of her. Some of her older, calmer ways returned and her insistence that her arm be provided *now* disappeared. She had also acquired a new symptom: regular, lumpy fecal soiling.

I met with the family soon afterward. During a phone call before the meeting, I learned that in talks with her mother, Betty defended her soiling by jokingly saying that the BM was her "little rabbit tail" and that she liked having one, like a rabbit. It wiggled and felt funny, like a tail.

In our meeting, Betty initially played and talked much as usual, but with the withdrawn, depleted air that Mother had reported. Turning to the frame dollhouse that is part of my playroom equipment, she created a scene in which a little girl moved through the windows to the outside and back in, eventually remaining outside. The rest of the family, some animals, and the furniture remained inside. She made similar puzzling movements with animal figures—a sheep and a rabbit in particular. Though low-key, the play was dominated by the theme of separation and loss.

Betty remarked about the rabbit and we played a hopping game with it. I said that her mother had told me how Betty was playing a rabbit game at home, pretending that she was like a rabbit and having her BM be a rabbit tail. She looked serious, listening. I spoke of how much a rabbit wants its tail, just as she wants both arms to be the same, as Millie's are. I said her mother and father love her just as she is and that they too know she wants both arms to be the same. Though it makes them sad, this is something they cannot do. Her mother, who was in the office, agreed, reiterating how special Betty is, just as she is. Betty went on playing with the doll figures without commenting on what I had said. Her play included a greater togetherness of the mother figure with the child figure, and she behaved with a familiar friendliness toward me.

Subsequent to that visit, the soiling ceased, not to return. Talk of the arm, of her feelings about Millie, and of other matters continued but without the constant demand for a new arm. Her subdued attitude together with episodes of sadness and anger, however, also continued.

Her sudden, unqualified demand for an arm like Millie's corresponded to a cognitive advance from preconcepts to more clearly conceptual thinking about her arm. Piaget described the sensorimotor organization of intelligence during the first year which eventuates in the beginning of verbal, preoperational intelligence with inner representational life during the second year. That early representational life is characterized by preconcepts in the form of blurred, inconstant images that can and do shift in content and significance under the impact of intense wishes and needs. Preconcepts become more definitive concepts under the limiting influence of experience in the real world of people and things.

Betty's affect, and her understanding, about her arm had passed through four distinct phases corresponding to the aforementioned shift from sensorimotor to preconceptual to early conceptual cognition. The first phase was one of cheerful accommodation to things as they are, based on sensorimotor experience of the arm and eventuating in a preconceptual knowledge of the arm, in which issues of permanence or impermanence were not considered. After Millie's birth, Betty's view of the arm continued to be dominated by wish and desire and by the unquestioned omnipotence of her parents. There was still no clear sense of the permanence of the afflicted arm. The pleasure principle, in this area, was not yet the reality principle. The final phase consisted of an attitude of subdued sadness based on an awareness of the permanence of the arm. In between there had been a period of both powerful desire for a new arm and intense anxiety that perhaps her mother could not provide the arm. Basic to all phases was the mother's frequent use of words for feelings, not only in connection with the arm but about all aspects of her life. Betty grew up with a vocabulary of feelings.

Betty's initial accommodation to the deformity was aided by the indefinite blurred quality of her concept of permanence. But faced with the awareness that her request to her mother might not be met, she became *anxious*, initiating movement toward what we term a more realistic attitude. This corresponds with her oedipal castration anxieties, which were also active at that time. Readers should note especially that Betty's final recognition that the arm will remain as is was accompanied by a *disavowal*, as described by Freud. Reality is accepted only with a parallel disavowal, an ever-renewable "rabbit's tail." The regression to soiling reclaims a desired body part; it is restitution for the lost arm.

Cognitive immaturity had permitted Betty to avoid confrontation of wish with a reality that could not satisfy that wish; when circumstances forced the confrontation, anxiety ensued, triggering a new sense of the real and a second, regressive, solution—the fecal rabbit tail.

I go on at length to make a simple point. We see in this case, in exquisite directness, the place of anxiety in instituting a regressive defensive solution to a conflict between wish and reality. Failure of such a solution, with continued disavowal, would set the stage for neurotic symptoms, an eventuality that fortunately did not occur.

The psychological events seen at that early date are similar in their dynamic progression to the events leading to neurosis in later life. Both anxious affect, with the expectation of a dread event, and depressive affect, with awareness that a dreaded event has occurred and is permanent, can be seen in this instance. We also see the place of preconceptual, preoperational thinking, which is so frequently found in the structure of neurosis. Even at an early age, anxiety serves a signal function, triggering the psychological process of a protective, adaptive nature.

CASE 3

Finally, I shall touch on the expression of anxiety in older children. I include this case because it is an example of traumatic anxiety—anxiety of such force that ego functions are massively disrupted.

Years ago, as an Air Force pediatrician, I was asked to examine a mute, trembling, and cowering 9-year-old boy, Jim, who lived with his mother and father. The father was an Air Force sergeant, a chronic alcoholic, and a tyrant. Jim's daily existence was dominated by a state of uncertainty and chronic anxiety that characterizes life with an alcoholic parent. The loving father of the morning often became the brawling, truculent, unreasoning father of the evening.

The day before I saw him had been a bad one. Jim's father had struck his mother before storming out and had not returned. Late that night, Jim awoke from troubled sleep and walked out of his second-floor bedroom and down the corridor. Looking over the banister to the living room below, he saw the figure of his father spread-eagled, unmoving, on the floor, and visible only because of the moonlight shining through the window.

Jim was immediately propelled into a state of terror, screaming, "He's dead! He's dead!" His father was, in fact, lying there in a drunken stupor. For the next 12 hours, despite the later awakening of his father and reassurance by his mother, Jim remained overwhelmingly, tremblingly anxious, mostly mute except for garbled statements that his father looked dead. I examined him at that time and instituted simple supportive measures. By the third day, the anxiety had lessened but he was now terrified to leave the house, a symptom that became fixed during the succeeding weeks.

Little imagination is required to recognize the dynamics involved. Chronic, barely repressed hatred, with wishes for his father's death as well as with relief that it might actually be so, erupted under the stimulus of viewing the unconscious body. The conflict between these reactions and the demands of conscience and, quite possibly, of reality provoked intense anxiety and guilt. The meaning of the visible, prostrate form of his father had had traumatic impact, given the intense but only partially conscious, ambivalent attitude he held toward his father.

Anxiety is the result of conflict. Karen, it is true, "learned" anxiety from her mother; anxiety, in her case, was the result of a disparity, or conflict, between expectation and actuality. She was taught to have such anxiety in the instance of actual or potential injury to her body. The teaching took place within the framework of a loving relationship. With Betty we saw the effects of an external conflict between Betty's wish on one hand and Mother's refusal to comply on the other. Jim's conflict was internalized; it reflected both an intense wish for his father's death and the strictures of conscience. Repressed death wishes erupted under the stimulus of viewing the immobile figure. At the time, however, Jim was aware only of the helpless dread. As is often the case, the anxiety became focused on an outer scene rather than on the inner state of conflict and helplessness. The process of moving an inner conflict to the outside is even more evident in the displacement onto the dangers of leaving the house, expressed in Jim's anxiety-binding, subsequent phobia.

My conception of anxiety in young children thus follows Freud's (1926) classic ideas as extended by Brenner (1982) and others. Anxiety and other negative affects, especially depressive affect, rest at the fulcrum of neurosis, instigating and promoting regression and defensive distortion as a means of resolving conflictual situations.

Certain special circumstances of childhood focus on the developmental issues related to an infant's distress/anxiety as I have described and on the place of anxiety in symptom formation; the remainder of this chapter is devoted to more extensive consideration of both.

One intriguing part of the classical approach to the problem of anxiety in children concerns early infancy, because our conceptualization, which stresses the psychological content of the anxiety condition, must also account for emotional experience and response during early infancy. The issue has a parallel in the issue of conflict in early life. It's an onset issue; if psychological content is not there at the outset, just when does it begin and how do we recognize it? The question is dangerously close to semantic scholasticism, similar to attempts to decide when life begins. My predilection is to assign the beginning of psychological content to nonreflective means–end behavior and to obvious intentionality. In its earliest forms, intentionality is noted at about 12 weeks; as a regular component of behavior, at 16–20 weeks.

But these are essentially one-way, linear activities; much like extensions of reflex motor activities, they are manifestations of sensorimotor intelligence, lacking any but the most fuzzy of mental representations. It is only with the acquisition of verbal capacity at 13–18 months that mental representation is unquestionable; even then it has a long way to go to achieve reversibility—the recognition of multiple possibilities—which makes its appearance with the operational thinking of 5- to 7-year-olds. Thus my choice for the age of beginning anxiety contrasted with undifferentiated distress is about 16 weeks though still reserving for the second year of life an experience of anxiety that approximates the experience of older children and adults.

What elicits distress? Pain, hunger, thirst, skin irritation, and other physical stimuli are obvious answers. Overstimulation—or understimulation—is a less obvious instigator of distress. To these possibilities we must add disruptions of sensorimotor anticipation, which occur with ever growing frequency during the first year of life. The scent of the mother's milk or the sound of the bottle being prepared signals an anticipated feeding. If the feeding doesn't occur, distress rapidly follows.

But the undifferentiated unpleasure of distress is not the same as human anxiety; it *is* the same as what is termed anxiety in animals. Human anxiety awaits the formation of mental representations and a rudimentary differentiation of self from other. This corresponds to Pribram's and Gill's suggestion (1976) of parallel processing by the right cerebral hemisphere with the limbic system in human emotion. An important transitional phase in the movement from distress to anxiety occurs with the formation of the affective object, that is, a regular linkage of emotion with the sensory experience of a particular person around 6 months of age. Anxiety proper, with anxious responses to the loss of a mother who is truly recognized as other, begins after 1 year of age.

I readily appreciate that such discussion may smack of word-chopping and seem of little consequence to the therapist of adults—a therapist of children and infants who is stirring the ashes of his chosen profession. However, a glance at an influential alternative to the Freudian anxiety model may stimulate readers' interest in what I have outlined; the assumptions involved in this model lead to drastically different views of psychological functioning, of psychopathology, and thus of psychological treatment, for what is behind the scenes of these discussions is both the conflict theory of psychoanalysis and what I, somewhat awkwardly, call the transformational theory of psychoanalysis.

Underlying recent challenges to the Freudian viewpoint is the poorly known affect theory of Tomkins (1962, 1963, 1991) as presented in his three-volume work. Tomkins sees affect as the primary motivator, dismissing drive theory. The basis of affect is neither a physiological or a psychological phenomenon. It is motor/muscle and skin sensory in origin, predominantly if not exclusively involving the muscles and skin of the face. Darwin (1973), as Tomkins and others have noted, described the universal facial expressions of a variety of affects as well as the similarity of emotional expression in related mammals. Cross-cultural recognition of the facial expression of distress, surprise, excitement, and joy were confirmed by Tomkins and coworkers, especially Ekman, Freisen, and Ellsworth (1972). Unquestionably, the facial expressions of a number of emotions are cross-culturally recognized; some of them are present in infants at only a few weeks of age.

Actors, trained to assume particular expressions, are regarded by others and by themselves as "feeling anxious, depressed, etc." (Tomkins, 1963). Tomkins claimed it is motor expression of the face together with associated sensory stimulation of the skin and other forms of feedback that evokes the psychological and physiological responses we term affect. A messy, unmeasurable, subjective psychology of meaning is thus sidestepped; observable, measurable phenomena (e.g., facial expressions) are made central, with all the attendant advantages for those seeking hard-science methodology. Tomkins does provide a complex and interesting elaboration of this basic paradigm, acknowledging, for example, the blending, substitution, and inhibition of affect. He is, however, vehement in his promotion of the peripheral origin of affect and in his denunciation of the relevance of drive, in the psychoanalytic sense, to motivation. Motivation is driven by affect and affect alone.

Tomkins's theory underlies the work of our best-known psychoanalytic interpreters of infant experience: Emde, Gaensbauer, and Harmon (1976); Stern (1985); and Lichtenberg (1989), the latter using Tomkins's work to support self psychology. It has fueled the rejection of drive theory and of the tripartite structural theory by these and other analysts.

Emde et al. (1976) provided the most thoughtful of these extensions of Tomkins's approach. They retained Tomkins's view of affect as motivator but moved away from the view of affects as sharply delineated entities. They presented a view of emotion as a continuous background of all activity, thereby supporting a continuing sense of self. They described a progression of the regulation of emotion from control by endogenous rhythms to social control to internal control, a view that correlates nicely with the traditional psychoanalytic view I illustrated with Karen and Betty. Anxiety retains a place in this system.

Stern (1985) shifted further away from the Freudian baseline, defining psychopathology in terms of various disturbances of a sense of self. Therapy consists of clarifying and defining the historical antecedents of these present-day disorders of a sense of self.

Lichtenberg (1989) presented a motivation theory based on separate systems (e.g., attachment, aversion, and sensual-sexual). The theory eliminates the tripartite model and the centrality of intrapsychic conflict, and it never mentions anxiety in either unmodified or signal forms.

All three of these models have clear implications for our theories of neurosogenesis and therapeutic action. Disturbances in the formation of the various motivational systems because of inadequate neural equipment or lack of appropriate interpersonal experiences is responsible for the failures or distortions of development that are the point of origin of psychopathology. Treatment lies in recognizing, defining and correcting the faulty organization of those systems. The contrast with the emphasis on conflict that has characterized psychoanalytic theory for the past hundred years is stark.

Anxiety in children, as in adults, has a spectrum of forms. At the extremes are traumatic anxiety—occurring in a state of helplessness —and signal anxiety—the consciously inapparent trigger of defense and symptom formation. Those distinctions are lacking in an anxiety-less theory such as Lichtenberg's (1989). Psychoanalytic theory is characterized by a transformational theory of affect, including anxiety. In psychoanalytic theory there is a place behind the scenes, a place outside consciousness, consisting of the vast mental space with the quality of unconsciousness where drives, defenses, and a variety of processes and principles, including the reality principle, operate. Transformations are instigated there also, for defensive and other purposes.

Drive derivatives, including affects, may appear in consciousness in a variety of forms and disguises. Among such potential transformations is the possibility that anxiety may appear in consciousness as anger, or anger as anxiety. An awareness of this potential is at the heart of the usual analytic therapeutic approach. Analysts seek to recognize and interpret defensive management of affect, including anxiety, as a means of entering into the psychological world of patients. This is more specifically true of analysts of children than of analysts of adults and constitutes the basic discovery, by Berta Bornstein and Anna Freud, that made child psychoanalysis possible. A model of affect presentation that is based purely on visible, conscious mechanisms leaves scant room for the insights that have made psychoanalysis viable.

As others will amplify, I doubt there is any aspect of psychoanalytic theory that is less clearly developed, more fully the object of interest and research, and more promising as a source of new psychoanalytic understanding than is affect theory. The tendency of infancy researchers to insist that advances in affect theory mean the end of drive theory and, possibly, of the tripartite model, is, I believe, unfortunate. It is often helpful to their research methodology to consider affect in this light as a means of isolating and focusing on affect as the subject of study. But that research methodology is not a requirement demanded by their research findings. There is good reason to believe that it will be the interactive accommodation of observational data from normal children and psychoanalytic data from disordered children and adults rather than exclusive attention to one set of data that will lead to useful change.

REFERENCES

Brenner, C. (1982), *The Mind in Conflict*. New York: International Universities Press.

Darwin, C. (1973), *The Expression of Emotions in Man and Animals*. New York: AMS Press.

Ekman, P., Freisen, W. & Ellsworth, P. (1972), *Emotion in the Human Face: Guidelines for Research and an Integration of Findings*. Elmsford, NY: Pergamon Press.

Emde, R., Gaensbauer, T. & Harmon, R. (1976), *Emotional Expression in Infancy: A Biobehavioral Study. Psychological Issues, Monogr. 37*. New York: International Universities Press.

Freud S. (1926), Inhibitions, symptoms, and anxiety. *Standard Edition*, 20:87–174. London: Hogarth Press.

Katan, A. (1961), Some thoughts about the role of verbalization in early childhood. *The Psychoanal. Study of the Child*, 16:184–188.

Lichtenberg, J. (1989), *Psychoanalysis and Motivation*. Hillsdale, NJ: The Analytic Press.

Pribram, K. & Gill, M. (1976), *Freud's Project Reassessed*. New York: Basic Books.

Stern, D. (1985), *The Interpersonal World of the Infant*. New York: Basic Books.

Tomkins, S. (1962), *Affect, Imagery, Consciousness, Vol. 1*. New York: Springer.

——— (1963), *Affect, Imagery, Consciousness, Vol. 2*. New York: Springer.

——— (1991), *Affect, Imagery, Consciousness, Vol. 3*. New York: Springer.

6 Learning to Be Anxious

Gerald I. Fogel

Everyone knows what anxiety is, which should make the subject an especially rich one for interdisciplinary study. However, interesting and crucially important aspects of a psychological subject—aspects that bear directly on one's ability to conduct effective and sophisticated psychotherapy—may also be the most difficult to bring an intelligible interface with neurobiological and psychopharmacological understandings. The latter disciplines require a quantitative empirical approach, relying on methodological reduction and precise definition. Problems that can be studied with measuring devices and psychological states that can be most precisely defined and described by the people who are the subjects of study yield the most accurate and replicable empirical knowledge.

I argue here, however, that a significant group of patients nowadays are especially difficult to understand and treat *because* of their abilities to describe and understand accurately their anxieties and other affective states. In a sense they know too much, and I believe that in their early lives they also needed to know too much too soon. They replicate their accurate findings too easily, too well, and too adaptively. They need to lose knowledge to regain a more spontaneous and rich psychological life, and often they do not realize what they lack and therefore long for. In order to accomplish change in the deepest sense, they must recapture and learn to tolerate and describe confusing and incomplete experiences that challenge and defeat their considerable capacities for self-articulation, experiences that include mixtures of unpleasurable affects that ordinarily are *impossible* to accurately define and precisely replicate, sometimes for long periods in treatment.

I have come to regard this increasingly prevalent phenomenon as a characterological style that I call *psychological-mindedness as a defense*. The phenomenon seems to cut across traditional diagnostic categories and therefore to assume a wide variety of forms. Such patients often appear to be ideal for analytic work, for they seem to share the practitioner's outlook and values. The interior life—comprising feelings, fantasies, and motives, as well as an apparent sensitivity to the same things in others—is centrally important to them, frequently a preoccupation. Self-reflection, rapport, and psychological insights are highly valued and manifestly pursued, and the analyst's initial instinct is to accept without question such patients' capacity to talk in rich psychological terms about themselves and others and their earnest and emotionally sensitive discussions of relationships, ambitions, conflicts, and values. Such persons appear pre-educated in regard to self-observation in the therapeutic setting. They are naturals—never merely isolated intellectualizers, shallow dramatizers, or simply avoiders or exploiters of other people. They appear involved with themselves and others in ways that are richly layered with meaning, personal and interpersonal connectedness, and psychological complexity.

Among the things that come naturally to them is the language of anxiety and depression. When one finally begins to catch on, however, their language of feelings and understandings is revealed to be the cornerstone of a subtle, egosyntonic adaptive-defensive system. Such people have something of the therapeutic layered into the core of their deepest selves, and their great gift to themselves and others (including their analyst and primary caregivers of the past) is the correct but premature understanding or interpretation. Experience is not disavowed, but is prematurely organized and synthesized. Psychological phenomena are identified and organized not only to reach spontaneously for and live out personal experience but to make it more tame or familiar—its boundaries more objectifiable and controllable—and to increase security and self-esteem or to gain the admiration and protection of others. Insights are proud possessions rather than, as they should be, simple tools in the service of living life. Like precocious children, which many of them once were, they usually have not learned to recognize and deeply experience important fears and other dysphoric experiences, from which they remain tuned out in various ways and to various degrees. Therefore, paradoxically, an important task they must accomplish in their treatment is more truly *learning to be anxious*.

CLINICAL VIGNETTE

After weeks of frank and profound doubts about whether I were the best possible therapist for him, Mr. A, a successful executive in his mid-30s, began analysis. The transition to the couch seemed uneventful and his hours were filled largely with descriptive details from his daily life—mostly concerns with job performance and personal relations—which he presented in an introspective and psychologically alive manner. He included feelings, motives, and fantasies, referencing the internal worlds of himself and significant others. He was a kind and soft-spoken man, neither overintellectual nor especially self-dramatizing, and he routinely considered possible sources for his fears and associated to details of their long history. He frequently felt anxious and inadequate but additionally was vulnerable to sudden unpredictable intensifications of such dysphoric states—usually when involved in some interaction with important authority figures in his life—and he had many insightful things to say about his conflicts in relation to authority. On the relatively rare occasions when he actually had one of his anxiety "attacks," however, he was deeply convinced that he was transparent to others, and that mortifying thought was almost intolerable to him. He felt like an open book.

Relatively early in the treatment he had an hour that was very different from all prior ones, although at the time I was not able to characterize it. He recalled a childhood memory of walking through the hallway that connected his bedroom to the living room and catching a glimpse—through the slightly ajar door to his parents' bedroom —of his mother dressing. Uncharacteristically, he lingered over the memory, painted a vivid impression, and provided evocative details. He described, for example, particulars of his mother's clothing, what parts of her body were visible, and architectural details, including the doorway, the layout of the hallway, and the rest of the apartment. Although neither he nor his mother explicitly acknowledged each other's presence or ever spoke of it, Mr. A felt that somehow, implicitly, this had been a shared, *mutually* gratifying experience. Importantly, however, I formed vivid images of the scene through his eyes, and *I* myself realized that this had not usually been the case in our work to that point.

His mood also impressed me. He seemed especially absorbed in the story. There was an air of pleasant nostalgia and unspoken pleasure in telling it to me. In retrospect and in light of subjects to be developed later in this chapter, I would say that part of the pleasure lay in the *implied* psychological mastery and the *illusion* of sharing this mastery while sharing the story, both in the early memory and in its re-creation in our relationship. That was to be the first of many shared moments from his past and present life and in our work that felt rich and real but that seemed to come and go without rhyme or reason or solid sense of fittedness into his life, life history, or analysis. Usually he did not seem aware of this. When the stories recurred, however, as I listened to the same details without additional understandings or new perspectives, they therefore gradually lost life for *me*. It was as if one owned a videotape of *Oedipus Rex* that for unexamined reasons one sometimes felt like viewing, usually enjoyed it when one did so, and also could enjoy sharing with a friend if one sensed the friend could appreciate it and get into it with one in a way that felt comfortable and compatible with one's own sensibilities. But these stories were sequestered somehow from Mr. A's own life and relationships and had a quality of almost being vicarious. His *own* oedipal complex was untouched; even insightful understandings had the quality of a skillful exercise in *applied* analysis. Mr. A had never discussed that moment with his mother, so her actual reactions or thoughts were quite unknown to him, and that fact did not seem especially noteworthy to him. Everything felt clear, seamless, and pleasant, but all understandings—his own or those between himself and his mother—were tacit, unspoken.

On that occasion I made no interpretation. Mr. A's reflections seemed stereotypical and obvious to me and he thought so too. I was impressed only by the absence of any connection of this vivid memory to the preceding or subsequent fabric of the analysis, especially in the transference. The question, Why now? relative to the moment, the session, current themes in the analysis, or resonances in our relationship was not raised. I followed my technical guidelines for newly emerging material that was neither yet understood nor sufficiently disturbing to require particular attention. Wait and see. I did not know then that there might be something prototypical here, that a likely link between the here and now and the early memory was the implied but actually *precocious and premature* psychological mastery in both moments, and his pleasure in sharing it, as well as an unspoken assumption that it gave me pleasure also.

The actual fate of that memory during that analysis is complex and as yet incomplete. Its appearance marked my first awareness that the psychological sophistication of what came before had been somewhat misleading and its *absolute inability to be integrated with anything else* a first clue in a puzzle that forms the subject matter of this chapter. The *integration factor* figures prominently in later discussion. At that moment, in retrospect, my data were not the story, but the fact that I could not *imagine* any way to make the story fit—in the deeper sense—into the larger story of his life or the narrative flow of his analysis. My first real theory developed when I noticed a possible pattern: that such moments were far more likely to occur on the last session of a week. I recall mentioning the incident briefly, shortly after it occurred, in a small discussion group on the differences between psychotherapy and psychoanalysis, when I speculated that in a treatment with less structured frequency, I would be far less likely to see such a phenomenon, and I estimated that it would be another year or two before the material was ripe enough for understanding or comment, a demonstration that in the field of analysis, evolution and timing were all. There was some truth in this formulation, but it was far too simple; Mr. A's behavior turned out to be generalizable to a wide variety of affects and situations, not simply separation and attachment or other issues raised by the symbolic comings and goings of his analyst.

For a time later on, Mr. A and I found one way to characterize the phenomenon usefully: the metaphor of the lullaby. As in "Rock-a-Bye Baby," potentially aggressive, overexciting, painful, or dangerous situations—contents with the power to disarm—are presented as coherent narratives in soothing tones that lull, reassure, and create an aura of pleasure, togetherness, safety, and mastery. Yet Mr. A could draw a complete blank, feeling inadequate and inarticulate when connections that would be psychological child's play for him under other circumstances took him by surprise. For example, the outer of the two doors separated by a small foyer by which patients may exit my office without going through the waiting room is sometimes incompletely closed by the former exiting patient—in other words, it is left *ajar*. When Mr. A noticed the ajar exit door on his way through a hallway to my waiting room and tried to bring it to my attention, he felt disconcerted, self-conscious, and inarticulate. He could neither comfortably treat the event as reality ("Would you mind closing the door?") nor fantasize usefully, produce associations, and thereby possibly connect the event to the prototypical ajar door in the screen memory. Pressed to explore *either* aspect, he felt even more helpless and inadequate, intruded upon, humiliated, and controlled. On another occasion, a childhood image of his mother's face framed by blue sky, the wind blowing a lock of hair across her face, suddenly appeared at an emotional moment during an hour. Pressed later either to speculate on why it was there or to associate to it, the same inadequate-angry-overwhelmed-uncomprehending feelings arose.

Progress in the analysis gradually gave us easier access to such contents, but the pattern was persistent and movement occurred in fits and starts. For example, later breakthroughs in his capacity to assert himself occupationally produced not only successes and triumphs but also signs of separation and mourning. During one hour, he spoke movingly of his young son's recent surge of new developmental attainments but also of a reappearance in the son of previously outgrown clinging behaviors and night fears. Mr. A spoke insightfully of the inevitable connectedness of all of these; of his newly acquired abilities to discern these complex inevitabilities and thereby be a better parent; and, more sympathetically, of his wife's (sometimes burdensome to him) difficulties separating from the child.

There were pride, rueful wisdom, and the explicit acknowledgment that his hard-won new capacities were a reflection of our good work together in the analysis. My gentle suggestion that he might be using these understandings to shield himself from his own identical conflicts and feelings was received as traumatizing—jarring and unusable; there was no gratification in his recognition of the inevitable awkwardnesses, fears, doubts, and uncertainties that accompanied *his* developmental evolution, especially in relation to me.

On that occasion, Mr. A recovered his aplomb and gradually began to articulate some of the components of his state of shocked and angry confusion, and we were even able to connect some of these thoughts to the material that preceded my traumatizing him. But a powerful wish and need persist that periodically assert themselves in order to subvert all of these possible pathways to a single scenario that, in effect, proclaims earnestly to me, "I am doing fine. Relax and enjoy it, for I do not need anything from you. There are no 'problems' here, so do not tamper with the situation in some ill-advised attempt to try to help me. You are, naturally, also pleased with the work we have accomplished. Don't we both have reason to be pleased and proud?"

TRAUMATIC MOMENTS

Psychologically minded people like Mr. A are *capable* of high degrees of self-reflection and are therefore capable of exploiting self-reflection for defensive purposes. They also, however, frequently need to retain both a level of integration and the subjective sense that things are all right that accompanies it by avoiding situations that challenge it. Like anyone else, they exploit areas of strength to avoid areas of vulnerability. The experience that is being avoided is usually brought about by some combination of uncontainable psychic intensity or conflict and an island of developmental unintegration experienced as emerging too rapidly or uncontrolledly—leading to a loss of integration, of regressive dedifferentiation, of overwhelmedness and disorientation, and of "losing it." I call such a moment, which has led to successful analytic work, *a traumatic moment*.

I toyed with various other phrases to characterize such a prototypical moment, but the interface with the subject of psychic trauma seems crucial. I want to highlight an essential therapeutic moment when the previously inarticulable becomes potentially capable of articulation. If I wanted to emphasize the everydayness of such an occurence—not predispose the reader to think of the more difficult patient—I might have called it a loss of balance or a moment of disequilibrium. To emphasize the potential for creative reorganization, a moment in an analysis when sound clinical intuition, tact, and timing correctly sense that analytic work is possible, I could call such a moment a capacity to be *usefully* overwhelmed.

There is an interface here with the so-called difficult character disorders, but I am discussing commonplace problems in highly analyzable patients. There is a spectrum, of course, but such patients, when they are doing deep and useful analytic work, must suffer periods when the only terminology we have available to describe what goes on in them is terminology that is familiar to us only from the literature on difficult patients and it is easy to be overimpressed with the variably problematic but surprisingly often transient nature of the regression and its so-called primitivity. When such patients' customary defenses are threatened, they utilize splitting and projective identification, become mortified, and suffer narcissistic rages and panic. Their anxieties are uncontrollable and primitive. They may evoke transient but powerful counterresponses in the analyst. Sometimes, the first sign that something useful is happening in such an analysis is revealed through a psychosomatic symptom, other forms of somatization, experiences that are transient but only classifiable by them as weird or strange, or some other term that means inarticulatable, or as impulsive, addictive, or perverse behavior or trends.

Certain so-called primitive phenomena and defenses are becoming increasingly the rule in all patients, and this is particularly well illustrated by this group. They all rely on some form of as-if behavior—a form of role-playing that is, if not simply compliant, certainly unauthentic to some degree by virtue of its defensive function. They also rely on a form of splitting that may be conceptualized variously as Kleinian splitting, Kohutian vertical splits, or Freudian disavowal or denial in fantasy. One's understandings and interventions depend not only on theoretical preference but also on intuitive clinical judgments regarding the usefulness in varying and constantly changing contexts of such technical procedures as tactful silences, simple empathic statements, painstakingly careful and detailed mutual clarifications, speculations, expressions of puzzlement or timely questions and wonderings, confrontations regarding the interpersonal or other defensive aspects of the disavowal, or, if sufficiently ripe clinical material is available, useful constructions, reconstructions, or interpretations. No simple all-purpose formula exists.

This is because these capacities for role-playing and compartmentalization of experience are combined with deeper capacities for rich personal and interpersonal experience in cunning and ingenious ways, and it is far from easy to tell at a glance what is the marrow and what is only skin deep. Capacities to tolerate regression and to use the analytic situation and the therapeutic relationship to contain and structure powerful regressive responses may be high. Symbolic experience is easy, however, and experience that is both adaptive and authentic as a defensive strategy can be a powerful egosyntonic barrier to allowing more archaic and proto- and presymbolic experiences to emerge. Much depends on motivational and other less tangible factors than are contained in DSM-III-R. Loewald (1952) was one of the first to point out that in every patient there is an inevitable coexistence of integration or developmental-lag psychological factors and object-instinctual wish-fear-conflict factors and also (1960) to point out an innate striving in psychic life for higher levels of organization and integration—a sort of developmental, ego drive. In the analytic situation, close attention to splits and enactments and to the traumatic moments when splits are challenged, enactments bracketed and articulated, and logical analytic developmental lines subtly derailed reveals clues that may lead us to the often invisible fault lines where the deepest and most useful therapeutic work takes place.

Obviously, my subject is wider than anxiety or affect. Consider some of the words I found myself using to describe some of Mr. A's traumatic moments and the feelings involved: uncertainty, inarticulateness, mortification, doubts, disorientation, puzzlement, confusion, awkwardness, spaciness, overwhelmedness, shock, panic, rage—an almost endless list, which is different for every patient. In classical analysis it has been for years a standard intervention that when an analyst senses the possibility of a silent or subtle resistance, the analyst inquires "Might you be feeling anxious about something?" I have almost deleted the word from my working vocabulary, however, because these patients leap on it—they always have some good and usually true set of higher-level thoughts about identifiable anxiety. Sometimes I have found myself falling back on Freud's structurally superseded theoretical terminology and think rather of unpleasure (or the modern equivalent—dysphoria), which leaves open a door that can contain a range of affects of varying qualities and intensities, a welcome ambiguity between the motive or drive, the sometimes ephemeral and difficult to articulate affects and bodily sensations, the vaguely experienced impulses to action, and the potential thoughts that want to emerge, organize, and define those experiences.

This phenomenon crosses classical diagnostic lines, and I have not the space for further detailed clinical vignettes. In the service of pondering the variety of phenomena that may be contained in such a moment, however, consider a universal experience familiar to us all: the common temper tantrum. Any single tantrum or potential tantrum may contain imperious demands; impotent and uselessly destructive rage; the rage and shame of mortification; *effective* incorporative or destructive rage (which may vary with the effectiveness of the behavior, its successful articulation, or its precision of application to its object); a variety of aggressively expressed sexual and psychosexual longings; frantic clinging; the isolation, helplessness, and overwhelmedness of total abandonment; furious wishes to be left alone; affects of desperation, dread, or inconsolable pain; experiences of madness or disorganization; and so forth. In simpler times Mr. A may have been regarded as having a routine obsessional neurosis with depressive features, but I regard as naive any interpretation in relation to Mr. A's material that took the reflexive or formulistic form of delineating a power struggle or a simple defensive reaction in relation to the so-called oedipal-level anxieties, or a dependency longing or wish simply to be held. When Mr. A loses it, sometimes the liberated aggression, pain, need, and fear take new, articulatable forms— sometimes not—and situations, fears, mortifications, self-states, higher- and lower-level object longings, and conflicts become more or less visible.

In addition, these more or less well defined contents must also be considered in relation to issues of authenticity or fit both within him and between the two of us. In other words, these episodes are more or less traumatic, self-defining, or authentic, and reintegration sometimes leads to new levels of awareness or integration and sometimes not. But I have many other patients who present with these same diagnostic and treatment enigmas in very different forms. I have another patient, for example, who deals with analogous situations—ones that Mr. A might wish to gently withdraw from and work on in his own way—by leaping boldly into the breach; he is a kind of counterphobic and manic (in the Kleinian sense) psychological cowboy who analyzes my countertransferences and parades his ability to express violent and sexual fantasies about me in ways that can be quite impressive. But as time goes on, these behaviors are more clearly revealed to be an avoidance of something deeper, subtler, and more difficult to get at. The most reliable affect signal of hidden intensity for this most articulate man has turned out to be a simple intrusion on his powers of self-expression—in the form of a subtle speech disturbance that he had all but forgotten from his early childhood. Space does not permit further examples, but the varieties of presentation are enormous, ranging across all styles and degrees of psychopathology.

THE DEVELOPMENTAL HISTORY AND
ITS RECONSTRUCTION

In work with such patients, the deadliest path is the formulistic interpretation or reconstruction, no matter if it is Kleinian, Kohutian, Lacanian, or Freudian. Most of the important work needs to grow first in the here and now of the transference and the transference-countertransference interface, and a good deal of work must often be done before meaningful reconstruction can take place. I sometimes do a lot of talking at various points in working with such sophisticated people as I struggle to create a context for collaborative work—for both analyst and patient trying together to make sense of what is going on. I do not hesitate to be uncertain or to say so. A highly individualized metaphorical language that is different for each patient must be mutually constructed if one is to catch the unique structural, existential, relational, and developmental variables that characterize each of them.

Patients discover their own ways to contain traumatic dislocation in language. One patient recently used the concept of swinging from one trapeze to another to characterize the ungrounded moment when one has risked leaving one compartment or mental set but is not yet safely connected at the other end. That man had actually spent long periods of his childhood in isolated play in which he enacted complex imaginary scenarios using shoe boxes. A woman told me recently that she felt like Magnus Pym, protagonist of the John Le Carré novel *A Perfect Spy*. Like Magnus and many of these patients, she had lived her whole life with the feeling of having many different lives and knowing how to lead all of them, but never feeling secure that she was the same person in all of them or that any one person knew all the parts of her. Le Carré's are stories of love and betrayal but also of confusions of commitment and loyalty, of people who have profound capacities for love, commitment, and wholeness, but who have not yet found a world good enough or constant enough for them to risk giving all of themselves to.

The childhoods of these patients often emerge quite slowly in the meaningful sense, and when they do, the here and now is usually thrown into astonishing new light as well, affirming that there had been too much knowledge and not enough uncertainty and mystery. My impression is that there had usually been much in the way of stereotypic understandings, generally legends or myths regarding childhood and parents, both of idealization and devaluation. Apparently always empathic, tyrannical, or intrusive parents are revealed to have been overwhelmed themselves in various ways, or much less together than *their* apparent psychological knowledge made it appear. These parents were *unauthentic* to varying degrees to the child, although the child was usually not fully aware of that factor at the time. Such patients often were responding to clues that the parents was not able to handle authentically difficult moments, and the patient responded by somehow utilizing their own psychological resources, placing them in the service of their parents' vulnerabilities.

My patient of the trapeze and childhood shoe boxes is nearing the end of a long analysis and recently returned from a visit to aging parents, having gained many new observations and perspectives. Long accustomed to thinking of his formerly idealized, dapper, and controlled father as impossibly judgmental and demanding, and his labile and insecure mother as needy, grasping, and always potentially entrapping, he had had new glimpses of them. He was impressed, for example, by the sincerity of their love for each other, by the love for himself and his mother that lay behind his father's hard corners and easily pierced vanity, and also by the newly visible solid flesh of his mother's body, formerly invisible to him in the face of the often spacey, chaotic, repellent, and frightening experiences that had dominated the interface between them so often in the past. Important for my thesis, however, he also described the several days since his return as dominated by a powerful feeling of *disorientation*. We were able to define that disoriented state as a logical consequence of the influx of so much new experience, and the patient was relieved to reframe the experience not only as a sort of shock (i.e., a trauma) but also as a likely preface to a necessary shakedown period during which he might be able to digest these new and exciting, but unnerving experiences. Disorientation was something that we could now see had characterized important parts of his childhood and subsequent life. Good reasons seemed now to come into view to uncover and begin to understand both why his parents were so often unable to provide an orienting context for understanding his experiences and why it had become important for his parents' psychological well-being that he either become able to orient himself or act oriented enough so as to not further distress or disable them in their capacities to be responsible parents. "I am beginning to see," my patient said near the end of a session, "that my parents are difficult people who were leading difficult lives in difficult times."

I believe that many patients may be understood in just such a way. Many of them grew up with basically loving and earnest, good-enough parents, but ones who were imperfectly equipped either to manage effectively their own difficulties and difficult lives. They were unable to prepare their children adequately for lives that they themselves had no chance to master or integrate in the face of rapidly changing and sometimes confusing times. A not uncommon strategy in our secular world is to claim psychological wisdom as holy writ—the psychological platitude as ethical imperative: Thou shalt be neither narcissistic nor unempathic nor treat others as part objects. Thou shalt not suffer low self-esteem; neither shalt thou not express thy feelings. In uncertain times, people need something to believe in, and parental wisdom has become infiltrated with values derived from various popular psychologies, so that parental anxieties are often disguised and contained in psychological observations and suggestions. In many psychologically minded patients, such parental interactions are the prototype for the premature or unauthentic interpretation. And such problems are undoubtedly contributed to both by the rapid and unpredictable cultural shifts and dislocations of recent years, during which children and parents have been less likely to share common values, traditions, understandings or even shared lives in a common location and by the seemingly more intensely traumatic and unpredictable qualities of life in today's world.

There is an interesting parallel to be drawn, I believe, within psychoanalysis, wherein the past thirty years or so have also been a time of rapidly evolving change. Competing theoretical paradigms offer us useful perspectives, but sometimes we feel incompletely prepared to comprehend fully the complex characterological pictures we actually see in our practices without falling back on our own preferred personal psychological platitudes and unknowingly indulge in individualized and stereotypic wisdom trips. Bear that danger in mind, and let me try to put my heretofore clinical and largely anecdotal account in a more formal psychoanalytic theoretical context.

THE THEORETICAL CONTEXT

My theoretical approach to understanding the clinical problem of learning to be anxious begins, as is often the case, with Freud. When I refer to anxiety, I do so, of course, in a broad, essentially *paradigmatic* sense. It is in that paradigmatic sense, for example, that I can make the statement that Mr. A's complex behavioral scenario is a transference enactment, a piece of his transference neurosis, a compromise formation that, among other purposes, serves to ward off anxiety. All of us implicitly understand that in this context, anxiety is a generic word that stands for specific fears yet to be elucidated and that although we can anticipate certain universal categories, we cannot predict the details that will eventually emerge.

The paradigm I have mainly in mind is the one that evolved out of Freud's initial conception (1926) of the *anxiety signal* in response to *situations of danger.* Here, Freud contrasts signal anxiety with automatic anxiety: signal anxiety connotes an intrapsychic communicatory process and the possibility of reflection, whereas automatic anxiety connotes psychic trauma, overstimulation, overwhelmedness, discharge phenomena, and an absence of the possibility of reflection.

Many believe that the creation of that theoretical paradigm in 1926 was the founding act of modern psychoanalysis, and I agree, because good defense or resistance analysis, which is what many of us still aspire to do, remains easy to relate to this formula, at least if we do not take it too formulistically.

Here are the elements in the formula: First, there is a feeling state—an *affect*—more or less available to awareness, which arises classically in response to unconscious conflict and which institutes defense. Second, there are *situations* to be dealt with that are represented psychically. These psychic representations of situations may refer to past, present, or future and to internal or external reality and may be conscious or unconscious. They also contain motives of all kinds (classically emphasizing sexual and aggressive ones) and cognitive discriminations of varying degrees of maturity, many of which motives and discriminations are organized within significant object relationships. We ordinarily refer to such psychic representations of situations as *thoughts* or *fantasies.* Where we find evidence of repetitive, persistent, life-controlling unconscious fantasies, we infer that they reflect underlying psychic structure. Third, there is a signal function, a communicatory or dialogic aspect, an element in an intrapsychic and interactional *process.* Finally, there is a continuum formed by psychic trauma: the non- or prereflective form one pole; mixed or more archaic mental organizations are in the middle; reflective mastery and insight form the opposite pole. Successful analysis reveals successively deeper layers combining all of these elements, regression alternates with progression; and therapeutic or developmental success is measured in relation to the latter polarity—widening the sphere of reflection, insight, mastery, and integration (i.e., structural change).

Although this paradigm remains useful to many psychoanalysts today, almost every category within it has expanded in ways that would have astonished and confounded Freud. There has been a gradual assimilation of object-relational, self-psychological, and developmental perspectives into the awareness of almost all psychoanalysts, for example. Therefore, regarding the first two elements, most of us have greatly expanded the number and variety of both the affects and danger situations with which we work, and we've also modified our ways of understanding Freud's classical categories. Jacobson (1983), and Gediman (1983) in useful reviews integrating structural and object-relational concepts, added annihilation anxiety to Freud's classic list, thereby creating a category to contain the important primitive object anxieties and various dangers to the integrity of the self that are such a common phenomenon in today's typical expectable analysis. As the aforementioned authors and others have demonstrated, the subject becomes additionally complicated because modern understandings of such dangers as fear of the superego, of castration, of loss of love, or loss of the object need to take into account characteristics of the entire mental organization—not merely the content of a fear—in order both to form an accurate impression of the structural and developmental level and to accurately assess the ways a patient may be accessible analytically and to what degree. The categories triadic, dyadic, and narcissistic are the clinician's most useful and most common generic terms for what was once referred to as oedipal, preoedipal, and symbiotic. The former terms always reference complexities and levels of organization of intrapsychic and interpersonal processes. Such process factors include complex ego, superego, object-relational, and existential variables that are relevant and constantly being reworked at every developmental level, as well as qualities of the psychic organization as a whole.

In clinical practice it is becoming increasingly accepted that triadic, dyadic, and narcissistic refer to qualities inherent in *everyone's* character. It appears that all patients now have varying degrees of preoedipal, narcissistic, perverse, psychosomatic, borderline, and even psychotic cores layered into their characters, and conducting successful analyses requires that we discern signals that thoughts or feelings relatable to any of those layers are present or imminent that can now become a useful piece of analytic work. It has become psychoanalytic cliché that the classic oedipal neurotic is a fiction, and therefore, any analyst who uses as a guideline for clinical judgment only the older content categories to determine whom to analyze or what to analyze and when is blind in regard to today's patients. We can see that

Freud's original elegant and simple theoretical paradigm has expanded considerably.

The third element—Freud's signal concept—heralded the beginning of a trend in psychoanalysis, in addition to mental *contents*, that has come to focus on complex hierarchical *processes* both in development and during treatment: a partial list would include not only intrapsychic processes but also internalization processes, developmental processes, interactional processes, and intersubjective processes. I conceive of the psychoanalytic process, for example, as an intrapsychic one that takes place in *relation to* a complex interpersonal and intersubjective relational field. When analysts consider such a complex field, they routinely take into account realities that earlier analysts did not recognize, had not yet conceptualized, or took into account only intuitively: not only may contents defend or screen other contents, but also contents can defend subtle aspects of process, and higher-level processes can defend lower-level processes or vice versa; in fact, any processes may defend or screen any other processes. New potential for misunderstanding and for deeper understanding arises in such a field—ambiguities that must routinely be taken into account. Ambiguities abound in the assessment of intrapsychic processes when the analyst must also take into account the interface with interactional and intersubjective realms, including the analyst's own intrapsychic processes. Our "database" here is a superordinate mental organization consisting of complex suborganizations in interplay and interaction with other complex organizations.

Analysts must also assess qualities of the whole psychic field in evaluating a process or group of interrelated processes. They do not, for example, adequately account for the vitality, authenticity, and direction of psychic processes by cataloging the contents of those processes. They evaluate not only structural characteristics of the field as a whole but also adequacy of developmental processes whether or not the field as a whole is maintaining a trend in the direction of greater integration. Analysts take such factors into account intuitively when they observe that some patients are able to exercise an observing ego and be held in the analytic situation, although by DSM-III-R criteria such patients are primitive, or preoedipal, or narcissistic, whereas others more manifestly seeming to fall into the higher-level categories may be astonishingly refractory in the same setting, and also in an assessment of such things as the stages or completeness of an analysis.

The point to bear in mind is that psychologically minded patients are capable of exploiting that very complexity in the service of defense. As with Mr. A, interpersonal psychological sophistication can defend narcissistic vulnerability; narcissistically sophisticated empathic and self-soothing capacities can defend object-instinctual intrapsychic conflict; and capacities for integration can defend subtle psychical splits and sectors of unintegration. From the analyst's side, analogous psychic processes may in one instance make an otherwise correct interpretation useless or destructive and at another time, convert a stereotypically clear but empty and lifeless analysis into a confusing but vital, passionate, and real one.

It is Freud's introduction of the polarities represented by psychic trauma and automatic anxiety on one side and signal anxiety on the other that represents, in retrospect, the most decisive stepping-off place for the whole modern trend to view structure and structuralization in ways that depart sharply from Freud's earlier, energic and materialistic, models. Freud's new model was rather primitive in this respect in 1926. Most analysts now agree that the symbolic function and the representational world constitute what is structured in structuralization, and they intuitively regard the capacity to integrate increasingly more differentiated aspects of internal and external reality as the obverse of neurotic distortion. The obverse of neurotic distortion for Freud in that earlier model was reflection—the secondary process—which he tended to equate theoretically with objective truth in the empirical sense. The capacities for insight or reflection on one hand and psychic integration on the other are actually related but separable subjects. Reflection and insight may correlate with underlying psychic integration, but the former refers to personal experience and personal conviction, whereas the latter refers to a more experience-distant estimation of qualities of the whole psychic organization. Mr. A is a good example of the importance of that distinction, for I believe I have much evidence that his attainments and capacities regarding structural integration are high, but that his tolerance for subjective experiences that *feel* unintegrated is what is at issue in our work and will determine much of its further course and outcome.

CONCLUSION

In summary, I believe that a sizable group of modern patients use their sophisticated capacity for psychological reflection and their talent for premature or precocious integration to ward off knowledge of more primitive conflict and islands of unintegration. Effective therapeutic work requires necessary traumatization—experiences of regressive dedifferentiation that undermine such patients' considerable capacity to know what they feel and think. Structural and process variables interact with content variables in complex and ambiguous ways, and estimates of the authenticity and fit of personal and interpersonal experiences and behaviors of both partners in the therapeutic encounter become necessarily involved. This greatly increases possibilities for mutual misunderstandings, pseudounderstandings, and more firmly grounded authentic understandings. Long periods of clarification and confrontation along self-psychological and object-relational lines must often precede effective construction and reconstruction, and the lines separating where such clarifications and confrontations end and subsequent interpretations, constructions, and reconstructions begin are often difficult to specify. Similar issues are usually eventually revealed in the patient's early life, when psychological and other too readily applied understandings were prematurely applied to offset helplessness and other unarticulatable experiences and during which the patient's talent for ambiguity, irony, self-integration, or responsiveness to others was, in effect, exploited at the expense of full psychological growth. Paradoxically, many patients who at the outset can compellingly and convincingly speak of their own anxieties and the anxieties of others discover in analysis that they actually had never truly learned how to be anxious.

REFERENCES

Freud, S. (1926), Inhibitions, symptoms, and anxiety. *Standard Edition*, 20:87–172. London: Hogarth Press, 1961.

Gediman, H. K. (1983), Annihilation anxiety: The experience of deficit in neurotic compromise formation. *Internat. J. Psycho-Anal.*, 64:59–70.

Jacobson, J. G. (1983), The structural theory and the representational world. *Psychoanal. Quart.*, 52:514–542.

Loewald, H. W. (1952), The problem of defense and the neurotic interpretation of reality. In: *Papers in Psychoanalysis*. New Haven, CT: Yale University Press, pp. 21–32.

——— (1960), On the therapeutic action of psychoanalysis. In: *Papers in Psychoanalysis*. New Haven, CT: Yale University Press, pp. 221–256.

7 Anxiety and Resistance to Changes in Self-Concept

Gloria J. Stern

Faced with a change in their self-concept, patients in psychoanalysis experience anxiety stemming from a sense of narcissistic vulnerability. Although the situation presents severe difficulties for individuals with narcissistic personality disorder, it can be heard as a *basso sostenuto* of resistance in many treatments. Patients develop resistance strategies to cope with the anxiety that threatens to arise in them whenever there is a shift in their narcissistic equilibrium. In cases of serious early trauma—for example, primal-scene exposure or sexual molestation—patients have disavowed identifications with key pathogenic objects. As relationships with those objects become manifest in the transference, the opportunity arises for reintegration of the self and other representations that the relationships inspire. Indeed, such a reintegration must take place for effective working through of the transference neurosis. However, previous to treatment, patients have created a certain narcissistic stability by keeping these self and object dyads apart from their sense of self, which both strengthens and weakens their self-concept. As the representations threaten to reenter the patients' self-concept, anxiety arises and becomes a source of new resistances to the working-through of certain transference paradigms.

Patients who are more traumatized frequently present with symptomatic anxiety disorders that are an expression of the trauma chronically reenacted. As they invest the transference with aspects of the disavowed self and object representations that are associated with the trauma, their anxiety disorder improves. Thus, there are antianxiety effects of the establishment of the transference. In the transference, the analyst is holding those frightening parts of the patient's self. But the threat of reemergence of severe anxiety causes tenacious resistance to reintegration of those unwanted parts of the self. As long as the analyst contains those disavowed aspects of the patient, the patient prefers to remain in a lengthy analysis rather than to separate. The patient has bought a temporary narcissistic equilibrium at the expense of keeping part or all of the unacceptable self and object dyad outside the self: inside the analyst. There is a partial repair but not a full working-through. The patient therefore depends, for a complete sense of self, on remaining with the analyst. It is only upon reintegration that the patient can stand alone and successfully leave the analyst.

Most difficult for the patient to reinternalize are unconscious sadistic aspects of self and object representations that were never adequately integrated in the first place. As they are identified with and expressed toward the analyst, they threaten to destroy the analyst, thus the self. Not every patient can take the risk of destroying the analyst-self, and this stalemates many treatments. Tortured by the potential for anxiety and a disruption in self-concept, the stalemated patient prefers the antianxiety effects of remaining in an incompletely worked-through treatment situation. The following extended vignette presents a patient who was able to reintegrate his frightening, aggressive imagos by the analysis of powerful resistances to anxiety associated with narcissistic disequilibrium. He was then able to separate and individuate from the analyst and successfully terminate.

CASE 1: MR. M

Mr. M, a 30-year-old lawyer, came for analysis of a panic disorder after several failed attempts with medication treatment. He had experienced claustrophobia in social settings, especially in airplanes, and a crippling writer's block. During his worst anxiety attacks, he visualized himself walking down the aisle of an airplane holding on high his bloody genitals, ripped out by his own hand, with all the other passengers looking on in horror. He had had the first of these experiences while he was on a trip and overheard the couple in the next bedroom having sex. Of historical importance, he had slept in his parents' bedroom for his first seven years. This set him up to be susceptible to fears of self-annihilation as well as to intense castration anxiety.

At the start of analysis, he was relying on his lover, an older woman, to quell his massive anxiety by doing his work assignments with him. This recapitulated the dependent, narcissistic-masochistic, performance-oriented relationship he had had with his mother when he did schoolwork, in which he fantasied himself an oedipal victor. Overwhelmed by the anxiety he now experienced while working, he was beginning to feel that his mother had not preferred him to his father.

His lover had been pressuring him to marry and have a baby despite the fact that they were in an embattled relationship. This caused him great anxiety. Envious of his lover, he expected to acquire her emotionality, her friends, and her creative phallic power. He hoped I would prefer him to my other patients, thus restoring a mother who preferred him. Fearing the loss of his lover, he succumbed to her demands: several months into the analysis he precipitously married and impregnated her, he said, "to contain the possibilities of the analysis before opening them up."

For a number of years he carried on a deadlocked sadomasochistic interaction with his wife and with me, endlessly reporting their fights to me in excruciating detail. He defeated interpretive attempts to deal with the severe marital discord. With me "watching" these fights, he reenacted the primal scene. I, not he, was now its helpless victim. By making me the victim of his primal scene, he was able to temporarily deny his own victim status. Although this intrusion into the transference of the patient's disavowed self-representation as passive victim had the dramatic effect of releasing him from the crippling anxiety attacks, it set up the central resistance of the treatment: the resistance to experiencing himself either as the victim or as the aggressor in the primal scene.

His first deep experience of himself as the victim came in response to a flash memory he had after watching the birth of his daughter. He suddenly remembered that at age four he was moved out of his crib into a bed in the room he shared with his parents. Jumping on the bed, he fell, cutting open his forehead, and then ran, streaming blood, into the living room. His extended family assembled there looked at him in horror. The patient was thrilled to have this as a memory "rather than a destiny." He used this memory to reassure himself that the danger of castration was not going to befall him in the future, for that incident—a real event of his childhood—had served as a symbolic castration, the paradigmatic experience for his later autocastration fantasies. On one hand, the memory gave him the opportunity for a dramatic reinternalization of himself as a victim: a victim of castration in the primal scene. On the other hand, his use of the memory served as a resistance to experiencing deeper, more disorganizing anxieties concerned with primitive aggression stimulated by the primal-scene exposure. These anxieties were not merely a straightforward fear of superego punishment for psychosexual impulses but had more to do with the fragile posttraumatic organization of self and object representations as they dealt with aggression.

During the mid-phase of the analysis he began masturbating to various aggressive transference fantasies. He envied me as the phallic female who had everything—ovaries and penis—whereas he was threatened with the prospect of having neither, because castration loomed in the act of intercourse. He both desired and hated me as the idealized phallic female, for I provided power by identification but made sadistic-narcissistic demands upon his performance in the analysis while he suffered. For several years he virtually abandoned sex with his wife. At one point, he dreamt that he was looking through the bars of a crib and felt he had a large foreign object inside him that he had to expel. He associated to me as someone who, having had a sex-change operation, was now a hairy man menacing him with anal rape. The feeling was so strong that he wondered if this were just a fantasy or whether he had ever been anally raped. Allowing himself to be identified as the victim of anal rape in the primal scene, he then wondered how much this was a wish rather than a fear. Working through it permitted him to form attachments to powerful men in the workplace —no longer fearing their possible homosexual implications—and he began to have enormous work success. Instead of wanting my phallic power, he now wanted me to admire his.

However, he remained stalemated in the enactment of the primal scene with his wife and me, chronically fighting with her and reporting to me, avoiding sex with her while fantasying about me. I interpreted that his avoidance of sex with his wife warded off deeper anxieties, and I confronted him with the need to reenter that arena in order to learn the basis for those anxieties. This conveyed that I could no longer participate in the tranquilizing addiction he had to analysis as an antianxiety agent, which compromised his adult relationship. It caused a shift in the treatment. As he experienced anxiety anew during sex with his wife, his deepest fears emerged: castration in the vagina dentata, annihilation by merger. He now made it clear that he was "enjoying" analysis as a sadistic attack by me. Here he made me the sadist, as he had previously made me the victim. Eventually he would have to experience himself as the sadist. After particularly pointed interpretations, he had dreams of sexualized aggression toward me, the beginning of his reintegration of his own sadistic impulses, which had originated in his confusion of sex with aggression when exposed to the primal scene. As he abandoned his passive-aggressive behaviors toward his wife, he set the stage for an intense reexperience of himself as the aggressor in the primal scene and finally felt his rage for me.

For years he had elaborated the primal scene in dreams of the Holocaust, the hermaphroditic self, and other representations; of fears of being gay; of a protracted sadomasochistic marital relationship; and of putting me in the position of witness-victim and anal rapist. At several nodal points he was dramatically able to reexperience himself as the anally raped, castrated victim of the primal scene. It was more difficult for him to become the aggressor. This happened late, in conjunction with separation-termination.

During the termination phase, by way of progressive emergence of the split-off part of his self-organization, he came close to an experience of narcissistic disintegration. The previously dissociated destructive self-object dyad that had been enacted in derivative ways throughout the analysis now became us, the pair in the room. Not able to imagine termination, he dreamt about the parental couple having sex; one eviscerated the other, then jumped out the window. In another dream, he saw me as a sadistic sergeant in boot camp murdered by a tortured recruit, who then suicided. At this point he could imagine only a murder-suicide as a way out of the sadomasochistic relationship of the treatment.

He became totally incapacitated. For two weeks he ranted and raved curled up on the couch in fetal position, saying, "You've finally got the whole man." He felt very small, physically hurt, and that he had glimpses of his parents' bedroom, a changing table. He wanted to kill his whole family. He cried profusely in session. I suggested that he must have had those feelings as a baby in the parental bedroom when he sensed that his parents were having sex and he could not speak. He now was astounded that he wanted to "push us onto tricky ground. Let's get out there where there is some danger for you too," he said, feeling direct hostility for me as never before. He wanted to slash me about the ribs, and this felt sexual. It frightened him.

In this patient, as a result of primal-scene exposure, castration anxiety and separation anxiety were condensed. He viewed parental sex as a destructive act, and to avoid being destroyed in its midst he withdrew into himself. This withdrawal was such an extreme form of separation that it too threatened annihilation. Caught between the possibility of annihilation within the primal scene and that of devastating separation as a result of withdrawing from it, he developed severe narcissistic defenses to deal with the anxieties. Through much of the analysis, he and I had been joined in an idealizing relationship, which was largely worked through. Termination would mean a complete separation. The prospect of being "alone" reopened the dangers of annihilation, and he was enraged at me for no longer protecting him. At the same time, his current work assignment required that he take a position in his own voice, meaning that he had to be visible. In the parental bedroom he had made himself invisible in part to avoid castration for his aroused libidinal wishes. Now in the spotlight, although he was at risk again, he felt whole, integrated, and able to speak in his own voice. He no longer required the counterphobic autocastration defense to ward off castration. With all this interpreted, he felt separated from me; he had shown me his core and survived.

This patient was able to terminate successfully. He completed an individuation process when he finally experienced himself with powerful affects as both the victim and the aggressor in the primal scene. In so doing, he felt an inordinate, disintegrating anxiety for several weeks, an experience that he had defended against in all the previous transference and extratransference resistance maneuvers of the treatment. His dream life presaged what then happened in the transference. If he had not experienced his aggression with anxiety in the transference, he would have remained in a timeless, frozen treatment, an interminable analysis.

CASE 2: MS. F

A second case example illustrates work in progress with a patient who was probably molested as a young child. She suffered from chronic lifelong anxiety, which interfered with her concentration as a writer; unstable self-esteem; and separation anxiety, which troubled her close relationships. As in the case of Mr. M, this patient's resistance centers on her inability to integrate into her self-concept both the victim and the aggressor of the molestation. She has been slow to allow herself to experience the kind of anxiety that comes with facing a disavowed self-representation arising from an early traumatic experience.

Ms. F, a 47-year-old married writer, came for treatment six months after the death of her mother, complaining of a generalized anxiety disorder mixed with depression. Childless, she had had sudden cessation of menses shortly after the death, and she now wondered why she had never made having a child a priority. In her 30s she had been in what she considered a lengthy failed analysis, which the analyst had terminated abruptly. During the early phase of that treatment she had left her first husband, experiencing him as angry and controlling. She then met her current husband, with whom she had chronic difficulties. Although the current husband was very nurturant of her and supportive of her writing, he made many dependent demands, refused to have a child with her, and was severely hypochondriacal. When she rejected him or was overly anxious and ambivalent, he flew into rages and occasionally struck her. Sexually he was quite aggressive, and they frequently playacted his taking her by force. She was a reluctant, nonorgasmic partner and was always thinking of leaving him. At the start of psychotherapy she was struggling with the writing of a murder mystery.

Initially, she required a lot of support in the treatment to mourn her mother and her lost procreative ability. In the early phase, a negative maternal transference evolved. She hated me and hated the way I expressed myself, which was not nuanced enough to understand her. Yet she suffered massive separation anxiety between sessions, on weekends, and especially when she had to immerse herself in the writing process. That anxiety disrupted her cognitive functioning and was interfering with her current project. Much of the early phase of therapy involved establishing me as a constant object for her. She was hypochondriacally preoccupied with her anxiety symptoms and was particularly unable to connect the eruption of symptoms to events. Coming late to sessions, she missed half to three-quarters of her time. We learned after many months that she was warding off extreme anxiety as she approached or waited in my office. She recovered the memory of entering the large walk-in closet into which her mother brought her when dressing, which she had found stimulating. As a result of this reconstruction, the patient began to arrive on time. However, her anxiety was then renewed on her way to my office. She now feared being waylaid on the way in—molested, perhaps murdered; I was becoming very dangerous to her.

In contrast to the first case, in which a victim self-image warded off anxiety, this patient had symptomatic anxiety as a resistance. For several years of psychotherapy, each time the meaning of molestation or murder threatened to enter the transference, the patient experienced anxiety that functioned as a resistance for long periods before she would allow the content to be revealed to herself. We were now over the resistant hurdle this anxiety had previously caused, and a flood of material related to fantasied or actual sexual molestation followed. A traumatically experienced tonsillectomy at age five was the screen memory for a possibly earlier molestation. She had recurrent images of a large object being shoved down her throat against her will. She had the fantasy of a huge tapeworm living inside her: How did it get there? How would she get it out? A daily bowel movement was a crisis: she feared she would not get out what someone had wrongfully put there. She could not imagine that anything sexual had ever actually transpired between her and her father, who died from a lengthy, debilitating illness when she was a postadolescent, but she was suspicious, because she had remarkably few memories of him. She did have pubertal memories of her older brother French-kissing her to "show her what not to do on dates"; she and that brother were found taking a shower together and were severely reprimanded.

The patient had a suspicion that she had been molested in early childhood. In her treatment process, she would take a cue from a current experience in which she felt a mixture of fear and erotic excitement and try to extrapolate to the past. She had extreme anxiety when she went to collect the mail in the package room of her apartment building, which led her to wonder whether the black mailman from her childhood had molested her. He had reappeared in one of her novels as a rapist-murderer. While her apartment was being reconstructed, she felt a thrill at the sight of a burly workman. Was it one of the endless series of workmen her family employed during her childhood? A man she hardly knew fondled her publicly on a dance floor and she felt passive, riveted in a do-with-me-what-you-will excitement. Is that how it happened? As this material emerged, she herself suggested the use of the couch. When I agreed it might be a good idea, she irrationally felt that I was forcing her to do something she did not want.

As she was making a transition from psychotherapy to psychoanalysis, her anxiety level rose and her trust in me deteriorated. This had a destabilizing effect on the treatment until she understood that she was reexperiencing me as the real or imagined molester. When she did begin to use the couch, she fantasied that a big zipper would open up her body and black snakes would leap out. She had the palpable sensation that I was her previous analyst, a heavy, older man, who in fantasy lay on top of her and whom she imagined she had to constantly push off. Phallic-exhibition themes emerged and she began to deal with previously denied competitive issues with women. Each time there was a separation or an opportunity for competitive victory, a molestation image, accompanied by anxiety and depression, arose. She became convinced that something had happened to her at age 2½ when her mother left her to go to the hospital to deliver her younger brother.

In the fifth year of treatment, for the first time she had the courage to inquire of relatives about family secrets that she had either known and repressed or never known. It turned out that her paternal grandfather had been a molester of his children and that one of her paternal uncles had followed suit. She began to deal with intense feelings of shame. It was also revealed to her that her mother had not been orphaned by a car accident, as she had been told: in fact her maternal grandfather had abandoned his wife, who then left her infant daughter, the patient's mother, in the care of her mother while she went to a nearby city for work. There she either suicided or was murdered; no one knew for sure. The patient undertook these researches haltingly over the course of a year. At each new discovery she suffered such anxiety that she was reluctant to go on to the next. Ultimately she sent away for police files, which referred to an autopsy report that she has not yet been able to bring herself to request. The patient wondered, "Am I so identified with my grandmother that if I find out what actually happened it will be as if it happened to me?"

For this treatment in progress I have made certain working assumptions: that the patient is identified both with the rapist and the rape victim and will the murderer and the murder victim and had previously kept both of these identifications outside her awareness. Keeping the facts of her grandmother's demise a secret has served to maintain these identifications extruded. She has suffered a great deal of narcissistic instability, attempting to deal with the incestuous and murderous themes in her fiction. Working through the victim side in the transference has led to marked improvement in her capacity to be alone, to work, and to be sexually and socially interactive. During the course of treatment she became aware of having identified with the aggressor when reading newspaper accounts of rapes, which went against her feminist values; she no longer does this. Early on she used predominantly avoidant defenses over competitive issues; that too has changed. I suspect that she will have a difficulty similar to the previous patient's when she truly integrates her aggressive feelings for me in the transference. In her sixth year of treatment she cannot yet imagine termination. She is still resisting identifying herself with her murdered grandmother and the murderer of her grandmother.

DISCUSSION

For these two cases I have relied on the writings of some key theoreticians on the subject of resistance and its relation to unconscious and conscious anxieties. Much of the work in these analyses that has not been the subject of this chapter was done along wish-defense lines, the resistances being conceived of and interpreted according to Freud's original contributions on the subject. Freud (1926) presciently noted both that resistance accompanies the treatment at every step of the way and that there are resistances to the uncovering of resistance. He described several forms of resistance: (1) the repression-resistance used by the patient to keep out of awareness those impulses and memories that would lead to painful affects, especially anxiety; (2) the transference-resistance, which both recapitulated and defended against the infantile wishes now experienced with the analyst in the treatment situation; (3) the resistance of secondary gains, due to some derivative drive gratification; (4) the id-resistance, or the tendency for instinctual expression to remain along habituated lines; and (5) the superego-resistance—the most difficult—which originated in a sense of guilt and need for punishment. Following Freud's metapsychology, the compelling reason for a reluctance to change would be fear of the emergence of a fantasied instinctual gratification loaded with the possibility of retribution. Recognizing the relation of resistance to forms of anxiety, a body of literature has grown up that emphasizes an oppositional relationship between the patient and the analyst, with the analyst seen as attempting to elicit warded-off instinctual material from a patient reluctant to experience anxiety.

When Sandler et al. (1973) reviewed the literature on resistance, beginning with Freud's 1926 paper and going through to the 1960s, he found that the concept of resistance had not changed. Yet many authors had insisted that resistance and defense, although closely related, were not synonymous. Sandler (1973) said, "Whereas the patient's defenses are an integral part of his psychological structure, resistance represents the patient's attempts to protect himself against the threats to his psychological equilibrium posed by the analytic procedure" (p. 78). Perhaps out of deference to Freud, he did not expand upon the ways that issues of narcissistic equilibrium might define resistance as distinct from defenses against the emergence of unacceptable drive derivatives. He did mention "unobtrusive" resistances that "infiltrate" the analytic situation, manifesting themselves as a lack of change in the patient (p. 79).

Sandler kept within Freud's format and added two more sources of resistance: fears of loss of the analyst as an important real person in the life of the patient and threats to the patient's self-esteem due to shame about infantile impulses (pp. 80–81). He then located the problem of resistance in preoedipal attachment issues and in concerns for narcissistic equilibrium. "Some structures may evolve in order to solve ongoing conflict. But they may persist and be utilized in order to maintain safety feeling even though the original impulses which entered into their formation are no longer operative in the same way. It is likely that the latter structures are those most amenable to change through . . . therapy" (p. 82).

In the first case presented in this chapter, an intermediate structure was created as the patient made me watch him reenact the primal scene. He simultaneously felt that I was watching over him in a manner that made it safe for him to continue the work of the analysis, ending in his ultimate reintegration of both the victim and the aggressor in himself. For Sandler, the structure of the patient, the structure of the resistance, and the structure of change in the relationship with the analyst coalesce in the concept of safety. Together patient and analyst construct new structure and new safety systems, thus keeping anxiety at bay and narcissistic disequilibrium to a minimum.

Loewald (1960) suggested that when the analyst's principal aim was to revive old wishes in the transference only to disappoint them, by definition the analytic situation was not only not safe but in fact was deceitful. As Friedman (1991) points out, by emphasizing the process that occurs between analyst and patient, Loewald places treatment in the context of normal psychology. Transference is not something the patient has to outgrow, but the passionate attachment of transference "bathes the world in new meaning" (p. 99). That relationship between patient and analyst engages the fantasy life of the patient in an interactive process. His wishes are progressively more structured as the higher-level organization of the analyst draws the patient along to greater degrees of differentiation. Loewald's theory rests on the assumption that patients have an innate desire to change and also that analysts are indeed motivated to influence that process in the context of a highly personal, new relationship in which dedifferentiation and redifferentiation contribute to a mutually enhancing experience. It was when I tired of performing the "container" function for my patient Mr. M that I was motivated countertransferentially to draw the patient to a higher level of functioning, which implies greater differentiation. My insistence that he must engage in sex with his wife in order to learn where his deeper anxieties lay moved him beyond his resistance. I was pushing him out of the primal nest, as it were. Loewald's (1960) description of the analytic process emphasizes the ecstatic, future-oriented, developing dialectic of internalization on a continuum from preoedipal to oedipal developmental tasks, making use of early ego and later ego states. An analysis conducted in the fashion Loewald suggests facilitates the normal narcissistic developmental line with a minimum of disequilibrium and anxiety and thus a minimum of resistance.

It was Kohut (1959) who most clearly developed ideas about treatment fostering the normal narcissistic developmental line; he reminded us of the profound influence of the analyst's theoretical bias—especially the analyst's way of thinking about technique—on the degree of resistance produced in the patient along the way. For example, it was critical for me to empathically receive the hatred of the second patient during several years of initial psychotherapy while I established myself as a real object for her. As I became less hateful to her, she was able to enter analysis and deal with me in the transference as the molester. In earlier treatment she had been immediately placed on the couch and dealt with only along classical lines; as a result she developed insurmountable resistance. Kohut (1977) ultimately decided that the central problem for all patients was historically a nonempathic fit between the self and selfobject, which could be corrected in the mirroring and idealizing transference by a finer-tuning of empathy between patient and analyst. He believed that this would cure resistance, eliminate aggression conceived of as due exclusively to early frustrations and their recapitulation in the transference, and allow for transmuting internalization and new structure.

What Sandler, Loewald, and Kohut have in common is the desire to redefine the psychoanalytic process in terms of the new meanings available to the patient involved in it. The three have clarified the motivation for the patient to do the difficult analytic work. They explicitly stress the real relationship of the analyst and patient and the preoedipal issues therein. The therapeutic optimism in their tone betrays a hope of overriding resistance. The meaning-giving function of the analyst and of the analyst as safe harbor provides the backdrop for new structural development. Implicit is the patient's desire to grow, stemming from primary autonomous functioning of the ego—a concept inherited from Hartmann—and the patient's desire to form an attachment—a fact observed by the developmentalists, who also adopt Winnicott's idea of the holding environment.

These conceptions of analytic process evolved theoretically—out of ego psychology and infant observation—and practically—out of a need to treat the patient's anxiety deriving from the narcissistic disequilibrium caused by the treatment situation itself. For the simplest changes in self-concept (which produce only a mild narcissistic disequilibrium), the safety system of Sandler, the empathic self-selfobject matrix of Kohut, and the exciting dyadic differentiating experience of Loewald all support the patient's self-esteem while the patient undergoes change, keeping anxiety to a minimum. Such change involves the loss of previously held self and object representations in return for internalization of transmuted ones. Both loss and internalization result in a reconfiguring of the self with attendant anxiety. At more benign levels of psychopathology, reconfiguring of the self centers predominantly on the vicissitudes of the libido. At graver and more frightening levels, where reconfiguring of the self revolves around the vicissitudes of aggression, the holding modes of Sandler, Loewald, and Kohut are necessary but not sufficient tools in allaying the profound anxieties of narcissistic annihilation. In order to more thoroughly understand the role aggression plays in generating anxiety about narcissistic annihilation, one turns to the Kleinian school.

Klein (1952) faulted Freud for skewing analytic theory in the direction of libido, his having aggression as an auxiliary concern. Freud had construed defenses mainly as against libidinal strivings. Focusing on anxieties associated with early fantasies, Klein found that she could alleviate anxiety in young children only by analyzing their sadistic fantasies; aggression had a major role in causing the anxiety. She also took issue with Freud for defining objective and neurotic anxiety as distinct from each other: the first due to threat from an external object, the second to threat from an instinctual demand. Freud (1926) alluded to the anxiety of the infant at the breast, in the form of its fear of an objective danger situation of object loss when missing its mother, no longer certain that its needs would be satisfied. Klein (1952) agreed that objective anxiety derived from the infant's complete dependence on the mother for need satisfaction. But, she argued, the infant feared that he himself had destroyed the providing mother by his sadistic impulses or was in danger of so doing. Thus neurotic anxiety was connected with the mother as an indispensable good object, both external and internal, and to the infant's earliest aggressive fantasies, which threatened to destroy both. This contributed to the infant's anxiety that the mother would never return. Klein focused more intently than Freud on how both internal and external reality were both functions of psychic reality.

This Kleinian theory vigorously addresses the anxieties that stem from the vicissitudes of aggression as they impinge upon narcissistic equilibrium. Whether or not one adopts Klein's concept of a death instinct, one cannot ignore the dramatic interplay of projective and introjective processes mobilized by the patient to deal with ragefully perceived objects internalized and reexternalized as persecutors that threaten to destroy loving and loved objects. At bottom, resistances are directed at the internal rearrangement of these self and object representations. That the struggle has been externalized to some extent in all patients accords them some measure of relief from anxiety. But patients achieve higher levels of integration only at the risk of reexperiencing the anxiety of reinternalization of the aggressor, with the attendant fantasies of damage or destruction to the self or the needed object or both. In his termination phase, as Mr. M reexperienced his entrapment in the primal scene: he both wished to destroy me in the analytic room and feared that he would do so. This was a terrifying but necessary reintegration during which his condensation of sex and aggression were most clear.

Kernberg (1975), much influenced by Klein, continues to address the thornier aspects of the treatment situation as they derive from the vicissitudes of aggression and early deformations of the ego. Central to his theory of pathological narcissism is his idea that the self-concept of the narcissist is a condensation of the ideal self, ideal other, and aspects of the real self. Such condensation gets projected onto the other. The resulting distorted object relation in a pure culture of pathological narcissism is thus the interaction between this defensively condensed self and its projection onto the other. Such an interaction defends the individual against an awareness of the other as a separate person in order to avoid dependence on the other, envy of what the other has to offer, and the rage this engenders. In pathological narcissism, the anxiety of experiencing envious, rageful disequilibrium fuels the most entrenched type of resistance—the resistance to acknowledging the analyst as a separate entity in the room. Mr. M experienced that kind of disequilibrium when he abandoned his narcissistic transference to me in the process of termination and truly accepted us as separate.

In more complexly evolved characters, multiple units of self and object representations colored by specific affective experiences are combined by the synthetic function of the ego to form a more stable self-concept. Even when this is the case, Kernberg (1976) points out that there can be problematical self and object representations—the "not me" (p. 122)—a dissociated, extremely painful, and frightening aspect of the self-experience induced by severe frustration or trauma. For example, Ms. F does not want to be identified with her murdered grandmother. This is a screen for her not wanting to be herself the molested child. Even in much less malignant situations, the patient is still reluctant to readmit into the self-concept the previously dissociated self and object representations, which form a nidus of resistance in the treatment. The patient experiences extreme anxiety as those units threaten to be reintegrated, since his narcissistic equilibrium has been bought at the expense of keeping that dyad outside the self, which both strengthens and weakens the self. It is along that spectrum that we find the insidious, infiltrating resistances.

In summary, the traumatized patient presents with anxiety and invests the transference with disavowed identifications, which acts as an antianxiety agent. The analyst may experience a counterresistance in response to frustration as the patient prefers to remain tranquil rather than face the reintegration required for change. Because such reintegration entails the reexperiencing of anxiety, powerful resistances may develop. Classical approaches to analyzing the resistance may lead to only partial results and a stalemated treatment. The analysts's empathic immersion in projected early ego states, especially as they involve the vicissitudes of the patient's aggression, is crucial to completion of the reintegration process. Only this will allow true individuation from the analyst and future freedom from symptomatic anxiety.

REFERENCES

Freud, S. (1926), Inhibitions, symptoms and anxiety. *Standard Edition*, 20:87–172. London: Hogarth Press, 1959.

Friedman, L. (1991), On the therapeutic action of Loewald's theory. In: *The Work of Hans Loewald*, ed. G. Fogel. Northvale, NJ: Aronson, pp. 91–105.

Kernberg, O. (1975), *Borderline Conditions and Pathological Narcissism*. New York: Aronson.

——— (1976), *Object Relations Theory and Clinical Psychoanalysis*. New York: Aronson.

Klein, M. (1952), On the theory of anxiety and guilt. In: *Developments in Psychoanalysis*, ed. J. Riviere. London: Hogarth Press, pp. 271–291.

Kohut, H. (1959), Introspection, empathy and psychoanalysis. *J. Amer. Psychoanal. Assn.*, 7:459–483.

——— (1977), *The Restoration of the Self*. New York: International Universities Press.

Loewald, H. (1960), On the therapeutic action of psychoanalysis. In: *Papers on Psychoanalysis*. New Haven, CT: Yale University Press.

Sandler, J., Dare, C. & Holder, A. (1973), *The Patient and the Analyst*. Madison, CT: International Universities Press.

8 The Patient's Anxiety, the Therapist's Anxiety, and the Therapeutic Process

Owen Renik

I use the term "anxiety" to refer to a mental state concerned with the anticipation of danger. The familiar physiological features of anxiety—tachycardia, perspiration, and the like—have their origins in the basic flight-or-fight responses, and they occur because the anxious individual has made an estimation of a current situation and reached the conclusion that either pain or loss of pleasure is imminent. Such estimations are inevitably based on learning that is rooted in prior experience.

The relation between physiological reactions and the estimation of danger in anxiety has definite implications for therapy. Not infrequently, a patient complains of anxiety in the form of a sense of dread that has no cognitive content. The patient knows that he or she is afraid and notices all the physiological signs that usually accompany fear, but is unaware of being afraid of anything specific. In its more chronic forms the experience has been called free-floating anxiety or generalized anxiety disorder; in its acute forms it is sometimes termed panic attack.

The way a clinician understands this sort of symptomatic presentation will have crucial consequences for the treatment. If one takes the patient's conscious experience at face value by assuming that a specific idea of danger either does not exist or is inaccessible, then analytic investigation may seem pointless, and anxiolytic medication or a similar form of intervention aimed at suppressing the signs of fear may seem the treatment of choice. The limitation of that therapeutic approach, however, is that if the patient has an underlying irrational judgment of danger, the judgment remains intact and can continue to exert a maladaptive influence. To the extent that its immediate impact on conscious experience is diminished, this is accomplished by the

121

costly method of interfering to a degree with the patient's capacity to create and respond to emotional signals.

My own approach, as already indicated, is to assume that signs of anxiety proceed from a specific idea of danger, even if that idea is not consciously available to the patient and even if the patient asserts vigorously either that no such idea exists or that he cannot possibly determine what it might be. Moreover, when an anxious patient is not aware of exactly what he fears, I direct all my efforts to bringing the ideational content of his fear into awareness in detail, because such detail gives the patient the opportunity to review the rationality of his judgment of danger. If the danger is real, then the patient is in a position to decide how best to deal with it; if it is not, then the patient can try to look into the causes for his irrational fear and eliminate it.

It has been my observation that the idea of danger that lies at the core of the mental state of anxiety can be quite unpleasant to think about. An anxious individual often has compelling motivations for remaining unaware of what he fears, and a significant part of the analytic treatment of anxiety disorders is usually concerned with addressing those motivations. In phobias, for example, the fear of which the sufferer is aware hides a more disagreeable and salient concern.

The foregoing considerations lead us to the concept of unconscious anxiety. If one uses "anxiety" in its strictly phenomenological sense, the term denotes a feeling state: either one is aware of anxiety, or it does not exist; unconscious anxiety, then, is a contradiction in terms. However, what a therapist wants to take account of are aspects of behavior designed to avoid the experience of anxiety (i.e., what might be called defenses against anxiety). For example, of a Don Juan who has deep-seated fears of being effeminate we might say his womanizing defends against his anxieties about his masculinity. The important clinical point is that a patient who is engaging in a successful defense against anxiety does not feel anxious; yet the potential for anxiety is very real and immediate, and the patient will indeed feel anxious just as soon as his defensive behavior ceases. It is convenient to describe this state of affairs by saying that the patient's anxiety is unconscious. However, it should be noted that used this way, anxiety becomes a theoretical concept rather than a phenomenological one.

Having established a perspective on anxiety, I now turn to the presentation of clinical material. Early in my psychoanalytic career, a teacher whom I admired very much referred his niece to me. He obviously liked the young woman a good deal and was distressed to have to acknowledge the severity of her disturbance. Several attempts at treatment with respected analysts had not worked out; she remained panicky and disorganized. It was clear that she was now being sent to me because, having just finished my residency and being more involved in general psychiatric practice, I was more up-to-date and comfortable with the use of medications.

I, too, found the patient to be very appealing. She was a medical student at the time she came to see me and I began working with her. She was pretty and very bright, but she lacked self-confidence in a way that seemed out of keeping with her considerable personal assets. Her manner was extremely self-effacing: she spoke hesitantly, and when she made an assertion of any kind, she would leave it incomplete, her voice dropping until she trailed off into a sigh or a nervous giggle. She startled easily and had the overall appearance of a frightened doe.

What she described and wanted help with was a life that appeared to be on the edge of disarray on every front: She suffered from frequent episodes of panic; often, at night, she woke up, dripping with sweat and with her heart pounding, but unaware of being frightened of anything in particular. She couldn't figure out what kind of medicine she wanted to practice; she was interested in psychiatry, but felt she wasn't nearly smart enough or personally together enough to consider it as a career. She believed she was not in the same league as someone like her uncle, for example.

She lived with a boyfriend to whom she felt inferior as well. He was more intellectual than she, better looking, and as fascinating and charming as she was dull. That he used drugs a fair amount and also hadn't settled on a career was inconsequential to her compared with his virtues. She ignored what seemed to me, from her descriptions of him, to be striking evidence of a powerful sense of insecurity on her boyfriend's part. For instance, she accepted as valid and never questioned his constant criticism of her. She expected him to break up with her any minute, and the thought of it made her desperate.

The rest of her social life was consistent with what I have already recounted. She shied away from people whom she respected, assuming that they would find little of interest in her. She gravitated instead toward those whom she regarded as more on her own level. These tended to be people who had in fact achieved a good deal less than she. When my patient inevitably became the object of their envy and resentment, she didn't see it for what it was and simply felt herself to be a dislikable failure.

This young woman was quite convinced she was a mess, and she felt hopeless and helpless about being able to change. Her impression of her situation had gained confirmation from her lack of success in prior attempts at psychotherapy. Agitated depression and panic disorder were the diagnoses that had eventually been discussed in connection with the possibility of trying psychotropic medication. The idea implicit in those diagnoses that something basic was wrong with the patient's emotional equipment made sense to her. She had felt underlying apathy and alienation as far back as she could remember. She was an only child. Throughout her childhood her mother had been troubled by what she regarded as my patient's sullen withdrawal. Relations between mother and daughter had been strained. The patient believed she had never satisfied her mother, which left her feeling hurt and as though there were something wrong with her. Her father, who became seriously ill when she was 13 and who died five years later, had seemed more accepting of her, but his preoccupation with business kept him largely unavailable.

Filled with therapeutic zeal, I considered that my patient suffered from massive defenses against anxiety, and I began by addressing these. In a number of ways, I directly challenged her view of herself. I brought out that she maintained her low self-esteem despite evidence to the contrary. She felt unintelligent and unattractive, ignoring that she had managed to do quite well in school and that there had always been men who wanted to go out with her. I pointed out that she constantly devised self-deprecating explanations for her successes, such as her claims that good grades were the result of hard work alone, not talent, and that she could get men's attention only by flattering them and accommodating them sexually. I showed her how her critical self-image was often self-fulfilling. Because of her expectation that she would be rejected, she inhibited herself, thus hiding her wit and imagination and actually making herself dull. If she never tried to be friends with people she really liked, her sense of inferiority would remain safe from contradiction. I confronted her with her idealization of her boyfriend, as well as her reluctance to reject his hypercritical accusations and call him on his own transparent defensiveness. When she denied competitiveness from her friends, I would ask her why she was overlooking the obvious.

Needless to say, she found ways of refuting my various efforts to call into question her negative self-image and the panicky confusion it generated. This phase of the work required persistence on my part, as well as attention to her need to see herself as a failure in therapy as elsewhere. In all of our investigations of her self-defeating attitudes and behaviors the foremost question concerned her motivation: what was her reason for remaining entrenched in a view of herself as second-rate at best?

We learned something about the answer to that question from what the patient felt as she began to move forward a bit in her life. Her customary ways of holding herself back became gradually discredited by our investigation of them. My approach was based on the premise that she could be more successful than she believed—an implicit message of encouragement that enabled her to risk a few changes. She stood up to her boyfriend more, made overtures to successful people she wanted to get to know better, and started to act less hesitant and be more expressive in general. Eventually, she selected a medical specialty (not psychiatry) and applied for a residency; she broke up with her boyfriend and began dating a responsible man who treated her well; her circle of acquaintances enlarged; and the panicky episodes virtually disappeared.

However, the patient was not entirely gratified by these achievements. In fact, she could not believe in them. She no longer felt a global sense of being overwhelmed and confused, but was suffering instead from misgiving in more specific forms. Her new boyfriend complimented her frequently and told her he loved her. Nonetheless, she was sure he would eventually tire of her neurotic insecurity and leave. Now she knew what kind of doctor she wanted to be, but could see that she didn't really have the right stuff. Sitting through courses in medical school was one thing; taking on actual clinical responsibility would be another. Being accepted into a prestigious residency filled her with dread of failure. In the company of more competent and more interesting friends, she constantly feared making a fool of herself. All in all, she felt that with my support she had managed an imposture and risen above her real worth to a place from which she was bound to come crashing down.

Her sense of being undeserving and expecting exposure constituted a particular feeling state with its own associations. Looking into it caused her to recall a period in her life that she had been putting out of her mind for some time. Her father's illness had made it necessary for him to all but retire from his business and spend much of his time at home. Mother worked, and father and daughter spent many long afternoons together alone talking. A tender and pleasurable intimacy developed between the two. Sometimes the patient's father gently complained that he had never been able to come up to his wife's expectations, whereupon the patient, who identified strongly with that very predicament, would be outraged on her father's behalf. She was convinced that she and her father had become closer than he had ever been with her mother. She treasured the closeness, but she knew she did not deserve it. It was wrong both to criticize her mother behind her back and to take advantage of Mother's absence and Father's neediness to capture first place in his affections. She always thought that one day her mother would find out what was going on and "bust my bubble."

Now we were able to form a picture of some of the motivation for this young woman's presenting complaints, as well as for her tenacious difficulty in accepting and making the most of symptomatic improvement when it did occur. To feel competent and satisfying and to be appreciated by a man had the meaning to her of being close to her father and of having unfairly supplanted her mother. In order not to feel guilty about it—as she had when she was a teenager—she had to avoid such success or, when she was successful, had to disavow and undo it with visions of imminent disaster. Above all, she could not feel that she was doing too well in her treatment, because that would cause her to have the experience of satisfying me, a man whom she admired and liked as she had her father.

I drew her attention to these matters and we discussed them at length. She reflected on the fact that it was natural for her to have wanted to be close to her father, that he himself had chosen to complain to her about the marriage (it was something she could not reasonably take responsibility for), and that her sense of having defeated her mother and taken the mother's place was probably exaggerated. She saw that her adolescent dread of having her bubble burst had to do more with losing her somewhat grandiose illusions about her relationship with her father than with actually having supplanted her mother.

These reconsiderations, however, did not have the liberating effect that might have been expected. My patient agreed that our work together bearing fruit had a forbidden and threatening significance for her, but again, that realization on her part, though apparently sincere, did not seem to alter the status quo. Time wore on and progress remained stalled. My patient had made a certain amount of symptomatic improvement, but continued to suffer from irrational and painful self-doubt and confining inhibitions. I suggested to her various ways of applying the considerable amount we had learned, but none of it seemed to make any difference. It began to look more and more as if our analytic efforts, despite their promising beginning, might end in relative disappointment.

Looking back on the next stage of the treatment, which constituted something of a turning point, my sense of it is best captured by a famous Morris and Becky story. Morris and Becky (a legendary Jewish couple about whom many wise and humorous tales are told) lived in a little room above their grocery store. The episode I have in mind concerns Morris and Becky in bed asleep. Morris is tossing and turning. Eventually, in rolling over, he bumps into Becky and wakes her up. "What's the matter, Morris?" she asks. "Oy, I'm so worried," he replies. "I don't know how I'm going to pay Mendel Cohen the $10 I owe him." "Go back to sleep," Becky says. Fifteen minutes later,

Morris is still tossing and turning. He accidentally kicks Becky and wakes her up again. "Morris, what now?" "Oy, I'm so worried. I don't know how I'm going to pay Mendel Cohen the $10 I owe him." "Go back to sleep." Fifteen minutes later, Morris is still thrashing around. This time he catches Becky in the ribs with an elbow, and again it's "What's the matter?" "Oy, I'm so worried. I don't know how I'm going to pay Mendel Cohen the $10 I owe him." "Go back to sleep." The same thing happens again and again. Finally, for the umpteenth time, Morris knocks into Becky and wakes her up, and when she asks him what's the matter, he answers, "Oy, I'm so worried. I don't know how I'm going to pay Mendel Cohen the $10 I owe him." Becky jumps out of bed, marches to the window, and throws it open. It's the middle of the night. All is dark and still. She screams out the window at the top of her lungs, "Mendel! Mendel Cohen! Mendel Cohen!" Finally, on the other side of the street a window is raised and a sleepy head appears. It's Mendel Cohen. "Nu?" he asks. "So who wants him?" Becky shouts, "Morris Schwartz is not going to pay you the $10 he owes you! She slams the window closed, marches back to bed, and says, "Now! Let *him* worry. *You* get some sleep!"

The clinical relevance of this story is, I hope, clear. It illustrates the important principle that sometimes if one person in a relationship suffers from anxiety, the other doesn't have to. And that's what was happening at the juncture my patient and I had reached.

Let's review the sequence of events so far. Initially, I had judged the patient's presenting complaints of confusion and panic to represent the results of an inhibition motivated by anxiety. I had demonstrated the irrationality of her low self-esteem to the extent that its function as a defense against anxiety was undermined. Her inhibitions then lifted a bit; she began to behave more in accord with her actual abilities. Her underlying anxiety emerged in the form of various fears of disaster based on the conviction that her newfound achievements were undeserved and would therefore prove illusory. We could trace the origins of her feeling of being undeserving and her fear of having her bubble burst to her adolescent guilt at having taken advantage of her father's illness in order to unfairly supplant her mother in his regard. She examined that guilt feeling and could see it was unrealistic —the product of a childish, wishful, omnipotent view of her own powers and responsibilities—a later edition of oedipal guilt, if you like.

With the accomplishment of such good analytic work on my patient's anxieties, why weren't the therapeutic benefits more conclusive?

Well, because the therapist had some work to do yet on his own anxiety. Like Morris, I was worrying in a way that made it unnecessary—impossible, actually—for my patient to worry, and my monopoly on anxiety was blocking our progress. The patient was a very appealing young woman, and the idea of helping her afforded me all sorts of gratifications; the prospect of failure invoked in me fear of all the corresponding frustrations and humiliations. Moreover, this was the niece of my highly regarded teacher. Instead of treating her with medications as was expected, I had chosen to try to succeed where senior analysts had already failed, and it was easy for me to picture my arrogance and competitiveness rewarded by the early dissolution of an apparently promising career.

The difficulty was that I was not aware of those anxieties because of my defenses against them, which took the form of *furor therapeuticus*. I was interpreting everything I could think of, and then some. Again like Morris, I had taken entirely upon myself the responsibility for a problem that in actuality my patient and I shared. I was so busy trying to contend with the limits of our understanding that I was not giving my patient a chance to feel some responsibility for her future and to see what she could come up with that might help.

Once I realized that my analytic technique was being driven unproductively by my own anxiety, I was able to adopt a more *que-sera-sera* attitude and—as Becky might have put it—let my patient worry a bit. A prompt and important consequence of that tack was that my patient began, for the first time in the analysis, to get angry at me. This was a very useful turn of events. All the while that I had been struggling heroically, she had been suffering but not been blaming me for it. In other words, my kindly preemptive worrying had been preventing my patient's negative transferences from emerging.

Now she began to feel disappointed in me and neglected by me. She wondered if I really liked her or cared about her. Perhaps I was self-centered like her mother—interested, ultimately, only in my own narcissistic gratifications. In retrospect, it became clear that as long as I had been trying as hard as I could to find the right interpretation, my patient had been blocked from experiencing this maternal transference. She had been seeing me, instead, as like her idealized father: a loving and devoted, if impotent, ally.

These developments marked the end of the impasse and ushered in the final, decisive phase of analysis, concerned with further insight into both the nature of the anxieties underlying my patient's inhibitions and her reasons for expecting that any attempt on her part to be successful would inevitably end in disaster. Eventually, she came to be quite uncomfortable with her resentful accusations of me. She realized that although it was understandable that she was disappointed and critical of my limitations, she really had no evidence for her derogatory supposition that I was self-centered and unconcerned with her welfare.

That realization made it necessary for her to face her concerns about her own childish narcissism and sense of entitlement. If the limits of what I was able to offer could not be attributed to neglect and lack of concern on my part, then her personal indictments of me weren't very fair. She felt very ashamed of her vindictive anger and the attacks she had made. The negative image of me that she had been entertaining was, after all, a mother transference, so that as she began to question her view of me and to recognize the self-vindicating function it had served for her, she also had to reconsider the view of her mother that she was transferring into the treatment relationship. For the first time, it occurred to her that her long-standing assumption that her mother really didn't like her might not be entirely accurate. Perhaps with her mother, as with me, it helped her feel more justified about her own angry disappointment to believe that the other person was mistreating her.

My patient's desperate concern that underneath it all she was a nasty, demanding little brat stood at the core of the anxiety that necessitated her many punishment fantasies and inhibitions. Exploration of her conflicts about her greed and hostility permitted her to achieve a new level of self-confidence and to enjoy and feel secure about the changes she had made in her life. On that basis, she eventually terminated her analysis.

The following summarizes points this chapter has tried to make about the patient's anxiety, the therapist's anxiety, and the therapeutic process. Anxiety is a perception of danger, elaborated into a feeling state that then serves as a signal to trigger defensive action. When the perception of danger is accurate and the defensive action appropriate, the capacity to feel anxiety is adaptive (e.g., it's a good thing to feel nervous when the light turns red while you're in the middle of an intersection!). That the capacity to experience anxiety is useful is one reason why we try not to interfere with it—for instance, by administering anxiolytic medication—if we can avoid doing so.

My purpose has been to call attention to factors of which I think a clinician needs to be aware in order to make the choice of treatment modality to best advantage. Certainly on one hand there are cases in which patients' experiences of anxiety are so intense that no investigative discussion is possible. None of us wants to fruitlessly prolong to patient's suffering in such an instances; thus medications are surely appropriate. On the other hand, it is also true that there are cases in which patients underestimate their own ability to look into that fearful state of mind, protesting vehemently about feeling too overwhelmed and too panicked to do so. The young woman whose treatment I've described did exactly that. In these instances the patient inevitably interprets the prescription of medication (no matter what the therapist's intention in prescribing is) as confirmation of his or her sense of defect, thus strengthening the conviction that anxiety is, ultimately, both outside the patient's control and unanalyzable.

Psychopathology exists when a judgment of danger is made that is unrealistic. Generally, what happens is that one applies conclusions about danger that one reached long ago, when judgment was immature and information incomplete. The unpleasant nature of what is involved in the anxiety makes one reluctant to think about it, so that one does not have a chance to review that perception of danger and then evaluate whether it is realistic under current circumstances. Usually, what one is most aware of is the distress caused by the defenses mobilized by the unconscious anxiety. Therefore, therapy consists of helping patients investigate their mental life in order that they can become conscious of their judgment of danger and then decide in a rational way what action, if any, is called for.

That, in brief, is what I have tried to say about the patient's anxiety and the therapeutic process. I have also suggested that the therapist's own anxiety plays a role in the therapeutic process as well—parallel, in fact, to the patient's anxiety. It is my impression that every successful analytic therapy consists of both a continuous emotional embroilment between therapist and patient and continuous efforts by the two participants to examine themselves and to understand the nature of their mutual involvement. Thus it is inevitable that therapists, like patients, need to identify their own defensive activities and bring into awareness the anxieties that motivate them. This means that the conduct of an analytic treatment is always, in some part, hard work, but at the same time, it guarantees that in all successful therapies, therapists as well as patients learn about themselves.

9 A Relational Perspective on Anxiety

Charles Spezzano

To position the relational perspective among the various points of view contained in this book, it is not accurate to specify as its foundational premises that anxiety is a consequence of a relationship, that anxiety requires a relationship to make it manifest in the infant, or that relationships create the characterological anxiety level of the developing child. To build a contemporary relational perspective on anxiety we have to assemble a specific set of arguments offered by various authors over the last 50 years. No single psychoanalyst's theory has been as foundational within the relational paradigm as Freud's work has been within the American ego psychology paradigm. Moreover, it is not possible, in assembling the building blocks of a contemporary relational psychoanalytic paradigm, simply to incorporate the entire edifice of any major theorist's writings. Fairbairn and Winnicott, for example, are the prototypical object relational analysts, and the British object relational perspective has contributed substantially to the emerging American relational paradigm. Nonetheless, in this chapter I extract and integrate relational elements of their work while leaving behind the remnants of Freud's drive theory that remained embedded. Similarly, when drawing on the writings of Bion, I ignore some of the more classical Kleinian elements in his theory. Coming from the other direction, I do not work as hard as, say, Mitchell (1988) does to bring all the work of Sullivan into the new American relational paradigm, because not all of Sullivan fits. Fairbairn, Sullivan, Winnicott, and Bion (among others) were transitional figures in the still ongoing shift in this country from American ego psychological to American relational psychoanalysis.

The relational paradigm is still being constructed, just as Freud can be seen, in retrospect, to have constructed his 1926 ego psychology over a period of 40 years—but it is being constructed by many analysts, who are providing the individual pieces of what will become, I believe, an American equivalent of what object relations theory has been in England: a middle school, here not between Freud and Klein, but between the interpersonal (Sullivanian, Ferenczian, self psychological, trauma-abuse) and classical (Freudian and Kleinian) paradigms. It combines elements of object relations theory with the new psychoanalytic theory of affect also being developed by many authors (see Stein, 1991, and Spezzano, 1993, for summaries and integrations of this work on affect), as well as elements of interpersonal, self psychological, and control-mastery theories. That is why this American school has drifted toward the label "relational" rather than the more established "interpersonal" or "object relational."

These arguments range across three domains of psychoanalytic discourse: ontological (the nature of psychological danger), developmental (what accounts for individual variations among adults in the intensity, frequency, or form of their anxieties and in their capacity to regulate it), and epistemological (how we and our analysands come to know the vicissitudes of their anxieties). In the rest of this chapter I explain the key arguments of the relational paradigm and how this paradigm has enhanced our understanding of anxiety in those three domains of psychoanalytic discourse.

PSYCHOANALYTIC ONTOLOGIES
OF DANGER AND ANXIETY

A tenet shared by all relational theorists (and one that is the antithesis of Freud's key theory of affect) is that the sexual excitement and rage that lead to so much human anxiety do not flow constantly out of libidinal and aggressive drives. Sexual excitement results both from certain bodily *activities* of the child *and* out of relational events. It is an intrinsically sought after experience. We do not learn to desire it. We desire it by our very nature as human beings, but the extent to which and the ways in which the pursuit of and experience of sexual excitement make a certain person anxious can only be understood only as the outcomes of a history of interactions with the environment, especially with other people in one's relational environment.

Rage is not understood by relational theorists to be sought after in the same way sexual excitement is; rather, it is thought to be an attempt to deal with other painful emotions. It is an emotion that occurs when a current event is represented unconsciously as involving a certain type of other person (malevolent, frustrating, etc.). Rage is an attempt to "kill off" bad feelings within ourselves; and where, if anywhere, we direct it in the environment is determined entirely by whom or what, in our unconscious representational world, we assess to be responsible for the affective pain that we cannot tolerate and by the extent to which we attribute ruthless or malevolent intentionality to the source of this pain.

By contrast, Freud's 1926 theory of anxiety (on which all classical and ego psychological theories are based) starts with an affect theory quite different from the relational theory of sexual excitement and rage. According to Freud's theory, the immature ego is endangered by the strength of the drives (they can simply disrupt the ego's adaptive functioning or, if the object of the drive is absent, then the pain will become intolerable). The anticipated consequences of expressing or acting on one's drives (alienating or destroying others with our ruthless sexual excitement and malevolent rage or being attacked by others or by our superego because of our rage). The key to this theory of anxiety is that the affects (sexual excitement and rage) that lead to anxiety are derivatives of endogenous drives. Libido and aggression flow out of the body all the time, and no contact with the world is necessary for sexual excitement, rage, or anxiety to occur.

Given a hypothetical sample of people born with the same endowment of libido and aggression, the factor that would account for most of the variance among them (even as adults) in the pattern, intensity, and frequency of their anxieties would be their varying constitutional endowments of anxiety-regulating ego functions. This is the closest that psychoanalysis comes to a purely biological account of differences between individuals in how much they suffer anxiety. There is no psychoanalytic theory that goes a step further and says simply that each of us is equipped with a certain level of anxiety for which no dynamic explanation is needed.

All other psychoanalytic theories move some distance away from this biological end of the purely biological to purely experiential continuum of accounts of anxiety and as, the term "relational" has become equated in the minds of many clinicians with progressive and contemporary psychoanalytic practice, it has been suggested that, surprisingly, classical theory is actually relational too. One author (Dunn, 1993), for example, has found a few places in Freud's writings where he speculated that, during evolution, the drives were shaped by the environment and so have a sort of anthropomorphic built-in awareness of the environmental limitations on their satisfaction and thus a preexperiential relational (in the sense of being conflictedly responsive to the satisfactional opportunities and constraints of environmental realities) nature. On this foundation Dunn attempts to ground the argument that Greenberg and Mitchell's (1983) division of psychoanalysis into drive and relational theories was based on making an unrelational straw man out of Freud.

While this recovery of Freud's phylogenetic relational theory may slightly mitigate the assessment that in Freud's writings individual biology ultimately determines individual psychology, Dunn's use of Freud's having once or twice said that over the course of human evolution the drives acquired an innate push–pull quality through contact with the environment conflates and confuses a phylogentically relational theory with an ontologically relational theory. Even if one allows the at least semi-Lamarckian notion of the gradual building into the drives (through experience) of a conflicted and anxious striving toward satisfaction, this would in no way address the issue of paramount concern in the contemporary drive theory versus relational theory debate: to what extent have any individual's unconscious motivations (and conflicts about them) arisen from and been shaped by biological or environmental stimuli? Or, more specific to the aims of this book, to what extent does each individual's interactions with other people during that individual's lifetime determine how anxious he is, when he becomes anxious, or the defenses he mounts against anxiety?

Dunn's argument that "internal and external phenomena reciprocally organise each other and attempts to conceptualize them as separate entities restrict the degree to which we can understand the nature of mental life" (p. 238) (a wonderfully clear, even if unintended, summary of the contemporary relational argument) would, if Freud had made that claim about the ontology and development of each individual's psychology, be a persuasive argument that Freudian drive theory is both biological and relational. Freud, however, only speculated that in the far distant past of the human race adjustments were made to the drives on the basis of environmental realities. Further, Dunn's argument implies that the drives generate their own anxiety because they have had caution, anxiety, or respect for the environment built into them over the eons, and this subverts Freud's own 1926 theory of the pivotal role of the ego in generating anxiety. I don't think Freud can have it, or be expected to have it, both ways: the ego brings the environment to bear on the drives and, thus, generates anxiety; but the drives are also, in and of themselves, carriers of phylogenetic, anxiety- and conflict-laden awareness of the environment.

In addition, the distinction between phylogenetic and ontologic/ developmental explanations of anxiety about one's own strivings is significant in how we formulate diagnostic thoughts about a patient's anxiety. For example, 31% of the women in the United States are likely to experience one or more episodes of the rapid heart beat, shallow breathing, and decreased blood flow to the extremities that we call "an anxiety attack" and that will disrupt their ego functioning to a debilitating degree, whereas only 19% of men typically suffer the same fate (Kessler et al., 1994). Following Dunn's phylogenetic Freud, we would conclude that women have been shaped by evolution to be much more anxious than men, and then we would argue that way of thinking reflects a contemporary relational attempt to understand the variance between men and women in prevalence of anxiety attacks. In fact, we would be confined to explaining everyone's conflictedness and anxiety concerning sex and aggression as largely, if not entirely, due to an unconscious unwillingness to know and accept the personal psychology of sexual and aggressive wishes with which evolution had endowed them.

Freud's account of the origin of individual psychic life is something of a theoretical Rorschach card. If one is intent, one can show that Freud was an object relational theorist, a self psychologist, and probably even an interpersonal theorist; but these efforts always involve overlooking the difference between having lived in Chicago and having once stopped over at O'Hare. Freud touched down everywhere on the psychological landscape, so it is not difficult to turn even libido into a relational concept. Such efforts to strip all post-Freudian theories of their radical quality, however, end up doing the same to Freud. If he held every conceivable position on human psychology, then he held no meaningful position (a point in every direction being no point at all).

Most readers of Freud's work, however, acknowledge that he had a distinct position. In my view, nowhere was Freud's "unrelational" position more clear than in his final theory of anxiety. Stein (1991), for example, acknowledges the relational spice in Freud's theorizing about anxiety without contentiously insisting that this transformed his drive and defense paradigm into the equivalent of a paradigm in which the main ingredient is the relationship between the ego and its objects. She points out that, in 1926, Freud observed how the ego treats anxiety as a threat to be defended against rather than simply as an informative signal of impending danger. Freud believed that to treat anxiety as a threat was to say that there must have been some very early episode of anxiety that reached horribly traumatizing proportions. Freud might have gone on to argue that early traumatic relational events must take place to account for a specific ego's vulnerability to those anxieties that he recognizes as being much more primitive and terrifying than oedipal anxiety. Freud did not do this. Instead he created a nonrelational account of the human capacity for panic attacks. He argued that there must be phylogenetic memory traces of primeval terrors or there must be an early and universal experience that leaves all of us with the vulnerability to become anxious about our anxiety and so fall into an escalating anxious cycle that ends in panic or breakdown. To fit his theoretical needs, this early experience would not only have to be universal (rather than a matter of individual development, which we will take up in the next section of this chapter), but also have to be so obviously an event that involves a flood of excitation that its traumatic quality would be virtually self-evident. One universal human event fit his needs: birth. Birth teaches the ego about how bad anxiety can get, and the ego never forgets.

Let me make a brief detour from Stein's account of Freud's thinking before arriving at what I believe to be her essentially correct conclusion about Freud's theory of primitive anxieties and panic attacks. Freud was purposely looking to be as nonrelational as he could at this critical point in his theorizing. That is what is unique and valuable in Freud's account of anxiety. He brilliantly and radically sidesteps obvious opportunities to embrace a relational perspective (that is, to say that vulnerability to primitive anxiety would not become a part of one's personal psychology unless one had, as a child, been trauma-tized in a relationship). He anticipates later theorizing about the importance of overwhelmingly anxious separations from the mother, but he finds a way to make even separation not a part of psychoana-lytic developmental psychology but a part of psychoanalytic ontology, a part of human nature. To be born one must of course "separate" from the mother, but that is not what Mahler or Bowlby meant by separa-tion. They meant separations as psychological, not biological, events and so as being managed by a mother in many different ways some of which would leave a child vulnerable to panic attacks and some of which would not. Freud, by contrast, left us with an analysand who, if subject to panic attacks, must be assumed to have a wired-in vulnera-bility to being overwhelmed by anxiety and consequently over-whelmed and traumatized to a qualitatively greater degree than most; or she must be assumed to have an excess of libido or aggression that triggers the universal vulnerability to panic.

Panic attacks, then, as Stein concludes, become, in Freud's 1926 theory of anxiety, "innate hysterical attacks . . . Freud has thus come full circle, and in this way he has bypassed the necessity of a psycho-logical and psychodynamic explanation of primitive anxiety" (p. 29). Freud flirts here with the relational nature of primitive anxiety but ultimately declines its seductions and favors the understanding of the pattern of anxiety in any adult psyche as much more a product of inborn endowments of sexual excitement, or of the universal experi-ences of birth excitation having met a constitutionally weak or strong ego, than a residue of the joint regulation of excitement, danger, and anxiety by a specifically endowed child and his specific parents.

What effect did this ontology have on the clinical work of American ego psychological analysts? It infused psychoanalytic treatment, at least in this country through the 1970s, with a debilitating pessimism. A significant number of patients seeking psychoanalytic treatment were assessed as unanalyzable because the high level (or "hair trigger") of their anxiety was taken as proof of a tragic mismatch between their temperamental anxiety level and their constitutionally endowed capacity to regulate anxiety. Some patients are fortunate enough to have been born with egos that could handle, through sublimation of libidinal and aggressive agendas and neurotic defenses, and with the aid of a functional superego, the inevitable anxiety we all experience as children during our first encounters with our endogenously unfolding endowments of sexual excitement and rage. Other patients, unfortunately, were not born with such egos and would, therefore, be unable to tolerate the classical analytic requirement that they be able to contain the anxiety caused by the inherent transferential pull on those warded-off drive derivatives to reemerge in full infantile force. While classical analysts might tactfully note a patient's anxiety being manifested in some form of resistance to the analytic process, they would believe themselves to have two choices: either maintain the analytic process by continuing to observe and interpret the resistance or temporarily abandon the analytic process by introducing a parameter designed to reduce the anxiety. Patients who could not tolerate the anxiety of the analytic process and who were likely to require constant help in the form of "parameters" would often be designated as "psychotherapy" patients or as in need of a preparatory, ego-building, preanalysis phase of treatment.

One of the major clinical consequences of the relational shift in psychoanalysis was the diminishing in importance (among relational analysts) of the analyzable–unanalyzable dichotomy, which, in turn, was due directly to the different role that anxiety was understood to play in the constitution of the human condition. *All relational theories argue that we were equipped (by nature, God, or evolution) with anxiety not only so that we could signal ourselves and energize ourselves in the face of perceived dangers, but also so that we would immediately communicate our sense of being in danger to others.* One of the most compelling accounts of this conceptualization of unconscious affective communication can be found in the writings of the philosopher Wittgenstein (1967). He argued that:

> we do not see facial contortions and make inferences from them—to joy, grief, boredom. We describe a face immediately as sad, radiant, bored . . . Grief, one

would like to say, is personified in the face. This belongs to the concept of emotion [p. 225].

Writing specifically of anxiety, Wittgenstein (1953) had argued earlier that "fear is there, alive in the features" of the face (p. 537). We do not have to turn the facial expressions, tones of voice, or hesitations in the flow of associations into an idea of anxiety. These are direct expressions of anxiety, and we immediately register them in that way. No inference is required. If a patient pauses, hesitates, changes tone of voice when talking to us, for us to characterize that as a resistance to the patient saying she is anxious is to assume, contrary to the relational assumption about the nature of anxiety, that the pauses and hesitations leave something out. By contrast, Wittgenstein can be read as arguing, as I have done (Spezzano, 1993), that the pauses and hesitations are a natural form of communication of anxiety in the analytic situation.

We don't need others to make us anxious, nor is even the newborn without any means for self-regulation; but, since anxiety is inherently a communication, every anxiety state is by its nature a relational event. This was a key proposition of Winnicott's psychology of anxiety. Believing that "unthinkable anxiety" (what we have come to call annihilation anxiety) is a routine part of infant life, Winnicott saw all of us as requiring analysis of the residues of such anxiety. When annihilation anxiety entered the transference, Winnicott would do and say whatever he thought was necessary to maintain the analytic process. For example, after six years of analyzing a woman at the usual five times per week, Winnicott (1971, pp. 58–64) agreed, when she found the end of the 50-minute hour intolerably terrifying, to see her once a week for three hours. He did not view this as a parameter, a break in the frame or a piece of supportive therapy, but as part of the analytic process. The analysand could not say why she had to have the longer sessions, but Winnicott had long believed that there were times in every analysis when the analyst would best facilitate the analytic process by taking the attitude that for one who knows another no explanation from the other is needed.

Whether the other person "gets" the communication of anxiety (it is always communicated, from a relational point of view), and what the anxious person unconsciously perceives the other to be doing once the other has gotten the anxious communications, will be a significant determinant of the further course of that anxious episode. There is, in other words, no way, from a relational psychoanalytic point of view, to be in a room with an anxious person and do nothing but observe that person struggling with anxiety. One is automatically a participant in the vicissitudes of the anxious state. It is natural and progressive, as well as pathological and regressive, for patients to need and want others (including the analyst) to see, understand, and help them regulate their anxieties.

There has been considerable confusion about Winnicott's technical implementation of this strongly relational ontology of anxiety. Winnicott is largely responsible for this confusion because (1) he repeatedly asserted that interpreting preoedipal types of anxiety would not do much good, but (2) he repeatedly reported his interpretations of those anxieties and sometimes said directly that such interpreting of them was crucial to effective analytic treatment of anxiety. He appears to have meant to communicate to his readers that (1) correct interpretation of anxiety is critical to its treatment; (2) the interpretation must come from a person represented in the mind of the patient as a particular kind of object; (3) this crucial object must be represented as having the intention of eliminating the anxieties that patient finds unbearable; and (4) to be represented that way in the mind of the patient there must be some tangible evidence of the therapist's willingness to help manage, and not just talk about, the patient's unbearable anxieties. For example, I began the analysis of one patient by moving back his sessions 15 minutes so that he would have time to feed himself quickly and change from his business suit into a sweatsuit before each analytic hour—and we both understood that this meant my waiting for him 15 minutes at the end of the day and so not being able to leave for my home until 15 minutes later than usual. I also interpreted this in two other ways: (1) as his need to feel connected to me as soon as he left his office rather than feeling frantic and alone in his rush to get to me and (2) as his need to see me actively helping him manage his anxiety of being overwhelmed by the demands of others on his time, rather than expecting him to manage it himself as the rest of the world, understandably, expected him to do. After six months I told him that I did not want to keep doing this unless it was still necessary, and we agreed to meet on the hour instead of 15 minutes after the hour.

Fairbairn also distanced relational psychoanalytic theory from the analyzable–unanalyzable dichotomy by his contribution to the relational theory of anxiety. He identified a universal unconscious conflict (one's love is bad and will alienate or destroy the objects one needs most, but one cannot make contact with those objects except through one's love and without an alive emotional investment in an object the ego dies) and a pair of dueling anxieties (loss of the object or loss of the ego). As a result of this anxious conflict, all human egos are split. There is not one class of patients with intact but intrapsychically conflicted egos and another class with structural defects (as American ego

psychology began to suggest in Fairbairn's day). "Consequently," as
Summers (1994) observes about Fairbairn's theory, "the fact that
structural defect is a component of psychopathology does not imply a
reduced accessibility to analysis" (p. 43). The analytic goals of healing structural defects in the ego and resolving conflict are not incompatible in Fairbairn's theory but are intrinsically intertwined. Thus, not
only did British object relational analysts begin in the 1940s (as
American relational analysts have begun) to analyze (and not provide
"supportive psychotherapy" to) a much broader range of patients, but
they saw establishing a personal relationship as essential to the analysis. Fairbairn (1954), for example, reported, quite matter of factly and
not as if he were introducing a "parameter," that in response to an
analysand's (who suffered hysterical anxiety) mentioning a play she
had attended the previous night, he had said something like, "Yes, I
was there too, and I saw you." Fairbairn saw such moments as opportunities to create the personal relationship that Freud had with many of
his patients and that Fairbairn conceptualized as essential for the
analysand to tolerate the anxiety of allowing the return of repressed
bad objects into the transference.

In fact, because Fairbairn saw sexual excitement and rage as affects
that had become bound up with a conflicted agenda of loving and
hating desired but frustrating objects, he brought into object relational
clinical theory the analytic attitude of Ferenczi that it made sense to
establish a sort of "friendship" with patients—we love and hate our
friends with an intensity seldom directed at anonymous strangers.
Because, however, his ego psychology provided Fairbairn with a
sophisticated understanding of how such friendliness would help open
up an analytic space within which the transference could fully
develop, he offered analytic love and friendship (what Winnicott
[1963] would later define as "understanding in a deep way and interpreting at the right moment" [p. 250]) rather than Ferenczi's maternal
love and friendliness. What Ferenczi seems to have understood intuitively, though, and what Fairbairn conceptualized more clearly, is
that the transferential possibility of opening up, in the analytic space,
one's unconscious representational world (built up over a lifetime of
affective-relational experiences) depends not only on a measure of
abstinence or anonymity but at least equally on what we might call
(paradoxically) a self-reflexive spontaneity on the part of the analyst.
It is this *analytic spontaneity* that allows the developmental story of
the patient to be *lived through the transference* in all its sexually
exciting and enraged detail—and this leads us directly into the
discussion of anxiety by relational theorists at the developmental level
of the psychoanalytic discourse.

THE DEVELOPMENT OF ANXIETY FROM
A RELATIONAL PERSPECTIVE

All contemporary relational theorists emphasize the importance of parent–infant reciprocity in affective development. The infant uses emotion to communicate internal states for which he or she is always at least partially "responsible." The relational analyst finds stories about the origin of a patient's anxiety that lay responsibility or blame solely upon either the patient or his parents as equally implausible.

Similarly, a relational analyst is likely to think in terms of a continuum of perspectives on anxiety. At one end would be "the infant's anxiety originates as a biological event inside the infant and then the anxiety level of the infant determines the object relationship." What is not at the other end of the continuum is "anxiety is a consequence of relationships," at least not if that is taken to mean that a hypothetically perfect set of parents could keep an infant from experiencing much, if any, anxiety.

What is at the other end is a pair of assertions that define a contemporary relational point of view about anxiety, such as (1) parents exert significant influence on the regulation and expression of anxiety, as well as on the extent to which neurotic and psychotic intrapsychic defenses have to be created by the developing child for anxiety regulation; or (2) the extent to which a child's constitutional anxiety level (tone, or predisposition) will evolve into the classic Freudian anxieties (about loss of the object, loss of the object's love, castration, or superego attacks) is largely determined by early relationships.

Ultimately, then, the twin questions of how anxious states originate and how they are regulated have been answered by relational theorists with the word "intersubjectively." Parent and infant, or analyst and analysand, construct what Beebe and Lachmann (1994) have described as dyadic modes of anxiety regulation, which include both interactive and self-regulatory psychological activities.

Consider, in this light, a case presented by ego psychological analyst Charles Hanly in *The Psychoanalytic Quarterly* in 1978. He argued that John Bowlby's relational theory and, by implication, relational theory in general, is flawed because it lays responsibility for an adult patient's neurotic anxiety on some failure by an attachment figure; the responsibility, Hanly feels confident, inevitably rests with the ego's failure to have regulated the patient's endogenously unfolding endowment of libido. He discusses a girl in her late teens who feels bad because she has found herself unable to turn to her mother for comfort and serious conversation. She would be stopped by feelings of resentment and suspicion toward the mother. What is the origin of this representation of the mother as an object of resentment and suspicion? Hanly demands irrefutable evidence that the mother had played any significant role in the formation of the maternal representation, but the patient does not recall abusive or malevolent treatment by the mother. So Hanly interprets the representation of the hated mother as having been constructed out of the patient's own *anxiously* disavowed hatred. To diminish the anxiety she experiences over her jealous and hateful intentions toward the mother, she projects this hatred and jealously into the mother and then reacts to the mother with resentment and suspicion, feelings less painful than anxiety.

This conclusion can be reached only if one starts not simply with a presupposition of drives, but specifically of libidinal and aggressive drives that *constantly generate* affects of sexual excitement and rage. Then, in essence, the patient can be presumed to be responsible for having infused all unconscious representations of others with her own disavowed sexuality and aggression. In turn, one can demand, as Hanly did, that to prove that anything relational contributed to her representation of her mother as worthy of suspicion and resentment the patient would have to come up with clear memories of malevolent actions by her mother.

A relational analyst would treat the account of her mother given by Hanly's patient as *plausible*, allow it to unfold, conarrate it with the patient, and let whatever evidentiary weaknesses plague the account expose themselves for mutual consideration by analyst and analysand. So where Hanly talked with his analysand about her vague sense that her mother had once made her very anxious by locking her in a closet as an idea that could qualify as a source of her current anxiety only if evidence emerged in the form of clear memories of such abuses, I would imagine myself making to such a patient statements such as:

> So you have this sense that your mother once locked you in a closet but you don't feel certain about that having happened.

> In any case you have ended up with a sense of her as having been dangerous and malevolent at times.

> You don't necessarily have to decide right now whether to treat that idea as a fantasy or a memory in order for us to recognize that you have been haunted by it.

> What matters right now is that in the place in your mind where there would ideally be an image of a mother soothing her anxious child you instead have an image of a mother who at best doesn't know when she is frightening her daughter or at worst is so angry that she wants to punish her daughter by making her anxious.

Hanly, to the contrary, was restating the drive-defense account of human development in which we do not want to know about our wired-in sexual excitement and competitive hatred and envy. The immature ego naturally flees from such awareness. In the analysis, while talking of her fear of being attacked by a sadistic man, Hanly's patient recalled a movie in which a mad psychiatrist plotted to take possession of his patient's brain by violent surgery. Then she made "a joking allusion" to the analyst that gradually was elaborated into an acknowledgment that she had cast him in the role of the depraved sadist who wanted to possess her brain. The analyst interpreted this as a defense against her *wish* that he become a depraved sadist so she could castrate him without guilt. Again, the patient was presumed to be the generator of her own affects. If there was sadism in her unconscious representational world and anxiety over that sadism, her sadism must have been causing her anxiety.

By contrast, contemporary relational theorists emphasize the importance of parent–child reciprocity in affective development. If there is sadism (and anxiety over the sadism) in a patient's unconscious representational world, then there must have been anxiety-laden sadomasochistic interactions in the patient's history. Might it not be the case that an excessively anxious infant provoked power struggles with a frantic parent trying to calm the infant down? No relational theorist would dispute that. Well, then, might not the child simply have represented the parent's urgent attempts to calm him down as a sadomasochistic encounter? Yes. The relational analyst does not view the parent as guilty until proven innocent but as having been a cocreator, even if a well-intentioned one, of the sadomasochistic self- and object representation that now haunts the patient's unconscious psychological landscape. The infant is "wired" to require others to do and not do various things in the face of her anxiety, which "things" will lessen the anxiety or increase it. Although the infant who becomes anxious easily and frequently will generate more anxiety and other negative feelings in parents, parents vary in their capacity to contain anxiety and in their methods of holding an anxious infant.

THE RELATIONAL ACCOUNT OF THE DEVELOPMENTAL ORIGINS OF UNCONSCIOUSLY PERCEIVED DANGER SITUATIONS

In addition to defining a relational perspective on anxiety in the way I have done so far, I make a distinction not made manifest consistently in the earlier chapters of this book, that between a person's general anxiety level or general tendency to become anxious and a person's unique hierarchy of unconsciously represented psychological dangers. For example, if a patient becomes anxious at the unconsciously perceived threat of humiliation, then his tendency to become quickly anxious about this specific threat would be best understood not simply as a reflection of a general tendency to become anxious quickly and easily (no matter whether the origin of that tendency is understood to be constitutional or relational) but also as a reflection of an early history of humiliations that left the patient constantly anxious that another humiliation was right around every corner.

The classical hierarchy established by Freud has become part of rote memory for all of us because it was assembled by one author. The relational hierarchy has never been assembled in one place, but I believe it is readily extractable.

At the base of the relational hierarchy is the anxiety of aloneness (abandonment anxiety and annihilation anxiety). This can be experienced from the beginning of life because it reflects the deprivation of a need to be physically close to other human beings. Winnicott posited that infants live on the border of this anxiety and require an adult close by at all times to keep their bodily and psychological state within tolerable bounds. In one of his earliest essays (Winnicott, 1949), he reported the treatment of a woman who seemed to function well in relationships and at work but who felt chronically discontented and lifeless. In an earlier analysis the patient had once expressed her anxiety in what the analyst had perceived as a hysterically resistant way by throwing herself off the couch. Winnicott interpreted this as a reliving of an incomprehensible anxiety of having her head crushed during the birth process. This interpretation communicated to the patient that Winnicott was able to think about such anxieties. His thinking made her aware for the first time of her own inability to think about the anxiety, that is, she was, for the first time, able to construct a representation of a not-thinking and not-knowing anxious self who was nonetheless not facing annihilation because she was linked to a person who does know.

Next in line developmentally is the anxiety of nonrecognition. This idea can be traced to Kojève and his lectures on the *Phenomenology of Spirit*, which revived interest in Hegel among French intellectuals (including Lacan) during the 1930s. Alexandre Kojève (1969) emphasized that a desire for recognition is specifically part of human psychology and not animal biology. For Hegel, Kojève argued, this desire is the moving force of human history. In relational psychoanalysis this desire is understood as a fundamental human need. Jessica Benjamin (1988) reintroduced this concept into contemporary psychoanalytic discourse and defined it as a need for "a response from the other which makes meaningful the feelings, intentions, and actions of the self" (p. 12).

As a result, relational analysts identify for their analysands moments when the analytic pair appears to have failed to connect and communicate: "I don't think we have figured out a way to talk about this that really brings it alive for both of us at the same time. When it seems to you that we have tried again and failed again you feel isolated and anxious." Or: "There is something about yourself and about our relationship that you are telling me by coming five minutes late to every analytic hour. It's like charades except you don't know how the message translates into words either."

Winnicott (1971) provided an example of such technical handling of anxiety in his report of his treatment of the woman, mentioned earlier, who wanted a session of indefinite length. During one of these interminable hours the patient was silent for the first half hour, sitting in a chair instead of using the couch and/or pacing around the office. She complained that she was not really trying to work at analysis that day and that she was a jumbled mess or a crash inside or drifting like clouds. When in the middle of talking about her life as not mattering, the patient suddenly thought of a postcard she had gotten in the mail. Winnicott understood her to be expressing her urgent need for the kind of recognition that holds one together and makes one matter, so he said about the postcard and the person who had sent it: "As if you mattered to her, but you don't matter to her or anyone" (p. 59). The patient responded by remarking that she now felt as if she had not made contact with Winnicott during the entire first two hours of the session. Winnicott understood this to mean that she now did feel in contact and felt this hypothesis to be confirmed when (1) she mentioned what we might expect a patient to say at the beginning of an hour, that she was grateful to him for having offered her what was a makeup session. He must have known she needed it, and (2) she reported being unable to remember the first two hours of the session. It was as if she had just arrived. Winnicott understood that psychic events often faded away inside of her rather than adding up to a sense of having been somewhere and done something. To avoid being brought to the place where anxiety about nonrecognition begins to turn into annihilation anxiety, she required recognition by the mother and the mother's holding in mind the child's experience. So Winnicott interpreted: "All sorts of things happen and they wither. This is the myriad deaths you have died. But if someone is there, someone who can give you back what has happened, then the details dealt with in this way become part of you, and do not die" (p. 61).

Advancing developmentally through the relational psychoanalytic hierarchy of anxiety-provoking danger situations we come to the object relational, paranoid-schizoid anxieties of Fairbairn and Klein (more accurately Klein as revised and relationalized by Bion). Fairbairn argued that we all, throughout life, want to be excited by others, but the dance of excitement has to proceed in such a way that the two partners avoid the anxiety of overexcitement and the anxiety of rejection. If an adult excites a child beyond that child's capacity to tolerate the excitement, then the child will become anxious. Or, if an adult is made anxious by a child's excitement over the adult and the adult rejects that excitement, the child experiences the episode as one in which he had been teased and frustrated. In either case, one's own excitement becomes dangerous. Similarly, taking Klein's portrayal of the infant as locked phylogenetically and ontologically into an anxiety-laden battle with her endowment of aggression and rage, Bion revised this into a developmental account in which two people in any dyad share the burden of containing the rage and continuing to think in the face of the rage. If that happens, then anxiety will remain manageable.

Fairbairn's clearest clinical example of interpreting this schizoid anxiety was reported in 1954. A patient he called Olivia suffered from anorexia and agoraphobia. He interpreted to her how her mother had become exciting and rejecting by repeatedly trying unsuccessfully (as Olivia had been told) to breast feed her. Then the father became the exciting and frustrating object by holding down the hungry and crying child (wrestling can be sexually exciting) but not calming her down (relief appears available but does not come). Her father's continued controlling interference in her life remained both exciting to (symbolically wrestling with him) and rejecting of her (he was rarely excited by what excited her). Fairbairn interpreted that Olivia had come to hate her own need for contact and so developed symptoms of not trying to take anything more inside and not going outside where people could excite her expectation of finally getting the needed maternal object only to fail inevitably to satisfy the very need they excited. Neither of Olivia's defensive strategies had brought an end to the anxiety because, when they quieted the anxiety of swallowing and destroying the object, they did so at the cost of cutting off the ego from its own excitement and desire and so left it to face the terror of psychic death.

Fairbairn's relational revision of Freud's structural theory (in which an ego struggles with two drives and one large object, the superego) into a psychology of an ego linked (in splitting or healing ways) with multiple objects through powerful affects was mirrored in the Kleinian world by Bion's relational revision of Klein. Coming to the analysis of individuals from group therapy, Bion assumed that a task common to all groups is the management of anxiety. The prototypical pathological way to manage anxiety is to evacuate it into another person, literally to communicate and interact with that person in some way that ends up with your being relieved and the person's being anxious. The healthy alternative is to communicate and interact in a way that catalyzes group thinking about the anxiety. In other words, when my anxiety approaches the level at which my own capacity for thinking about it is about to break down, I can either try to involve others in thinking about it with me or I can try to pass the feeling state off to them. I have noticed, for example, after studying Bion, that in discussing their "significant others" analysands sometimes unconsciously want me to be the one who holds in mind, contains the anxiety associated with, and thinks about whatever representation of the other causes them the most anxiety. If I talk about the other in the light of that representation which I have "taken in" from them, the patient will begin to defend the other by emphasizing alternative versions of him or her, ones that do not make the analysand so anxious as the version I have been left to deal with. I now make that interpretation: "I believe that we have worked things out here, without realizing it, so that I am thinking of the version of your fiancee that you find impossible to think about [perhaps because it makes the analysand want to kill her or leave her], while you live in your mind with a less disturbing image of her." If the analysand then wants to obtain immediate relief from the conflict by adopting an "OK, then I will break up with her" attitude, then I point out that his vulnerability to being made anxious by certain unconscious images of women will not be healed by his deciding this issue one way or the other. The immediate issue is the anxiety he avoids by dissociating, compartmentalizing, and evacuating one particular image of her into my mind and wanting me to think about that version of her.

Finally, we come to the most developmentally advanced anxieties: Klein's depressive anxiety and Freud's oedipal anxiety. A contemporary relational understanding of these anxieties focuses on the way in which the existence of one configuration of self in an affectively defined relationship to a specific version of the other threatens the existence of another such configuration. Linking mommy and me through sexual excitement threatens my identificatory link with daddy. A configuration of me hating the mother, whom I blame for my discomfort and pain, threatens the configuration of me loving good mother who soothes and excites me.

HOW ANALYST AND ANALYSAND KNOW
AND TALK ABOUT THE VICISSITUDES OF
THE ANALYSAND'S ANXIETIES

Psychoanalysts of all persuasions implicitly, if not explicitly, claim to be able to come to know two things about a patient's anxieties: (1) when they emerge during analytic hours, and (2) their origin. I will consider these two epistemological claims in that order.

As for knowing when anxiety emerges during analytic hours, the focus, somewhat obviously, has not been on overt panic attacks, which are evident to both patient and clinician when they occur, but rather on the appearance of what have traditionally been called "resistances." The major forms that such resistances have been said, by ego psychological analysts, to take are (1) pauses in the flow of associations, (2) changes in topic, and (3) prolonged periods of talking about unconfictual ideas. Since it is easy to run into trouble when making claims that one knows how other analysts work, I will say here only that when I thought of myself as working from a classical, ego psychological, resistance analysis theory, I would simply note the pause, the appearance and disappearance of a certain idea in the flow of the patient's associations, or the apparent prolonged absence of anxiety and conflict. Now, instead, I am likely to say:

I think you are letting me know that something has made you anxious.

When you start to talk angrily about your brother and then shift quickly to speculating empathically about the reasons for his making demands on your time, I find myself thinking that you became anxious about your rage at him heating up. I'm left with the image of him as entitled and demanding while you go on to describe the other side of your image of him, which emphasizes how weak and pathetic he is. So, I then find myself thinking that's what you want: I'll hold the rage at him, while you feel the sympathy.

When the patient becomes too anxious to think, we assume that a breakdown has occurred in the effort of the two people to hold the patient's anxiety in mind, think about it, and keep it from becoming overwhelming. By contrast, in the clinical situation a nonrelational theory "sees" such breakdowns as evidence of flaws in the analysand's intrapsychic drive-defensive compromises; and sees inhibitions of and disconnections from (inability to know and think about one's) sexual excitement and rage as ways of controlling anxiety. Further, negative transference is understood as "emerging" when the analyst correctly works in ways that do not distract, gratify, or comfort the analysand as exemplified in Owen Renik's chapter in this book when he understood his patient's suddenly feeling neglected, disappointed, and angry (when he switched from actively interpreting her anxieties to letting her worry about them herself) as an "emergence" (rather than a cocreation by the analytic pair) of those affects.

Read by many relational analysts, this vignette displays a certain pattern recognizable in ego psychologically weighted accounts of the analyses of patients' anxieties. The analyst realizes he or she has been too actively interpretive. The analyst does not disclose this realization to the patient but simply backs off and lets the patient do the work. What then "emerges" is a negative transference that combines accounts of victimizing analyst and victimizing parents. Finally, these accounts collapse under the weight of their own hyperbole, and the analysand sees herself, both developmentally and transferentially, as the source and maintainer of her own anxieties and hatreds.

A relational analyst in such a situation would be expected to respond to the realization that he had been carrying the anxiety for the analytic couple by saying, "We appear to have created a way of working in which I have been worrying about how to get you going" or "I'm wondering if my offering you all these ideas about how you seem to miss evidence of your own competence and attractiveness reflects some sort of unconscious agreement we arrived at early in the analysis—an agreement in which I'll feel the anxiety and you'll feel the helplessness."

For example, in treating a woman in her 20s (who entered analysis stuck in a life of minimum-wage jobs despite apparent intellectual and family resources that might easily have opened up possibilities of education or training for more enjoyable and profitable work), we would routinely, during the first year of the treatment, run up against the idea that not much was going to be different about her life unless she got some sort of post-high school education. Usually our conversational journey to this increasingly familiar point in the analysis was accompanied by her feeling stronger and happier. When, however, we actually reached that point, she would become intensely anxious. She would become mired in the impossibility of her untying the knot that bound her—the strands of which included a father to whom she could not concede control by asking for tuition money, the necessity of working to pay for analysis, and the scholastic incompetencies that she recalled from high school.

After several trips down this dead end, I described our situation in this way: "*We* talk for a time about your impasse in your relationship with your father and how it keeps you from moving forward, but I'm thinking now that *we* are creating the impasse in your life right here, or at least keeping it alive, by acting as if *we* are both waiting for the emergence in our sessions of an inspired plan that will allow you to make an end run around this dreaded conversation in which you ask your father for the money to return to school." She responds with frustration that she knows this. "I know that you know the conversation with your father hangs you up. I'm saying something different, that you and I together retreat from that conversation like an army regrouping to come up with a new strategy. But there is no new strategy. That's just wishful thinking." She asks if I think she likes coming in over and over to tell me that she has failed again to open up the dreaded conversation with her father. I answer that it seems she finds doing that less anxiety provoking than asking her father to give her the money to go to college. Shortly after this session, she, with heart pounding, does ask for and get the money. Then we begin to deal with her anxieties about her intellectual deficiencies and her anticipation of further defiant-girl-versus-controlling-father battles in the classroom.

Beginning to intervene in a merry-go-round phase of the analytic work by talking in terms of "we have become stuck" opens a particular door to understanding the anxieties of the analysand—a door that relational analysts favor—through which, for example, we might see how the analyst and analysand have been wishing together that life would offer the analysand some way to circle around her worst anxieties rather than facing them. It is, in fact, hard for me to imagine the value of making the distinction between a nonrelational and relational analysis of the vicissitudes of anxiety if we do not include the technical distinction between including "we" statements among our interventions and limiting ourselves to the traditional "I" and "you" structure of interpretations.

So, to the question "How do we know that the analysand has become anxious during an analytic hour?" relational analysts answer that the analysand tells us. Here is a clinical example flowing directly out of this relational perspective. I told a male analysand in his late 20s that, although he was manifestly talking critically of his mother (as he often did), today I thought I heard in his material some indications of his feelings of affection for his mother and even allusions to ways in which he had expressed that affection when he was a child.

The patient started to express his agreement with my interpretation, but as he did so he seemed to became inarticulate, stretching his words, needing to take deep breaths between phrases, clearing his throat loudly as if the phlegm, as he put it, kept "flooding into him." From a perspective that patients are mostly involved in intrapsychic struggles of which the analyst is observer, the analysand's odd behavior at that moment might be understood as a resistance. From a relational perspective, by contrast, one always treats such behavior as a communication: while starting to think and talk about a particular self- and object representation (in this case it was his being "difficult," his mother's being a good and sympathetic manager of his "difficultness," and his feeling gratitude to her), he became anxious. He did not, because of the anxiety, resist talking about his mother in the way he had begun to do—anymore than, if you and I were walking across an intersection talking about my mother and I suddenly interrupted myself to shout at you that we were about to be hit by a truck, it would make sense to conclude that I had begun resisting talking about my mother. The analysand talked about his mother in a particular light, became very anxious, and so started to communicate the anxiety.

Reading and rereading the work of Bion as contemporary relational Kleinian theory has instilled in my preconscious thinking the tendency to conceptualize clinical events in this way. As Hinshelwood (1994), a contemporary Kleinian analyst, has argued, it was as a result of Bion's work that "Kleinian practice was changed forever by the realization that the patient is communicating more than a disguised message—he or she is communicating a plea for help with a mind that is no longer capable of the important messages, disguised or otherwise" (p. 115).

It is not the recognition that pauses and interruptions reflect anxiety that distinguishes relational interpretive work from classical interpretive work. Rather, the difference is that, following Freud, the classical analyst views the patient as having stopped communicating, perhaps even having stopped relating to the analyst or having interrupted the analytic process, because of the anxiety, whereas the relational analyst understands the patient to be switching from communicating representational content to communicating pure anxiety. The relational analyst does not, therefore, expect that the patient will ultimately work through such resistances or even come to understand that he is trying not to know about some unconscious content. Instead, the relational analyst expects that if he does not note the communication of anxiety and identify this as all that is important for the patient to be communicating at that moment, the patient will experience increasing anxiety and despair. The relational analyst will try to find words for the anxiety without worrying that he is bypassing the patient's resistance to finding the words for himself.

So far I have been addressing the first of the two questions I raised at the beginning of this section: how do we know when anxiety or panic has emerged during analytic hours? In the example from my work, however, I have also begun to take up the second question, that of the origins of anxiety and panic. I attributed the onset of the analysand's incipient panic attack to the interpretation I had offered.

The interpretation brought to mind a representation of the grateful son linked to the loving mother. Because some patients unconsciously have categorized their hatred as untamable and murderous, they do not want to bring to mind (that is, bring into the same psychological field with their hatred) the good maternal object. They fear destroying the one on whom they depend for life. So they attack those psychological functions that keep the good maternal representation out front and in harm's way: their own capacity to think and communicate. In this case, the patient found relief in understanding that he would rather suffocate himself than talk with me (and so bring fully alive) his gratitude to his mother, his love for her, and his feeling of being loved by her. These aspects of his relationship with his mother had to be muted to keep them away from his rage and hatred.

I told the patient that in talking about his gratitude toward his mother he appeared to have started to feel as if he were choking on his words. He said that, now that he thought about it, he had felt as if he might not be able to talk and breathe at the same time. My mind wandered to the current pathophysiological psychiatric theory of panic disorder known as the suffocation false alarm hypothesis (Klein, 1993), which suggests that patients subject to panic attacks were equipped at birth with a pathologically oversensitive version of the normal human capacity to sense when one is suffocating and to react to this as the life-threat that it is. Like neurophysiological and biochemical accounts of anxiety, fear, startle, alarm, and arousal, psychoanalytic accounts also recognize that being overwhelmed with panicky feelings is not simply a gradual build up of anxiety beyond a certain threshold, but is a distinct clinical event.

I said something to the patient using the words "suffocate" and "panic," which further helped him elaborate the feeling state. Then I mentioned the sense of suffocating as a common experience in moments of sudden panic. That was a technical error, I now feel, based on a countertransferential wish to calm his anxiety about the terrifying conflicted relationship with the mother by being the scientific father (as his own father, a physicist, had become represented in my mind). He responded by saying sarcastically, "The patient is falling asleep." I then told him about what I thought I had been doing to calm him down and that he was telling me it was not only not useful but left him with the sense that I also did not want to keep the anxiety alive and so he would be better off just going to sleep.

He was quiet for a minute and then said, "I have sometimes had the fantasy that I was Einstein in another life." I said, "Perhaps if you are a great and famous man your mother will forgive you for not caring about her every minute of every waking hour." He cried here: "She couldn't have loved the ungrateful little bastard that I really was." I said, "And you relieve yourself of the enormous burden of constantly caring for the mother toward whom you feel gratitude by breaking apart the image of you and her that you felt me trying to hold up to your mind's eye."

We now were able to understand the transferential meaning of his worrying that he was not as interested in what we were talking about as he imagined that I imagined he was. I too must care about him only because he keeps alive in my mind a representation of him as constantly and unwaveringly excited, interested, and concerned about me. He hated that idea. "Oh shit," he said, "I don't want to think about that. I need a place to rest." I added, "So when I force you to think about the mother toward whom you feel love and gratitude, you break up your own ideas about that mother whom you love and you choke on the broken pieces." As I was saying this, however, I fumbled over a couple of words, and he laughed and said, "Hmm . . . you don't want her either." I laughed and asked, "I wonder if we do not want good mommy or if we want so badly to keep her safe from the not caring that we choke our own words when those words would bring her alive here in the room and burden us with either devoting ourselves to her or suffering self-hatred." He said, "I think sometimes about calling her and then I feel dead." I wondered, "Maybe you find in your mind the idea of calling her precisely when you feel nothing, dead, toward her, when she doesn't matter much to you."

He was able after this to remain aware, for the rest of the hour, of the hateful complaints he wanted to launch against mother and against me. Of even more lasting importance to him, however, was, I believe, his eventual realization that, even more than he was made anxious by moments of hating what he loved, he was terrified by the regularity of the experience of not caring about those whom he also loved. Narcissitic self-absorption, the moment of not relating, had become his great crime against his mother and me.

CONCLUSION

To sum up briefly, the contemporary relational analyst in the United States, drawing on the work of such authors as Fairbairn, Winnicott, Bion, Greenberg, Mitchell, and Hoffman, understands anxiety as not only an intrapsychic motivational signal but also a communication to the other, as an emotional system that becomes structured in each individual through a series of developmental relationships, and as a mode of relating to the clinician during the analytic hour.

REFERENCES

Beebe, B. & Lachmann, F. (1994), Representation and internalization in infancy. *Psychoanal. Psychol.*, 11:127–166.

Benjamin, J. (1988), *The Bonds of Love*. New York: Pantheon.

Dunn, J. (1993), Psychic conflict and the external world in Freud's theory of the instinctual drives in light of his adherence to Darwin. *Internat. J. Psycho-Anal.*, 74:231–240.

Fairbairn, W. R. D. (1954), Observations on the nature of hysterical states. *Brit. J. Med. Psychol.*, 27:116–125.

Freud, S. (1926), *Inhibitions, Symptoms and Anxiety*. Standard Edition, 20:87–172. London: Hogarth Press, 1959.

Greenberg, J. & Mitchell, S. (1983), *Object Relations in Psychoanalytic Theory*. Cambridge, MA: Harvard University Press.

Hanly, C. (1978), A critical consideration of Bowlby's ethological theory of anxiety. *Psychoanal. Quart.*, 47:364–380.

Hinshelwood, R. (1994), *Clinical Klein*. London: Free Association Books.

Kessler, R., McGonagle, K., Zhao, S., Nelson, C., Hughes, M., Eshleman, S., Wittchen, H. & Kendler, K. (1994), Lifetime and 12-month prevalence of DSM-III-R psychiatric disorders in the United States. *Arch. Gen. Psych.*, 51:8–19.

Klein, D. F. (1993), False suffocation alarms, spontaneous panics, and related condictions. *Arch. Gen. Psychiat.*, 50:306–317.

Kojève, A. (1969), *Introduction to the Reading of Hegel* (assembled R. Queneau; ed. A. Bloom; trans. from French J. H. Nichols, Jr.). Ithaca, NY: Cornell University Press, 1980.

Mitchell, S. (1988), *Relational Concepts in Psychoanalysis*. Cambridge, MA: Harvard University Press.

Spezzano, C. (1993), *Affect in Psychoanalysis*. Hillsdale, NJ: The Analytic Press.

Stein, R. (1991), *Psychoanalytic Theories of Affect*. New York: Praeger.

Summers, F. (1994), *Object Relations Theories and Psychopathology*. Hillsdale, NJ: The Analytic Press.

Winnicott, D. W. (1949), Mind in its relation to the psychesoma. In: *Through Paediatrics to Psychoanalysis*. New York: Basic Books, 1975, pp. 174–193.

——— (1963), Dependence in infant care, in child care, and in the psycho-analytic setting. In: *The Maturational Processes and the Facilitating Environment*. New York: International Universities Press, 1965, pp. 249–260.

——— (1971), *Playing and Reality*. London: Routledge.

Wittgenstein, L. (1953), *Philosophical Investigations*. New York: Macmillan.

——— (1967), *Zettel*. Berkeley: University of California Press.

10 Does Anxiety Obstruct or Motivate Treatment?

When to Talk, When to Prescribe, and When to Do Both

Steven P. Roose

With increasing frequency clinicians are using a combination of medication and psychotherapy as the preferred treatment strategy for a wide range of patients. Consequently, analysts and therapists are often referring patients for psychopharmacological consultations—sometimes in the hope that medication will lessen the intensity of depressive or anxiety symptoms, thereby facilitating the induction of psychotherapy, or sometimes with a wish that medication will unblock a stalemated treatment. Transcending the unique circumstances of each consultation are those beliefs held by analysts that underlie a sometimes subtle and sometimes overt adversarial relationship to medication. Indeed though medication and psychotherapy are often combined, giving two types of treatment simultaneously does not mean that the modalities have been either practically or theoretically integrated. In fact, combined treatment, though often effective, can be a treatment in conflict.

As both a psychoanalyst and psychopharmacologist, I have had the opportunity to do many pharmacological consultations for patients in psychoanalytic psychotherapy or psychoanalysis. The focus of this chapter is on the many facets of the consultation process and how I decide whether or not to recommend medication.

EVOLVING ATTITUDES TOWARD MEDICATION

In the late 1950s when psychotropic medication first became available for the treatment of psychiatric disorders—primarily schizophrenia and depression—the new treatment modality was greeted at times with skepticism but more frequently with outright rejection by the psychoanalytic community. Medication was characterized as a treatment that only relieved symptoms but did not affect the underlying psychic conflicts that were then considered to be the etiology of psychological illness. It was reluctantly conceded that the reduction of florid symptoms, albeit superficial, could be useful to the degree that it controlled behavior disruptive to the development of the transference, thereby facilitating the analytic treatment that constituted the definitive therapeutic process (Sarwer-Foner, 1960). However, it was strongly believed that psychological treatment, specifically psychoanalytic treatment, is deep and curative and should be left undisturbed whenever possible. In contrast, medication, though possibly necessary to treat severe symptoms that interfered with the analytic process, was considered an undesirable intrusion that should be implemented only as a last resort. Even when effective, medications were to be considered, at best, a necessary evil.

Even though the early psychoanalytic literature reflected an unfavorable view of combining medication with psychotherapy, data from many double-blind, placebo-controlled studies consistently demonstrated the benefit of medication in the treatment of schizophrenia and affective disorder. Subsequently, more recent studies, especially in affective disorders, indicated that though medications alone have a robust effect—for example, in the prevention of recurrent depressive episodes—combined treatment was often superior to medication alone with respect to certain dimensions of psychological and social functioning (Weissman et al., 1979). Furthermore, the development of a therapeutic relationship decreased the dropout rate for patients taking medications that had proven effective for their illness. It should be noted, however, that in those studies, medication was combined with either interpersonal, cognitive, or supportive psychotherapy and not dynamically oriented treatment.

Concern about the possible negative impact of medication on psychotherapy was directly addressed by a secondary analysis of data from one collaborative study of depression (Rounsaville, Klerman, and Weissman, 1981). As concisely summarized by Kahn (1991):

The researchers tested the hierarchical view that therapy is superior to drugs and that drugs interfere with therapy. They distilled four traditional hypotheses of negative interactions: 1) drugs could be a negative placebo, increasing dependency and prolonging some kinds of psychopathology; 2) drug relief of symptoms could reduce motivation for further therapy; 3) drugs could eliminate one symptom and create others by symptom substitution if underlying conflicts remain intact; 4) drugs could decrease self esteem by leading the patient to believe that he or she was not interesting enough for insight oriented work. They also examined the reverse position that psychotherapy could be harmful in patients sick enough to need medication, either by promoting regression or by encouraging the patient inappropriately not to use drugs. Careful statistical evaluation of outcomes in large samples receiving different treatment combinations revealed no negative interactions. On the contrary their work supported the theory that two treatments are additive, not conflicting.

In recent years a number of psychoanalytic authors have themselves concluded that combining medication and psychotherapy may have a synergistic, beneficial effect. In the course of reviewing the treatment of a patient with masochistic personality, dysthymic disorder, and probable panic disorder, Cooper (1985) concluded that "retrospectively, pharmacological assistance earlier might have provided a much clearer focus on her content related psychodynamic problems and would have made it more difficult for her to use her symptoms masochistically as proof that she was an innocent victim of endless emotional pain." Esman (1989), reviewing psychoanalytic concepts of obsessive-compulsive disorder in the context of recent research developments, concluded both that "recent findings raised serious questions about the conflictual origins of the obsessional character" and that the therapeutic efficacy of psychoanalysis has been "less than dramatic." His view that "a one dimensional model" of obsessive-compulsive disorder is no longer tenable leads to the conclusion that combining multiple modalities of treatment is more consistent with the revised concept of this illness. One statement on the issue of medication and psychoanalysis that is remarkable perhaps not so much for its content but because of its source, was made by Anna Freud, who commented that during a visit to the New York Psychoanalytic Institute, she was "surprised at the almost complete rejection of drugs during psychoanalytic treatment . . . as far as I am concerned I have had great help from medical colleagues used to the administering of modern drugs with three patients in severe states of depression. In all of these cases the therapeutic use of drugs did not in any way interfere with the progress of analysis; quite on the contrary it helped the analysis to maintain itself during phases when otherwise the patient might have had to be hospitalized" (Lipton, 1983).

Thus much has changed in the psychoanalyst's attitude toward medication. Especially with respect to schizophrenia and melancholic depressions, psychoanalysts have long recognized that somatic treatments are the primary modality of therapy. Combining medication with psychoanalysis or psychoanalytic psychotherapy is no longer an uncommon form of treatment. However, despite such seemingly open recognition that medication and psychoanalysis can be an effective

and compatible combination or, indeed, that medication has supplanted psychotherapy as the primary treatment for certain disorders,
there still exists a competition between different models of the mind
that strongly influences our treatment choices and makes our eclecti-
cism perhaps more apparent than real. For example, that competition
is manifest in the way many clinicians artificially divide psychopathology, to wit: Axis I disorders are biological, or hardwired
(i.e., not derived from psychic conflict), and, therefore, not amenable
to psychotherapeutic interventions. In those disorders, somatic treatments are necessary. In contrast, Axis II disorders result from psychic
conflict and therefore are amenable to interpretation, implying that
psychological treatment and not medication should be the primary
modality of treatment. It should be recognized that such a division has
no empirical basis, but serves only to promote any misguided competition within our field.

The following clinical example illustrates how theoretical beliefs
can adversely affect the consideration of combined treatment. I was
asked by an analyst colleague to see a patient in order to evaluate
whether medication might help reduce the high level of anxiety that
was interfering with the analytic process. The patient had originally
sought treatment because of anxiety, fears, and phobias and had been
in analysis for some 18 months. The analyst observed that, not surprisingly, the patient had marked intensification of anxiety at times of
interruption in the analysis, such as weekends or vacations. The
patient also had a persistent fantasy that the analyst looked sick and
was going to be out for an extended period of time, or if there were a
phone call during the session that it would be some family emergency
that would take the analyst away from the analytic situation.

The developmental data that the analyst considered critical were
that the patient's father had been a diabetic requiring repeated hospi-
talizations before he died when the patient was 10. In spite of both
adequate interpretation of the transference and in fact some modification of analytic technique in an attempt to be reassuring, the analyst
felt that the patient's anxiety seemed intractable and voiced concern
whether the patient had sufficient ego strength to be analyzable.

I saw the patient in consultation, made a diagnosis of generalized
anxiety disorder, and recommended a trial of medication. I discussed
these recommendations with the patient and the analyst, but I heard
nothing further from either party for three months. The patient then
came to see me again and reported that following my recommendation, she and the analyst concurred that the consultation had been an
acting out designed to force a separation from the analyst, that is, to
create just what she had feared most. Initially, that clarification had

seemed quite helpful, for she was now able to realize that many times when she felt abandoned by friends or family, in fact she had engineered the rejection. The high level of anxiety persisted, however, and so she was now willing to try medication. It was my belief that the patient's pursuit of medication at this time was motivated by her belief that her persistent anxiety was endangering the analytic relationship because she was becoming an irritating disappointment to the analyst. Though I tried to persuade both the patient and the analyst that the transferential meanings of the consultation or the use of medication should be considered separately from the clinical indication for medication, in this case a medication trial never got started. I think that the analyst's feeling that if the patient needed medication it meant that this was no longer truly an analysis, coupled with the patient's desire to do nothing to endanger her relationship to the analyst, made combined treatment an impossibility.

THE PSYCHOANALYST IN CONFLICT WITH MEDICATION

Over the years the consultation process has forced me to consider some of the factors that interfere with the psychoanalyst considering the use of medication in patients with anxiety disorders. Of course there is the other side of that coin, namely, the overprescription of medications by psychopharmacologists in an attempt to eradicate any unpleasant thought or affect. Clearly such practice exists and if to a lesser degree, only because there are fewer psychopharmacologists than there are therapists. But my major concern has been to understand what is brought into play when a psychoanalyst considers how to conceptualize and treat anxiety; to do this, it is necessary to recognize the central role that the metapsychology of anxiety has in both psychoanalytic history and current clinical practice. First, it is believed that dysphoric affects, anxiety especially, are what motivate patients to seek treatment. Patients do not come in complaining of unconscious psychic conflict, but rather they seek treatment because of pain in the form of anxiety or depression.

Second, within the theory of the signal affects, anxiety in particular is a signifier of psychic conflict. In many ways, following the affect is the most reliable, available, and direct royal road to the unconscious, or, more precisely, the unconscious conflict. Because affect is so strongly bound to psychic conflict, it is safe and most often rewarding —among the myriad of paths that one could choose during an analytic session—to follow the affect. Thus it is not hard to understand the *analyst's* anxiety about any outside intervention that would perturb the patient's anxiety because it could deprive the analyst of a guiding light in the course of treatment.

Third, if it is so that anxiety and depression are tightly bound to psychic conflict, then it follows that if they emerge during the course of psychoanalytic treatment, it is a favorable sign because it means that the treatment is getting closer to the core unconscious conflicts. In some ways it is analogous to the inflammatory process, which is the critical first step of the healing process: inflammation necessarily leads to pain and discomfort, but it lays the foundation for subsequent repair.

In cases of hysteria, Freud originally thought that strangulated affect was itself the causative agent of psychopathology. According to his theory, treatment must be directed to the abreaction of the affect; that is, the core of the curative process necessarily involves a powerful and direct transformation of the affect. But the advent of the second theory of anxiety that defined anxiety as a signal had two significant implications with respect to focusing treatment directly on affect: (1) it is no longer critical to treat the anxiety itself, because anxiety is not the cause of the problem but rather a by-product of psychic conflict, and, in fact, (2) reducing the anxiety is actually counterproductive, because the psychoanalyst loses a valuable clinical guide to the unconscious.

There is yet another significance that anxiety holds for psychoanalysts—one with darker implications. There is long-standing belief that if in response to interpretation patients do not engage in the working-through process but rather react to the deeper knowledge of their unconscious conflicts with even more intense and persistent anxiety, this is indicative of weak ego. The implication of all this is that the patient does not have sufficient ego strength to tolerate the regression necessary for the analytic process to make fundamental structural changes. Thus, if severe anxiety means that the patient is unanalyzable and therefore the treatment should be stopped, it is understandable why the analyst may unconsciously minimize both its intensity and its chronicity. This is even more so because the analyst does not consider anxiety to be a treatable disorder in its own right, but rather a symptom of unremediable weakness.

Given all of the foregoing considerations, it is not surprising that historically, analysts have been drawn to the belief that suppression of anxiety through medication is not only unnecessary but actually at odds with the analytic process. In addition to both the danger of undercutting the patient's motivation to pursue treatment and the loss of a valuable indicator of psychic conflict there is yet another powerful reason that steers the analyst away from treating anxiety: fear of gratifying the patient. The underlying belief is that to quickly relieve patients of psychic distress is to gratify their infantile wish that their every want be satisfied instantly. To experience and work through psychic pain develops strength of character. Patients in analysis will understandably yearn for the analyst to be the omnipotent and totally gratifying parent that they never experienced. Just as certainly, the analyst must interpret the patient's desires rather than gratify them. At times it can seem as if the patient's insistent desire for immediate relief from suffering actually stiffens the analyst's resolve not to gratify the patient. Thus, countertransference rigidity that can develop in response to the patient's perceived demands weighs against the consideration of medication as a possible treatment. The worst extreme of that attitude transcends psychoanalysis and represents part of a long tradition in medicine, namely, an attitude toward pain and suffering that is Calvinistic, paternalistic, and, at worst, sadistic. For example, doctors do not prescribe sufficient amounts of analgesics, for it is common practice for physicians to titrate to the lowest possible dosage of analgesics, leaving the patient always on the edge of pain or in anticipation of pain. The practice is often rationalized by the bizarre and unfounded belief that patients will become dependent on such analgesic medications.

THE DECISION TO MEDICATE

It thus appears that the psychoanalyst has many theoretical and technical obstacles to negotiate before considering a medication. But it is not necessary to abandon the analytic position or a psychodynamic model of the mind in order to overcome those obstacles. Rather, we must be careful to keep separate the concepts of meaning and etiology. The sections in this volume present two concepts of anxiety. The first considers anxiety as a brain-generated physiological tone rather than a product of psychic conflict, a consideration often misrepresented as proposing that there is a form of contentless anxiety. Even if, in its origination, anxiety is a brain state without content, as meaning-seeking and meaning-creating creatures we attach a meaning and a cause to every feeling. The psychic content we couple to a physiological tone may produce accurate or inaccurate and misleading understandings; indeed, this may play a part in the distortions of our life narratives, which are an essential part of neurotic conflicts. Patients who believe that a persistent anxiety was "caused" by their inadequate mother, who could not offer comfort, may unwittingly be reversing cause and effect. In fact, it may have been the child's anxiety that rendered that child unable to be comforted, thereby creating an "inadequate" mother. But whatever the veracity of our self-interpretations, it is critical to acknowledge that identifying and understanding meaning are not equivalent to establishing etiology.

The second concept emphasizes anxiety as a psychological event generated by structural conflict, the separation individuation process, or the transference. Of course it is acknowledged that all psychological events ultimately have a brain substrate, but the origin of anxiety is in the psychological sphere, and brain mechanisms simply follow. Although the first concept emphasizes brain mechanism, and the second psychological meaning, they are nonetheless competing theories of etiology. There has been no shortage of attempts to integrate the two theories, but many such attempts seem forced—or motivated by a desire to keep peace in our field (i.e., there is room for everybody) rather than to represent serious model building.

In any case, neither is it necessary to know the origins of anxiety nor do we need a resolution of theoretical conflicts in order to develop a system for guiding the pharmacological treatment of anxiety. Rather, we must put aside establishing the meaning or etiology of anxiety and focus on phenomenology. The data establishing the efficacy of medication in anxiety syndromes came from studies that included patients based on the phenomenology of their symptoms: the chronicity, the form, and the intensity but not the presumed etiology or meaning of anxiety. Of course the anxiety had meaning to these patients, and like all patients, they were given to elaborate conscious and unconscious fantasies to explain what was happening to them. But in these studies and in our clinical work, meaning is not the critical dimension, but rather, what should guide the clinician as to whether medication will be helpful to a specific patient is the phenomenology of their psychopathology. In short, if a patient meets diagnostic criteria for an anxiety syndrome (e.g., panic attacks), medication should be considered as part of the treatment. It is not that every patient of this kind must or should be on medication, but in all such patients, medications must be given serious consideration, and if not recommended there should be a good rationale why not.

Actually, psychoanalysts have already come to this position regarding treatment of melancholic depressions. Many analysts might still maintain that they can determine both the cause and the dynamic meaning of depressive symptoms, but would nonetheless absolutely concur that rapidly effective somatic therapies are the treatments of choice.

But what about patients who have anxiety symptoms but do not meet diagnostic criteria for an anxiety disorder? And what about patients in whom anxiety is not a symptom at all but simply part of the normal range of affective responses? Are these the patients with whom we should only talk and not medicate? In such patients the efficacy of medication has not been studied and consequently there are no data available to evaluate the risk-benefit ratio of their use. Therefore, as a general principle there is no basis on which to recommend medication, although clinical judgment for an individual case may dictate otherwise. Even if we affirm that there are patients with anxiety with whom we should only talk and not medicate, we must recognize as well the following: Even though medication in the strict sense has not been systematically studied in such patients, ironically we seem to have become culturally acclimated to the use of pharmacological or behavioral interventions to lessen acute situational anxiety, for example, through nicotine, alcohol, or vigorous exercise. These are the antianxiety medications of everyday life. We all know that patients in analysis can sometimes develop magical rituals in order to lessen anxiety surrounding the analytic session: how many patients go to the bathroom both before and after the session, or how many patients always get a slice of pizza on the way to the office?

In short, one systematic approach to decide the question of when to recommend medication for the treatment of anxiety says that if the patient has the phenomenology of an anxiety disorder that has been shown to be medication responsive, then a trial of medication is indicated. But it should be emphasized that the effectiveness of a biological treatment no more proves there is a biological etiology to the illness than an effective psychological treatment proves there is a psychological etiology. Effective medication treatment is not evidence that favors any theoretician; it only helps the patient.

CLINICAL EXAMPLES

The material that follows illustrates some of the points raised in this chapter. It is also intended to suggest that sometimes, sequencing treatments (i.e., giving medication prior to initiating psychoanalysis) should be considered.

Case 1

A patient was referred by an analyst colleague for a medication evaluation because of chronic symptoms of anxiety. The patient had been in analysis for two years, and the referral was made at this point because of the analyst's growing conviction that the chronic, persistent level of anxiety was making it difficult for the analytic process to deepen. That concern became crystallized when yet another interpretation, which was initially believed by both the patient and the analyst to be accurate and illuminating, nonetheless had no impact on the patient's anxiety symptoms.

The patient was a 28-year-old woman who had originally entered analytic treatment because of feeling that her life was not progressing; she felt stuck. As the analyst noted, there was a striking parallel between the patient's assessment of her life as she entered treatment and his own assessment of the analysis at the time of referral. The patient was a doctoral candidate in fine arts; she had completed her course work but, not surprisingly, was stuck regarding her thesis. She worked in an art gallery primarily as an administrator but recognized an opportunity to move into the creative and program end of the business. However, she was too anxious to pursue that opportunity. She had been living with a man for three years, a relationship that she curiously described as mutually helpful.

She reported no separation problems either beginning school, on sleepover dates, or going away to camp or college. She dates the beginning of her symptoms from her second year at college, when, as her courses seemed to become progressively more difficult and the demands on her more complex, she found her work slowing down because of increased anxiety. Though she continued to make a significant effort, her grades slipped and depressive symptoms emerged for the first time. She did have an active social life during college, including multiple girlfriends and two serious boyfriends, and enjoyed vacations and other activities outside schoolwork. She said that when she was not feeling anxious, college was a very happy time for her.

Her family history was notable in that her mother was clearly a phobic woman who had led an increasingly restricted life. A dominant theme in the analysis consisted in uncovering the extent to which her mother was phobic, restricted, and impaired and the impact of her mother's illness on the patient's life. The father was a successful attorney and in her view a decent and caring man who had been drained by her mother's insatiable need for reassurance and consequently had little left over for the children. She had an older brother with no obvious psychopathology.

The patient had begun analysis in September; the next June she had her first indisputable panic attack. It happened when she was at a movie with her boyfriend, and the analyst could not find anything in the content of the movie to account for the attack. The patient experienced shortness of breath, palpitations, sweating, trembling, a sense of depersonalization, and the fear that she was going to die. She had her boyfriend take her to an emergency room, where she was told that physically she was fine and had probably had an anxiety attack. During the preceding week her analysis had been focused on the theme of separation and abandonment precipitated by an upcoming business trip by the boyfriend; he was going to be away for a week, which was a very unusual event. Obviously in the background was August, which would be her first extended separation from the analyst. The analyst told me he had hypothesized there would be many more such anxiety attacks as his August vacation drew near, but surprisingly there was only one other attack in July; there were two attacks in August. Both the analyst and the patient anticipated that the attacks might disappear when analysis resumed in September, but instead the attacks settled into a steady pattern, occurring about twice a month. Though not occurring frequently, the panic attacks were of sufficient intensity and were chronic enough so that an increasing pattern of restriction developed in the patient's life. She was going away less on the weekends, and at one point during the winter did not take a vacation (which the boyfriend very much wanted to do) because she did not want to miss sessions. She had an increasing feeling of safety in the session and had the fantasy of increasing her sessions to five times a week or more. The analyst was increasingly concerned about the pattern and persistence of these attacks and equally concerned that the analytic sessions were becoming quiet—almost soothing for the patient—whereas outside the office her life was closing down.

It is apparent that, in the brief material presented, I concentrated on the phenomenology of the symptoms and the patient's behavior. At this point I made no attempt to explore unconscious fantasy or meaning. This was consistent with the purpose of the consultation, which was to decide if a medication might be helpful.

The patient met diagnostic criteria for both generalized anxiety disorder and panic attack disorder and I discussed medication options with her. She had come to the consultation hoping that something could stop the attacks, but approached medication with a sense of foreboding. Though she felt that it was the right thing to do, she believed her analyst would now think of her as sick—parallel to how her father thought of her mother—and consequently he would patronize her and tolerate her, but would not really like her. She had a conviction that men at best support their wives but really enjoy themselves elsewhere, which was connected to her concern that on his first business trip the boyfriend would have fun, opening his eyes as to the nature of their relationship. Further elaboration revealed that it was not that she believed men are so selfish, but that she was "damaged" like her mother and could not get any better. If she failed on medications, it would seal her fate, and so, ironically, her fear that the medication would not work was almost strong enough to prevent her from trying it.

Generally a patient's fantasies about medication are not routinely elicited by a psychopharmacologist, but my active pursuit of the foregoing material obviously had to do with my interest and perspective as an analyst. I had not necessarily pursued such material in patients who were referred for a second opinion about medications but were not in analysis. For patients in analysis, however, the exploration of the meaning of taking a medication, including fantasies about the analyst's reaction to such medication, seemed necessary for the effective administration of medications and often provides valuable material for the analysis itself. In retrospect I think that practice has been a mistake. Taking medication may have an important dynamic meaning for any patient regardless of what treatment the patient is or is not in. Considering that approximately 50% of all medication prescriptions are not taken as intended, probably more attention should be paid to the meaning of medication to the patient, whether it be an antihypertensive or an antidepressant.

The patient began alprazolam, and the panic attack syndrome improved significantly. Consequently, she could no longer use its presence to reinforce her identification with her mother. Why did the analyst wait 14 months after the onset of panic attack before considering medication? It was not an issue of diagnosis, for the analyst had diagnosed the patient as having panic attacks before she was sent to me. Rather, I think the delay resulted from the analyst's focus on the dynamic meaning of the symptoms instead of diagnosis.

The analyst's view of the meaning of the panic attack was dictated by his belief that since the first panic attack had come in the setting of a separation, the patient's anxiety had to have its origins in experiences and fears of separation and abandonment. However, two events coinciding in time do not establish a cause-and-effect relationship. Regardless of what was the real meaning of the patient's anxiety, if there was one, only when repeated interpretation of the meaning had no effect was medication considered.

Case 2

The following example illustrates a case in which pharmacological treatment and psychological treatment were sequenced rather than combined. The patient was a 26-year-old medical intern who was self-referred and who presented with complaints of obsessive checking that were "making my work hell." The patient reported that sometimes toward the end of high school she remembers being extra careful about things: always checking and rechecking to make sure that her homework was in her book bag; checking the setting on her alarm clock three times; or, to be sure she had brought the right books home from school, opening her bag three times. Most of the obsessive checking was school related. Though these habits would exasperate her friends and family, she was not an obsessive person who led a restricted life. Quite to the contrary, she was very social, spontaneous, and involved with and enjoyed a wide range of activities, including varsity sports and the theater club.

After high school she attended a prestigious university, but again, compulsive checking of class schedule, her papers, the spellcheck on the computer, and so on led to an increasing sense of frustration and helplessness. In her first two years of medical school the checking and rechecking patterns continued, but of course in that setting she was seen as hardworking, careful, and conscientious and was a straight-honors student. Inwardly, however, she realized she could not "break the grip on this" and was frightened and at times panicky. When she began clinical rotations, her performance began to deteriorate because she could not work fast enough, her case presentations were poor because she was too inclusive, and she was never able to get to the point. The outstanding reputation she had earned in the first two years carried her through her clinical years, but when she began her internship things began to fall apart. She was never able to leave because things were not sufficiently checked and put in place, and when she did manage to go home, she was in agony because of the certainty that she had left something undone and harm would come to one of her patients. She was clearly no longer a bright star but an intern with whom neither the residents nor the medical students wanted to work. She was increasingly depressed, frustrated, and anxious.

She had been involved with a man for the past two years, a fellow medical student, although the relationship had been markedly strained by her increasing irritability and depression. With almost palpable pain and pleasure, she told of a vacation taken two months prior to seeking treatment during which they both enjoyed themselves and she felt quite loving and cared for.

The phenomenology of the patient's symptoms met DSM-III-R criteria for obsessive-compulsive disorder, and I suggested that medication could be of help. She revealed that since her second-year psychiatry course, she believed that she had some type of obsessive-compulsive syndrome and that she wanted to "get the nerve" to try medication. I further told her I found it striking that her restrictive compulsions had always been directed toward inhibiting her career. We agreed that she would begin a trial of clomipramine and that we would reevaluate the situation after a number of months. On medication the compulsive pathology markedly diminished. Her checking behaviors were not totally absent but much more manageable, and she no longer had the fantasy that a patient admitted to her service would trap her in the hospital forever.

The patient continued on medication alone for four months and then asked to see me again. She had now begun her residency and wanted to talk about success. Specifically, she felt that being freed of the compulsive rituals had changed the question from whether or not she would fail to how good she could really be. In subsequent sessions, competitive themes and what can be generically described as oedipal conflicts emerged. I recommended analysis, to which she agreed, and, still on medication, she entered analytic treatment.

What were the origins of this patient's obsessive symptoms? Were the checking behaviors and the oedipal conflicts significantly related? I do not know, nor did I think I had to know in order to recommend medication. Medication would provide the most direct relief from the obsessive symptom, and that was the basis for its recommendation. Furthermore, the effect of the medication allowed the patient to enter an analysis that was focused on dynamic issues instead of immediate relief of symptoms.

SUMMARY

In conclusion, I have tried to make the case that medication treatment in patients with anxiety symptoms is a decision that should be based on empirical observations rather than metapsychological considerations (i.e., on the basis of phenomenology, not theory). This requires that the psychoanalyst suspend certain traditional beliefs. Though the administration of medication concurrent with psychoanalytic psychotherapy or psychoanalysis raises a whole new spectrum of technical problems (e.g., should the analyst administer the medication or should the treatment be split), in reality, combined treatment raises the kinds of issues with which psychoanalysts have always struggled. Our goal is to help our patients and not primarily to protect psychoanalysis or prove a theory of the mind. The introspective process that should precede a psychoanalyst's recommendation of medication is a paradigm for the open spirit of inquiry that is essential for the health of our profession.

REFERENCES

Cooper, A. M. (1985), Will neurobiology influence psychoanalysis? *Amer. J. Psychiat.*, 142:1395–1402.

Esman, A. H. (1989), Psychoanalysis and general psychiatry: Obsessive compulsive disorder as paradigm. *J. Amer. Psychoanal. Assn.*, 37:319–336.

Kahn, D. A. (1991), Medication consultation and split treatment during psychotherapy. *J. Amer. Acad. Psychoanal.*, 19:84–98.

Lipton, M. A. (1983), Editorial: A letter from Anna Freud. *Amer. J. Psychiat.*, 140:1583–1584.

Rounsaville, B. J., Klerman, G. L. & Weissman, M. M. (1981), Do psychotherapy and pharmacotherapy for depression conflict? *Arch. Gen. Psychiat.*, 38:24–29.

Sarwer-Foner, G. J. (1960), *The Dynamics of Psychiatric Drug Therapy*. Springfield, IL: Thomas.

Weissman, M. M., Prusoff, B. A., DiMascio, A., Neu, C., Goklaney, M. & Klerman, G. L. (1979), The efficacy of drugs and psychotherapy in the treatment of acute depressive episodes. *Amer. J. Psychiat.*, 136:555–558.

Epilogue

Morton F. Reiser

Reading this volume of papers should evoke in psychoanalysts a special version of the experience addressed as the volume's central theme. Why not feel anxious when confronted with more information than can be integrated and translated into cogent clinical guidelines? Collectively, the chapters make it clear that anxiety is both protean and ubiquitous: protean because we observe, measure, gauge, conceptualize, describe, and experience it in so many (vastly different) ways, and ubiquitous because we encounter it (in one form or another) throughout the animal kingdom, in all patients, and in ourselves.

The clinician's burden is heavy in terms of having to act (or choosing not to) without the security of complete knowledge and understanding, and doing the best one can under the circumstances. But as the foregoing text also makes clear, anxiety can and should act as a stimulus for growth and development. Books such as this one represent one of the profession's most effective ways of coping: by offering the opportunity to digest and reflect at leisure and, it is to be hoped, enabling us to emerge afterword with deepened, if still incomplete, understanding. In turn, enriched understanding will inform future clinical and research efforts.

In my opinion, one of the most impressive, and hence most challenging, aspects of the volume is the striking asymmetry between the nature of the empirical data on the two sides of the neurobiological (brain) and the clinical psychoanalytic (mind/psychosocial) sides of the mind/brain–body divide. For the most part we are faced with two incompatible (biological and mental) domains of data, causing pragmatic observational problems. The preclinical biological disciplines— being graceful, elegant, and precise in both method and theory— produce data that are relatively objective and satisfying compared

171

with those generated by the clinical psychological disciplines. Data produced by more clumsy, pragmatic clinical efforts, although becoming less subjective nowadays, are still relatively imprecise and frustrating; thus it remains far from clear how to fit the two sets together. This is obvious as readers compare the earlier with the later chapters, noting the progressive fogging up of the window as the subject matter moves from one domain to the other.

Such practical difficulties are compounded by fundamental conceptual problems that concern the nature of the observed phenomena themselves. The very idea of mind and body as being separate entities is an artifact resulting from fundamental differences between the languages, concepts, and methods of inquiry used by the mental and the biological sciences. That is, the biological sciences deal with material phenomena (matter and energy), and the mental sciences deal with meanings, which are without material quality. Ordinarily, units from the two realms are not interchangeable, and we are also able neither to translate across domains nor to base linear causal sequences on covariant (concomitantly observed) psychological and biological phenomema. Therein lies the challenging importance of this book, however: Anxiety, which is the quintessential example of affect, belongs to, and is manifested in, *both* domains. It is at once both a psychological and a biological phenomenon. The fact that affect is accessible to study *and* subject to influence both by subjective introspective psychological methods and by objective biological methods means that it should be possible in principle to develop empirically based psychobiological-social models of affect that will facilitate translation/integration across domains. (I return to this topic later.) Already we know, from information contained in these chapters and found elsewhere as well, that data from the two realms can be regarded as complementary rather than antithetical and that psychosocial and pharmacological modalities can be combined effectively in treatment, even though much more study and experience will be required before many of the important theoretical details and treatment principles can be worked out.

To my mind this book should end, as it began, with an evolutionary perspective. Accordingly, this epilogue picks up again that thread so brilliantly spun by Myron A. Hofer in chapter 2. Therein Hofer traced the evolution (from single-celled motile bacteria to *Homo sapiens*) of "a means to detect signals, a way to discriminate those that denote danger, and the capacity to initiate behavior that results in avoidance of that danger." Mankind, after the development of consciousness, was able to have the aware psychological experience of anxiety and to develop psychological and behavioral ways of dealing with it. Finally, having developed the capacity for symbolic communication by means of language, individuals gained the capability to communicate information about that experience to other individuals and, eventually, even to succeeding generations by way of the printed page—as in this volume.

Of course, in the unicellular organism the physiological and behavioral response are one. Following through on that evolutionary perspective I would add that as evolution progressed, the (danger-sensing) physiological-behavioral (reaction response) mechanism—originally tuned outward for signaling external danger (as Darwin, Pavlov, and Freud all appreciated)—eventually developed so as to be tuned inward for signaling internal danger as well. And with the development of memory, it became possible to compare and match new sensory input with information stored from previous experience. It seems clear that it was the competitive survival advantage in the form of the capacity to anticipate danger and react on the basis of prior experience that supported and enhanced the evolutionary development of cognitive functions and their linkup through corticolimbic circuits with the physiologic-stress central nervous, neuroendocrine, and neuroimmune response systems. Emotion, as the product of that linkage, belongs to both mental and biological domains. From this perspective, mind/brain–body in humans can be regarded as a unitary apparatus capable of responding to both external and internal—physiological and psychological—challenges. In principle it is not difficult to appreciate the basic unitary psychobiological nature of the apparatus and its role in adaptation and survival—of both individual and species. In practice, however, as noted earlier, it is not that easy. The development of highly specialized languages, methods, and concepts becomes clear as the chapters progress through the neuroanatomy, neurochemistry, and genetics of the danger response system; that system's experiential ontogeny in childhood and adult development; and finally, its expression as symptom and the challenges that that expression presents in treatment using talk; drugs; or both, if ways of combining the modalities are indicated.

Once again, in principle, it seems clear that we should endeavor to avoid spurious antitheses generated by the subspecialization Tower of Babel. As physicians and individual therapists, it behooves each of us to (1) understand and treat the individual rather than the disease by using whatever techniques seem best suited to meet that individual's needs and (2) make referrals based on the skills, rather than the biases, of the therapists available in the community. This, I believe, represents the clearly agreed upon message at the conclusion of the conference.

Much more research is necessary, but to be of most value it will have to cope with the problems inherent in multidisciplinary communication and collaboration, because such communication and collaboration across highly subspecialized disciplinary boundaries is becoming ever more difficult as the frontiers of knowledge and know-how advance ever more rapidly. To profit fully—both in research and in therapy—from the new knowledge that is sure to come, cross-disciplinary students will have to be specially educated and trained to communicate and work in more than one language and more than one discipline. This is not practical in today's real world. Yet the opportunity to learn more is wider than ever before. While indications are that all cogent disciplines may participate, there also exists that corresponding but grossly underrealized need for academic and practical cross-fertilization and collaboration.

Index